To
Francesca

THE ITALIAN AMERICANS
THROUGH THE GENERATIONS

THE ITALIAN AMERICANS THROUGH THE GENERATIONS

Proceedings of
The XV Annual Conference of the
American Italian Historical Association

Held at St. John's University, New York

October 29-30, 1982

Edited by
Rocco Caporale, Ph.D.

The American Italian Historican Association
1986

Volume XV in the series of Annual Proceedings of the
American Italian Historical Association

LIBRARY OF CONGRESS CATALOG CARD NUMBER: 85-071556

ISBN: 0-934675-15-5
ISSN: 0743-474X

Published in the United States of America by
The American Italian Historical Association
209 Flagg Place
Staten Island, N.Y.
Manufactured by General Hall, Inc.

New York City
August 21, 1986

CONTENTS

Part IV. Images of Italian Americans: Collective and Individual Traits

Part V. Education as a Frontier

Epilogue. The 1982 Covello Award Paper

Introduction   THE ITALIAN AMERICANS
THROUGH THE GENERATIONS
Rocco Caporale
St. John's University

The Fifteenth Annual Conference of the American Italian Historical Association was held at St. John's University, New York, from October 29 to 31, 1982. Several years had passed since the Association's successful meeting at Queens College in New York in 1975; once again the choice of the metropolitan venue proved attractive to a large number of members and provided the incentive for a stimulating conference.

The theme of the conference aimed to provide latitude for a variety of papers, while providing opportunities for exploring the intergenerational variations that clearly emerge from the most recent studies conducted by Italian-American scholars.

Regretfully, nearly half of the papers presented at the conference could not be included here due to limitations of space and costs. The essays selected for publication have been grouped into five parts. The first part focuses on personages and events which precede the Civil War and the large scale immigration period of 1880 and thereafter. The details on the life of Beltrami, Spinola and various Italian expatriates of this period shed considerable new light on this little researched area of Italian-American scholarship. The second part focuses exclusively on Garibaldi, in consideration of the centenary of his death. The three papers suggest that there is considerable material to be researched and divulged on this "hero of two worlds" in order to better comprehend some unknown features of the pre-immigration decades.

Part three presents four case studies of various aspects of the political, unionistic and social assimilation of Italian-Americans in different areas of the USA during the decades of large-scale immigration. The principal actors of this profound cultural transformation of a peasant people into sophisticated Americans were very ordinary folks, who emerged to play vital roles.

Part four reflects some of the more pressing preoccupations of the Italian-American community of the third and fourth generation. The problem of image, the personality traits associated with *Italo-Americanità* and the pressure to resolve age-old psychological complexes are brought in sharper focus, effectively contributing to the ongoing social catharsis which the Italian-American community has been experiencing in the past two decades.

A major area of this self analysis by the Italian-American community is examined in the last part of the book, namely education, as the ethnically-specific new frontier of Italian-Americans, who traditionally have assigned it third place, after family and work.

The epilogue contains the Covello Award winning paper of the year written by Doctor Daniel David Cowell, M.D., Associate Director for Medical Education, National Institute of Health. Cowell (anglicization of Covello) skillfully traces the development of funeral practices from the semi-magical customs of southern Italy to the conventional, rationalized format of urban America and views it as a crucial indicator of change and cultural transformation over the generations.

This collection of twenty excerpts of significant moments, peoples and trends in the several centuries' saga of the Italian-American experience strongly suggests that a systematic and comprehensive history of the Italian-American experience, from Columbus to our days, is conceivably within the capability of our scholarly community and ought to be set as a goal of the Association.

The role and contribution of Italians to the establishment of American civilization, from explorations, to the search for political identity, to the creation of labor unions, customs, religious practices and popular images, have not been given proper visibility in the conventional history of this land. Beyond the contribution of a few admirable Italophiles, the task of redressing this condition falls upon the scholars of the Italian-American community.

There may be, however, a lurking temptation to "play" the scholar within the safe compound of a national association, while avoiding the inevitable *rendez-vous* with the whole American society. Early in this new phase of the Italian-American experience, Giovanni Schiavo has provided an excellent model and strategy of work. As Italian-Americans move into the fourth and fifth generations it becomes imperative that the intellectual resources of the community be mobilized toward the production of a comprehensive socio-cultural history of the Italian-American experience, such that its findings become integral elements of the American tradition, not to be ignored any longer by American scholars, and so that its volumes be considered the standard reference for those interested in appreciating the significance of five centuries of Italian presence in the American continent.

This volume is intended to be a small contribution and a step toward this highly desirable goal. I would like to express a vote of thanks to Prof. Salvatore LaGumina and Prof. Remigio Pane for their help as members of the editorial committee and to former AIHA President Frank Cavaioli for his support in the preparation of the Conference and its proceedings.

New York   Rocco Caporale
August 21, 1986   St. John's University, New York

PART I

Explorers, Patriots and Expatriates

Chapter **1** GIACOMO COSTANTINO
BELTRAMI AND THE INDIANS OF
NORTH AMERICA
Luciano G. Rusich
College of Staten Island, CUNY

So many comprehensive and authoritative biographies of Beltrami have been written that to repeat what has been said before would seem superfluous.[1] Yet, it is necessary to sketch an outline of his life, previous to his arrival in the United States, in order to clarify the circumstances which brought this enterprising and cultured man to brave the wilderness of America.

Giacomo Costantino Beltrami was born in Bergamo in 1779. Bred to the law, at the age of 28 he became chancellor of the Department of Justice at Parma and Udine. Later he was appointed judge of the civil and criminal court of Macerata. Because of his fine intellect, solid preparation, professional competence, and untiring zeal in carrying out his functions, his superiors proposed him for the presidency of the Court of Forlì. But the fall of Napoleon and of the Kingdom of Italy prevented his appointment. When the Austrians occupied the Marche, he resigned and retired to his estates at Filottrano. In 1821, accused of being implicated in the carbonarian plots in favor of a constitution, he had to choose between incarceration or exile. Although ill, and hardly able to stand upon his feet, he chose exile and fled from Italy. He went to France, Belgium, Germany, and England. There he resolved to visit the countries and the peoples of the far away but free American continent. He sailed for the United States from Liverpool and landed in Philadelphia on December 30, 1822, after a very difficult and trying voyage.[2]

From Philadelphia he went to Baltimore, Washington, Pittsburgh, Cincinnati, and Louisville. Then he stopped at the confluence of the Ohio and the Mississippi rivers. It is here that Costantino Beltrami made the decision which, for better or for worse, changed his whole life. Initially he had planned to take a steamboat down the Mississippi to New Orleans and from there to proceed to Mexico. But, while waiting for the steamboat *United States* to carry him there, it so happened that another ship, the *Calhoun,* bound for St. Louis, stopped at the junction. Among its passengers were General William Clark, superintendent of Indian affairs at St. Louis, and Major Lawrence Tagliaferro, the Indian agent at Fort St. Anthony (Fort Snelling). Beltrami met them, became their friend, and in the conversations that ensued, they re-awakened in him the interest in Indians and Indian lore he had had since adolescence. With that impulsiveness which was so characteristic of him, he decided to accompany them in order to learn as much as he could about Indian customs, habits, rituals, and daily life. Together they went to St. Louis where General Clark remained, while Beltrami and Major Tagliaferro continued the voyage to Fort St. Anthony on board the steamboat *Virginia*.

On May 10th, nineteen days and 729 miles after leaving St. Louis, the *Virginia* arrived at Fort St. Anthony. The arrival of a steamboat, the first, to such an outpost of civilization as Fort St. Anthony had, in Beltrami's words, "marked a memorable epoch in this Indian territory, as well as in the history of navigation generally."[3] To the Indians who viewed with awe the "monster vomiting fire," the steamboat was an object of reverence and fear, and "all the persons on board were in their eyes something more than human."[4]

Beltrami stayed about two months at Fort St. Anthony. He was made welcome and treated as a friend by the family of Colonel Josiah Snelling, commander of the fort, who gave him the opportunity to explore the surrounding territory and to go hunting. Most important, he was able to spend considerable time among the Indians, studying their ways and collecting their artifacts.

On July 2nd, an expedition led by Major Stephen H. Long arrived at Fort St. Anthony. The expedition had been organized by the Government of the United States, ostensibly, with the purpose of exploring the St. Peter (Minnesota) River to its source and the Red River basin as far as Pembina (N.D.), near the Canadian border. At the same time the expedition had the task of collecting all types of information, military and scientific, necessary for the defense and colonization of that sensitive and vaguely defined border area of the United States. Beltrami saw in the expedition a unique opportunity to push on to the north and asked Major Long to be allowed to join it, "simply in the character of a wanderer who had come thus far to see Indian lands and Indian people."[5] Grudgingly, Major Long gave his consent and Beltrami left Fort St. Anthony with the expedition on July 9, 1823. They remounted the St. Peter River and during the trip Beltrami never failed to take due note of its most important tributaries, to record for us their Indian names, and to describe anything Indian he came across. This became nearly a mania with him for the duration of his journey.

On July 22, the expedition reached Big Stone Lake, left the St. Peter River, and the next day arrived at Lake Traverse. After a few days' rest during which they were entertained by the Great Chief Wanotan of the Sioux, the expedition headed toward Pembina. Pembina had been for years the center of brutal competition between the Hudson's Bay and the North West companies for the monopoly of the fur trade. According to Beltrami, the real actors and victims of this competition had been the *bois-brûlés* — the result of the unions between French-Canadian colonists and Indian women — whom he describes as an "execrable race" because of the atrocities they committed during the "war" between the two companies.[6]

In Pembina, on August 8th, Major Long fulfilled one of the main purposes of the expedition by formally taking possession of the settlement on behalf of the United States. Beltrami witnessed the ceremony and dutifully reported that "The boundary which separates the territories of the two nations [the United States and Great Britain] was formally laid down, in the name of the Government and President of the United States."[7] The next day, following some differences with Major Long, Beltrami left the expedition and struck out on his own plunging into the wilderness in search of the sources of the Mississippi, accompanied only by two Chippewas and a *bois-brûlé*.

The *bois-brûlé* who acted as an interpreter left him at the confluence of the Thief and the Red Lake rivers. Shortly afterwards, the two Chippewas abandoned him after a scuffle with a band of Sioux. All alone and without any experience on how to paddle a canoe, he capsized and then decided to reach Red Lake by towing his canoe up the river. Fortunately, after four days of this exhausting exercise, he met a party of friendly Indians, one of whom agreed to guide the canoe to the lake. At Red Lake, Beltrami had a chance to rest in the tent of the Chippewa who had guided him. Impatient to continue his journey, he pushed on with the help of another Chippewa and another *bois-brûlé* as guides. After a series of portages he reached a small lake which he called Lake Julia, in honor of his friend Countess Giulia Medici-Spada, and proclaimed it to be the northernmost source of the Mississippi. He continued south encountering a number of small lakes which he named after friends, but unfortunately the names he gave them subsist only in his map. Finally he identified Bitch Lake — later named Itasca Lake by Schoolcraft — as the western sources of the Mississippi. Having completed the task he himself had chosen, he returned to Fort St. Anthony dressed in animal skins, sewed the Indian way, and with a hat made of two pieces of bark. He had lived in the wilderness for nearly three months unflinchingly meeting its challenge, and he had come back to civilization with a wealth of information concerning its geography and its Indian population.

The narration of Beltrami's explorations was published in English under the title of *A Pilgrimage in America Leading to the Discovery of the Sources of the Mississippi and Bloody River; with a Description of the Whole Course of the Former; and of the Ohio.*[8] The book takes the form of thirteen letters, addressed to Countess Geronima Compagnoni. The majority of these letters deals exclusively with the observations about the Indians he made while visiting Fort Armstrong, Fort Edward, and Fort St. Anthony, and while travelling with and among them in their territories. The first Indians with whom he came in contact were the Saukis. According to Beltrami the Saukis numbered only 4800 members because of the endless little wars they would wage against their enemies the Ottawa, the Winnebago, and the Potomawa who lived around the shores of the Erie, Michigan, and Huron lakes. Then he met with the Jacovas who lived on the shores of the Jacova River and with the Foxes who, at that time, were only 1600 individuals divided into four tribes. Later, in the Prairie du Chien, he came across the Winnebago, a group of 1700 people subdivided into seven tribes, and the Menomenis or Folle Avoine who consisted of only 1200 people. Of all these groups of Indians, he described the physical and psychological characteristics; he related their history and legends; he explained their customs and ceremonies; he classified their languages. Not only that, but in passing from one group to another, he also observed and pointed out their differences in appearance, language, customs, dwellings, apparel, and artifacts.

Particularly detailed and interesting are his observations on the Sioux and Chippewas, the two most important and numerous Indian nations of the area who were always fighting each other over territory. According to the information Beltrami gathered from Wabiscihouwa, a Sioux chief and Eskibugekogé, a Chippewa chief; this fighting had been going on for more than three thousand moons. So:

> Reckoning twelve moons to a year, as they do, more than three thousand moons, adding the complementary days, bring us pretty nearly to the time of the conquest of Mexico by the Spaniards.[9]

Betrami also speaks of the Assiniboins, brothers of the Sioux, and explains how the two peoples were originally one and they were known as Dakotas. But as he remarks:

> One finds Helens everywhere. The Dakotas had theirs, and she was the cause of as great evils as the beautiful Greek.
> Ozolapaîda, wife of Winahoà-appà, was caried off by Ohatam-pà, who killed her husband and her two brothers, who came to reclaim her. Discord and vengeance arose between these two tribes, the most powerful of the nation. The relations, friends, and partisans of each, took up the quarrel; one act of revenge begat another, until the whole nation was drawn into a bloody civil war, which eventually divided it into two factions, under the names of Assiniboinà, the partisans of the offender's family, and Siowaé, those of the offended; — like the Bianchi and the Neri, the Uberti and the Buondelmonti, &c. &c.

When they wanted greater extent of country they split into two nations, the Sioux and the Assiniboins; but separation and distance did not put an end to their wars, which continued for a long period of time; it is but lately that they have made peace. The event which gave birth to their divisions happened, according to their calculations, about two hundred years ago; and the identity of their language, manners, and habits, adds weight to their respective traditions. I can vouch for the authenticity of these details, though they are perfectly new and totally unknown even to the garrison of the fort.[10]

Continuing his descriptions of the Sioux, he notes that they are all united by a loose confederation of tribes. Each tribe makes war at its own discretion and manages its own tribal affairs. To decide on issues of interest to the whole Sioux nation, they convene a general council, usually in a forest. On such an occasion each tribe sends a deputy, and any resolution of the council which deserves to be transmitted to posterity is recorded on a tree by means of hieroglyphics (picture writings). Then, the deputy of each tribe carves the "armorial bearing" of the tribe he represents, to indicate his approval.[11] Beltrami is really puzzled, however, when it comes to explaining the religion of the Sioux. He confesses his inability to form any kind of judgement on the subject. The only thing he ventures to say is that they "have traditions without divinities, ceremonies without worship and superstitions without religion: the homage they pay to the sun and the moon, if it deserves the name of religious worship, is certainly the only one which exists among them."[12]

With respect to the population density of the Sioux nation, he relates the information obtained from the Great Chief Wanatá and gives a list of the bands that compose the Nation and of the tribes which compose the bands. For each of these units, he indicates the name of the chiefs, their territories and their numbers which totalled 44,950 people. Then he continues describing their camps and their daily lives without forgetting even the most trivial detail. He enriches his own observations with the information obtained from the Indians themselves and from Mr. Renville, one of the guides of the Long expedition who was born and raised among the Sioux.

Also the observations on the Chippewas, the Sioux's traditional enemies, take up quite a few pages of the *Pilgrimage*. This is so for two reasons. First, after the Sioux, the Chippewas were the most important Nation of the area, both in numbers and in territory. They were "scattered over those immense regions from Lake Ontario to Lake Winnipeg, near Hudson's bay, a tract of about two thousand miles from east south-east, to north-west."[13] Second, because he had been in closer and more intimate contact with them than any other Indian tribe. During his lonely search for the sources of the Mississippi, his guides had been members of this Nation. He had been received in their tents, had shared their daily lives, and had been allowed to participate in their ceremonies. Just to give an idea on how close he had become to the Chippewas, it would be sufficient to note that they admitted him to their tribal council and asked his counsel on such an important matter as organizing a punitive raid against the Sioux who had killed the chief's son-in-law.

Fortunately, he was wise enough to suggest that the only one who could advise them was their agent at Fort St. Anthony, Major Tagliaferro. In spite of those who wanted immediate revenge, his suggestion was accepted, but this personal involvement in their tribal life nearly cost him his life. Twice he escaped assassination, thanks to the help of Woascita, the beautiful daughter of Cloudy-Weather, the Chippewa chief. Once he saved his own life and the Chief's, only after a strenuous hand-to-hand combat against two drunken Chippewas who had attacked them.[14] This episode marked the end of Beltrami's life in the wilderness. The day after, accompanied by Cloudy-Weather, he started his voyage to return to civilization.

In conclusion, even a cursory reading of the headings in which each letter of the *Pilgrimage* is subdivided shows the wealth of information gathered by this courageous Italian explorer. Nothing escapes his observant and keen eyes, especially for that which concerns the social organization, the daily life, and the culture of the tribes he visited. Everything is taken into consideration: their origins, their social structure, their laws and traditions, their religious beliefs and superstitions, their marriages and their funerals, their dances and their medicine, their warfare tactics and their peaceful pursuits, their sacrifices to appease the world of the spirits and their sacred festivals to thank them, the leisurely life of the summer months and the hard toil of the winter hunt, the prerogatives of warriors and the unhappy conditions of women. In addition he gives us an idea on how limited their scientific knowledge was. For instance, he relates that they divide the year into twelve moons or months. He lists the name of each moon in the Sioux and Chippewa languages and observes that:

> The Indians have no division of the week. They reckon the days only by sleepings. They divide the day into halves and quarters, measuring the time by the course of the sun from its rising to its setting.
>
> Though the Indians are completely ignorant of geography, as well as of every other science, they have a method of denoting by hieroglyphics on the bark of certain papyriferous trees, all the countries with which they are acquainted. These maps want only the degrees of latitude and longitude to be more correct than those of some of our own visionary geographers.[15]

He stresses that the course of the sun directs them by day and the north star by night. When neither are visible, it is the color and the position of the grass, of the tree tops, and of the moss that direct them when they travel. Finally he informs us that their knowledge of arithmetic is so rudimentary that in their languages there is no word for million and billion. Their largest number is one thousand.[16]

Another important source for the study of Indians in the American continent is Beltrami's *Le Méxique,* in two volumes.[17] Written in French the book has never been translated into Italian or English and it may be considered a continuation of the *Pilgrimage.* Like the *Pilgrimage,* it takes the form of thirteen letters addressed to Countess Geronima Compagnoni and it contains observations and impressions of his travels in Mexico. The first letter is dated Tampico, May 28th, 1824; the last one is dated Alvarado, May 24th, 1825. The book includes very interesting descriptions of the people, the geography, the climate, the vegetation of that country. Most important for the historian, it tries to give an accurate picture of the political and moral situation of the Mexican Nation, in the first years of its independence.

The book has a manifest political intention. Beltrami states that he has travelled to Mexico, moved by feelings of admiration for the Mexicans' strength of character, their love for freedom, their art, and their republican institutions.[18] And he concludes with a "good-bye" to the Mexicans expressing his hope that his work has helped to vindicate them from the calumnies with which the enemies of their independence have tried to smear their national character:

> Good-bye also to you, peoples for a long time slaves and always worthy of being free! Good-bye, Mexicans! May I have avenged you of the calumnies of your detractors, frivolous or malicious, by an impartial account of your customs, of your arts, of your new and old institutions! May I have joined to my best wishes and hopes, the expression of some useful truth![19]

As far as the Indians of Mexico are concerned, Beltrami was of the opinion that the history of ancient Mexico, written under Spanish domination, was full of inaccuracies because of ignorance and prejudice.[20] Therefore, he made it a point to look for original documents which could help him rectify them. He found an ancient record consisting of fourteen pictures surrounded by glyphs, painted on specially treated agave leaves, bound together to form a book. According to Beltrami, the fourteen pictures represented and the glyphs narrated the history of the fourteen kings of the Mexican Nation — the Aztecs — who ruled before the conquest. They were made by the Indians under the supervision of father Toribio de Benavente

(Motolinia), in order to save from destruction a record of their ancient history. With the help of other documents researched in the Mexican archives and of the works of Fray Juan de Torquemada,[21] Beltrami tries to interpret these pictures and in so doing he devotes a whole long letter (Letter X) to the writing of a short history of the colonization of the Valley of Mexico by the various Indian peoples who settled there, up to the time of the Spanish conquest. This letter gives an excellent idea of their political organization, their religion, their art, and their traditions. As far as the glyphs are concerned, however, he confesses his ignorance and tells the reader that he leaves the glory of their interpretation to some scholar who has the patience and the talent to do it.[22]

In *Le Méxique* he also mentions the finding of a copy of the *Commentary on the Sunday Epistles and Gospels (Postila sobre las Epistolas y Evangelios Domenicales)* written by Fray Bernardino de Sahagún in Nahuatl and expresses his hope that this finding will greatly improve the understanding of this language and help discover the origin of the people who spoke it.

> . . . to conclude, I want only to notice, with Leibnitz, Vico, and others, that languages are the only monuments of the moral and civil history of primitive people; consequently, it is in the language, especially of the Mexicans [Aztecs], that philosophers may find a guide which may lead them to know, or at least to conjecture, their origins and their migrations. From the origins of the Mexicans will come forth, perhaps, some plausible inductions on the origin of the other American peoples.[23]

With the Louisiana Purchase (1803), the United States acquired an immense territory, still uncharted, inhabited by Indian tribes whose contacts with the white man had been minimal. For what concerns the northern Mississippi-Missouri area, attempts had been made to explore it by William Clark and Meriwether Lewis (1804) and by Lieutenant Zebulon M. Pike (1805). Further attempts were interrupted by the 1812 War, the last war in which Indians allied themselves with a foreign colonial power against the United States. After the war, the exploration of the upper part of the Mississippi River basin resumed with William Cass who explored the wilderness of Minnesota and Wisconsin (1820). The exploration of these territories had been accompanied by efforts to deal with the Indian population who lived in it. In 1815 the United States signed the first treaty with the Sioux; in 1819 Congress, for the first time, appropriated a fund ($10,000) to civilize the Indians; and in 1824 the Bureau of Indian Affairs was established in the War Department of the United States Government.[24]

This interest in the Indians was dictated by practical and moral reasons. Practically, the United States Government aimed to safeguard the settlers, defend the Canadian border, quell intertribal warfare, and protect the Indians from the ruthless practices of the fur traders that caused a state of constant tension between Indians and whites. Morally, the American people, among a lot of controversy on how to solve the Indian problem, aimed to acquire "a more accurate knowledge of their actual condition, and devise the most suitable plan to advance their civilization and happiness."[25] So, together with the foundations of forts, such as Fort Howard at Green Bay, Fort Crawford at Prairie du Chien, Fort St. Anthony at the junction of the Mississippi and Minnesota rivers, to attain its practical goals; the Government of the United States established Indian agents and sent missionaries like Jedidiah Morse to observe and inspect the various Indian tribes, in order to fulfill its moral commitment.[26] This is the historical background in which the *Pilgrimage* should be read and its great contribution to the knowledge of the Indians evaluated.

The very same reasons that made Beltrami's search for the sources of the Mississippi an object of criticism, controversy, and discussion — such as the fact that he did not have with him competent people to chart his exploration, to witness his discovery, and to give its geographical coordinates — helped him collect information about Indians. Because he was alone, he was not considered a threat. Because he was an Italian, namely, one who did not belong to any of the white peoples they knew and mistrusted, he did not arouse their suspicions. Because he was brave, generous, and an excellent marksman, he aroused their admiration. Because he approached them as human beings, he gained their friendship and trust. They called him Tonka-Wasci-cio-honska (the Great Chief from a Far Country) and Kitci-Okiman (the Great Warrior) and they did not hesitate to take him into their confidence.[27] On his part, Beltrami did not betray this confidence and accurately and faithfully reported what he heard and what he saw. He did not have any interest to do otherwise. He did not belong to any of the nationalities or interest groups who, in those territories, were fighting for land, furs, commercial privileges, or souls. Furthermore, and even more remarkable, he did not succumb to the romantic myth of the noble savage. Beltrami sees and describes the North American Indians, objectively, as members of the family of man, with flaws and virtues, and in the context of the history of mankind. Consequently, he constantly reminds the reader of the similarities — in attire, artifacts, customs, ceremonies, religious practices, attitudes — which exist between them and the peoples of ancient and modern times. He is not blind to their shortcomings, but makes us aware that some of these shortcomings are not peculiar to the Indians, indeed they are very common also to the white men.[28] As a matter of fact, when compared with the white traders who cheated them, the Indians are definitely superior. And Beltrami cannot help accusing the white men of having a corrupting influence over the Indians.

. . . the Indians will revenge themselves, but will not descend to the office of accuser. There is great dignity and magnanimity in the silence they observe with regard to the traders, who are not ashamed to cheat them in every possible way. This is one powerful cause of their constant and increasing hostility to civilized people. The Red men, who are most in contact with the whites, are uniformly the worst. The Red women are completely corrupted by their intercourse with the white men. They have all the vices of both races; nor can they find a single virtue to imitate in men who come among them only to sate their sensuality and their avarice.[29]

Neither can he help lamenting the obtuseness of most of the whites who do not recognize how many noble minds are concealed under the rude exterior of the Indians, "notwithstanding the vices which their contact with civilized nations has already planted in their hearts."[30] Of course, this does not mean that he is idealizing the Indian. While he expresses his admiration for the pride, the dignity, the courage, the endurance they display on many occasions, he condemns them for the cunning, unreliability, cruelty they exhibit in others. He is especially critical of their contempt of women. In his opinion, it is this contempt which retards their civilization and increases their ferocity:

. . . The man who feels no moral sensibility, no moral attachment, towards that being whom heaven has destined to participate in our consolations and our difficulties, in our smiles and our best affections; towards the being by whom we are born in pain and reared with extreme tenderness and self-denial, —who enables a man to live again in his posterity, and whose graces, and love, and genuine friendship, constitute the very extract and essence of human happiness—such a man must inevitably be a barbarian or a brute, and his soul dead to every sentiment of virtue.[31]

In conclusion, however, he must confess that even though he has described the Indians and their culture exactly as they appeared to him, he cannot pass judgement on them. They are unique. They present the white observer with so many extreme contradictions that any fair judgement is impossible. In Beltrami's own words:

In their manners, their customs, and their ceremonies, we see traces of the ancients, the moderns, all times, and all nations; but they resemble no other nation in the world. After such a

contrast of sentiments and actions, of propensities and devo-
tions, I leave it to those who can compress everything into a
system, to decide on the character and the religion of the Indians. I hope they will be more fortunate than he who while attempting to catch the moon in a fountain was drowned in it
himself.[32]

Concerning the Mexican Indians, in *Le Méxique,* Beltrami aligned
himself with the Mexican *indigenistas* who tried to rehabilitate the high Indian cultures as a worthy component of the glorious past of the Mexican
nation.[33] In so doing, he followed the footsteps of two other Italians,
Lorenzo Benaducci Boturini and Gian Rinaldo Carli. The former had
demythicized pre-conquest Mexican history by applying Gian Battista
Vico's theories to his *Idea de una nueva historia general de la América
septentrional* (1746).[34] The latter, in his *Delle lettere americane* (1780), had
already defended the Indians of the charges of natural inferiority levelled at
them by the Abbé Corneille de Pauw in his *Recherches philosophique sur
les Américains* (1768).

Like Boturini, even though to a much lesser extent and not as a professional historian, also Beltrami tried to contribute to the knowledge of the
history of ancient Mexico by collecting documents. He offered to the attention of the scholars the codex he had found with the *Commentary on the
Sunday Epistles and Gospels.*[35] He even made it available to the members
of the Academy of Sciences in Paris. In London he showed it to Lord
Kingsborough, a famous expert on Mexican history, so that he could derive
from it any type of information useful to his work.[36] Apparently, nobody
paid attention to it. Nor did the Academy of Sciences pay more attention to
the other ancient manuscript containing the history of the first fourteen
Aztec rulers, Beltrami had sent them.[37] Unfortunately, the originals of
both works were lost. What is left of them is their descriptions in *Le Méxique,*[38] in the *Revue Encyclopédique,* and a copy of the *Commentary,*
printed in Milan in 1856 by the types of Bernardoni, under the title of
Evangelarium, Epistolarium et Lectionarium Axtecum, with glossary and
notes of Bernardo Biondelli.[39]

Like Gian Rinaldo Carli, he defended the intelligence of the Mexican
Indians, by citing the success of the College for Indians in Tlatelolco, under
the wise and benevolent guidance of Fray Bernardino de Sahagún,[40] and
vindicated them from the unwarranted accusation of being malingerers and
lazy. Beltrami's argument was, how is it possible to consider lazy and
slothful a people who built a highly civilized nation and, without the help of
work animals and metallic tools, created a thriving commerce, a flourishing
industry, an intensive agriculture, and exquisite works of art in stone and
precious metals.[41]

From what has been said so far, it is obvious that Beltrami's work should have constituted a valuable source of information on North American ethnology. Unfortunately it was not so, or perhaps it was so, but he was given no credit. For instance, in the studies contained in the *Annual Reports of the Bureau of Ethnology to the Secretary of the Smithsonian Institution* which avail themselves also of information gathered from travellers and explorers like Beltrami, he is mentioned only a few times. Namely, concerning the funeral ceremonies of the Chippewas, in a study of Harry Crécy Yarrow;[42] as regards the socio-political organization of the Sioux, in a study by Garrick Mallery;[43] and with reference to the Indian names of months and rivers, and in respect to the population of the Fox Indians, in a study by Albert Ernest Jenks.[44] In many other studies which deal with the ethnology of the tribes Beltrami had written so much about, he is not even remembered. Of little consolation is the fact that Hubert Howe Bancroft took into consideration also Beltrami's *Le Méxique,* in the writing of his impressive *The Native Races of the Pacific States of North America,*[45] and that the famous German anthropologist Theodor Waitz who knew Beltrami's work on Mexico listed it in the bibliography of his monumental *Anthropologie der Naturvölker.*[46] The fact remains that professional ethnographers nearly completely ignored or were not aware of Beltrami's work. Yet the information it contained is so varied and unique that even in more recent times some literates found it useful. For instance, Professor William J. Peterson, of the University of Iowa, used the *Pilgrimage* as the main source for his article on Minnesota history which describes the momentous voyage of the *Virginia,* the first steamboat to navigate the waters of the upper Mississippi into Indian territory (1823).[47] Professor Allen E. Woodall, of Pittsburgh University, refers to Beltrami to confirm the authenticity of the Indian legends and tales that inspired some of the short stories of William Joseph Snelling.[48] Professor Margaret Murray Gibb, in her important study on the influence of Fenimore Cooper in France, cites Beltrami's *Découverte* (Letter VII) to characterize the *coureurs de bois.*[49]

Naturally, this brings up the topic of the influence Beltrami's works had in the literary field. In a letter he wrote from his villa near Heidelberg, he complained that without giving him any credit, James Fenimore Cooper had used his descriptions of Indian life in his novels.[50] Some of his American biographers state that Cooper acknowledged his debt to him.[51] To the best of my knowledge, however, to this time, there has not been any detailed study of the extent to which the American novelist used Beltrami material, either directly or indirectly. Quite different is the case of René de Chateaubriand. As August P. Miceli, Beltrami's most recent American biographer, puts it: "Chateaubriand paid Beltrami the double compliment of quoting from the *Découverte, etc.,* with and without attribution."[52]

Referring to a study made by a scholar, Ernest Dick, who compared the Chateaubriand and Beltrami books, paragraph by paragraph,[53] the author of *The Man with the Red Umbrella* concludes that of 180 pages of the *Voyage en Amérique,* Chateaubriand borrowed almost 59 pages from Beltrami's *La Découverte* and gave him credit only for a little more than 2.[54]

> The appropriation from Beltrami covers a considerable part of the *Voyage,* particularly the sections on animals (castors, bears, deer, buffaloes, reptiles), Indian customs (marriages, children, funerals, dances, hunting, war, calendars, medicine, language, religion), Indian tribes (the Natchez, Hurons, Iroquois, and other Indians of North America), and the itinerary along the Ohio and Mississippi.[55]

Nor was Chateaubriand's borrowing limited to his *Voyage en Amérique,* also the *Mémoires d'Outre-Tombe* and his novel *Le Natchez* contain pages and passages borrowed from Beltrami, without any credit given.[56]

At this point, one question arises: Why only literates took into consideration the writings of this intelligent, cultured, and versatile man, while ethnographers nearly completely ignored them, in spite of the wealth of ethnographical information they contained? Perhaps because literates found in them excellent material suitable for further creative elaboration, while scholars considered them unreliable and amateurish. After all, Beltrami did not really belong to their community. Perhaps because the "experts" concentrated their attention and their criticism mainly on the geographical aspect of Beltrami's work, since his claim to fame rested principally on the exploration and discovery of the sources of the Mississippi. Very likely, however, the reason — or one of the reasons — may be that when the State of Minnesota in 1868 officially recognized the worth of his work as an explorer, by naming after him its largest county and an island, in a sense, it was too late to fully appreciate his contribution to ethnography. His observations and considerations on the Indians, disregarded up to that point, had lost their originality and had been superseded by the works of subsequent travellers and ethnologists. Furthermore, by that time, his books had become very scarce, especially in Italy, where Austria had ordered their sequestration, so very few people were able to verify and give him credit for the work he had done.[57]

In 1898, Albert E. Jenks, speaking of the Siouan names for September and October, in his study on the wild-rice gatherers, observed that "as early as 1828 Beltrami cited the names of these two months."[58] While Mr. Jenk's recognition is to be commended, Beltrami's work certainly deserves more credit than a mere acknowledgment. A careful reading of the articles which appeared, up to 1900, in the *Annual Reports of the Bureau of American Ethnology,* especially those dealing with the Sioux and the Chippewas, reveals that Beltrami had already said as early as 1828, much more about Indians than the mere names of the months in Siouan. He had described and had tried to explain Indian cultures going back to their very origin. Some of his statements may seem obvious today; but their proper evaluation should take into due consideration some of the "fashionable" theories of his times. Then, just as important as the theory that the Indians had come from Asia through the Strait of Bering, was the theory that they were the survivors of the mythical Atlantis. Others saw in them the descendants of one of the Lost Tribes of Israel. The matter of their origin and of their civilization became even more complicated when the Mayan ruins of Yucatan and Guatemala began to astonish the world. Some ventured the theory that these ruins had been the center from where all civilization had moved westward to China, Egypt, Greece, and Rome. For instance, in 1807, Guillermo Dupaix, the pioneer Mayan archeologist maintained that the Maya Indians had come from Atlantis or from some other land to the East of it. The scholarly Brasseur de Bourbourg, translator into French of the *Popul-Vuh* (1861), the Mayan epic, also held the theory of Atlantis to be true.[59] The Viscount of Kingsborough lost his money and his freedom in publishing the nine volumes of the *Antiquities of Mexico* (1831-1848) with the sole purpose of proving that the American Indians were the descendants of one of the Lost Tribes of Israel.[60] So, when Beltrami states that the Indians came from Asia through the Strait of Bering[61] and gives his reasons for this statement, he is doing much more than repeating a possible and known theory. He is making a considerate choice among equally important and, at the time, probable alternatives.

Similarly, when he correctly states that the mounds of St. Louis were the work of American Indians, he runs against the wild speculations of some of his contemporaries who considered them to be the work of a mythical super-race which supposedly flourished before the Indians came; or of the survivors of the sunken, and yet ever present, Atlantis; or, as others ventured, the work of Egyptians and Phoenicians wandering far from home. It took the magistral work of the American archeologist Ephraim George Squier, *Ancient Monuments of the Mississippi Valley,* published in 1848, to silence these fantasies. Incidentally, Squier is the same archeologist that in the Royal Library of Paris, in the autumn of 1855 found another copy of Sahagún's *Commentary on the Sunday Epistles and Gospels,* apparently similar to the one Beltrami had brought from Mexico and uselessly put at the disposal of the Academy of Sciences of Paris for examination, as early as 1830.[62]

In conclusion, Beltrami's *Pilgrimage* and *Le Méxique* are much more than simple narrations of things seen, heard, and done during a trip of exotic exploration. They contain more than enough ethnographic data to list them among the first works of ethnography written on the American Indians.

Notes

1. Of these the most important are: Vertova Camozzi, *Costantino Beltrami da Bergamo-Notize e lettere pubblicate per cura del Municipio di Bergamo e dedicate alla Società Storica del Minnesota* (Bergamo: Pagnoncelli, 1854). Eugenia Masi, *Giacomo Costantino Beltrami e le sue esplorazioni in America* (Firenze: Tipografia di G. Barbera, 1902). Augusto P. Miceli, *The Man with the Red Umbrella: Giacomo Costantino Beltrami in America* (Baton Rouge, Louisiana: Claitor's Publishing Division, 1974).
2. All information relative to Beltrami's life in the United States has been derived from his: *A Pilgrimage in America, Leading to the Discovery of the Sources of the Mississippi and Bloody River; with a Description of the Whole Course of the Former, and of the Ohio* (Chicago: Quadrangle Books, Inc., 1962. This is a copy of the first edition in English, published in London in 1828). We shall refer to this book as *Pilgrimage*. For the chronology of the events, however, the author of this study has relied on A.P. Miceli's *The Man with the Red Umbrella*. . .
3. *Pilgrimage*, p. 199.
4. *Pilgrimage*, p. 200.
5. *Pilgrimage*, p. 302.
6. *Pilgrimage*, p. 350.
7. *Pilgrimage*, p. 357.
8. See note 2. Before the English version of his travels, Beltrami had published another, more reduced, account of his travels in French: *La Découverte des Sources du Mississippi et de la Rivière Sanglante: Description du Cours du Mississippi, etc.* (New Orleans, Impr. par Benj. Levy, 1824). We shall refer to this book as *Découverte*.
9. *Pilgrimage*, p. 236.
10. *Pilgrimage*, p. 209-210.
11. *Pilgrimage*, p. 211.
12. *Pilgrimage*, p. 212.
13. *Pilgrimage*, p. 227.
14. *Pilgrimage*, p. 449.
15. *Pilgrimage*, p. 275.
16. *Pilgrimage*, p. 276.
17. Giacomo Costantino Beltrami, *Le Méxique*, 2 Vols. (Paris: Crevot, 1830).
18. *Le Méxique*, I, pp. ix-x.
19. *Le Méxique*, II, p. 369. Translation by the author.
20. *Le Méxique*, II, p. 88-89.
21. *Le Méxique*, II, p. 88.

22. *Le Méxique,* II, pp. 87-88.
23. *Le Méxique,* II, pp. 176-177.
24. Harold E. Driver, *Indians of North America,* 2nd Ed. (Chicago and London: The University of Chicago Press, 1975), p. 482.
25. Jedidiah Morse, *A Report to the Secretary of War of The United States on Indian Affairs, by Jedidiah Morse* (New York: A.M. Kelley, 1970), p. 11. Originally printed in New Haven in 1822.
26. To solve the Indian problem, Mr. Morse, in his *Report,* advocated missionary action, intermarriage, and education, especially for Indian women (pp. 74-75). Beltrami, as a commentary to Morse's *Report,* suggests that before any missionary action is undertaken the Indians should be fed, first, and foremost (*Pilgrimage,* pp. 471-472).
27. To the point of confessing to him that they often amuse themselves by "gulling the credulity" of white traders with imaginary tales about Indian life (*Pilgrimage,* p. 418).
28. *Pilgrimage,* p. 189.
29. *Pilgrimage,* p. 224.
30. *Pilgrimage,* p. 30.
31. *Pilgrimage,* p. 245-246.
32. *Pilgrimage,* p. 299.
33. For example: Fray Benito María de Moxó, Servando Teresa de Mier, Carlos María de Bustamante, to cite only a few who were Beltrami's contemporaries.
34. Benjamin Keen, *The Aztec Image in Western Thought* (New Brunswick, N.J.: Rutgers University Press, 1971), p. 234.
35. Beltrami's letter to the President of the Academy of Sciences of Paris, dated April 25, 1830 (from *Costantino Beltrami da Bergamo . . .* , pp. 100-102).
36. *Le Méxique,* II, p. 88.
37. Beltrami's letter to the President of the Academy of Sciences of Paris, dated May 10, 1830 (from *Costantino Beltrami da Bergamo . . .* , pp. 103-104).
38. *Le Méxique,* II, p. 175.
39. *Costantino Beltrami da Bergamo . . .* , p. 35.
40. *Le Méxique,* II, p. 120.
41. *Le Méxique,* I, pp. 227-8.
42. "A Further Contribution to the Study of the Mortuary Customs of the North American Indians" in *First Annual Report of the Bureau of Ethnology to the Secretary of the Smithsonian Institution 1879-1880* (Washington: Government Printing Press), pp. 190-191, 197.
43. "Pictographs of the North American Indians — A Preliminary Paper by Garrick Mallory" in *Fourth Annual Report . . .* (1882-1883), pp. 104-105.
44. "The Wild-Rice Gatherers of the Upper Lakes" in *Nineteenth Annual Report . . .* (1897-98), Part 2, pp. 1051, 1090, 1121, 1122.
45. "Notizie di G.C. Beltrami sugli Indigeni Americani." in *Atti del XXII Congresso degli Americanisti* (Roma, 1926), p. 695.

46. *Anthropologie der Naturvölker—Die Amerikaner, Ernste Hälfte, Dritter Theil* (Leipzig: Friedrich Fleischer, 182) p. xx.
47. "The 'Virginia,' the 'Clermont' of the Upper Mississippi." *Minnesota History,* 9, (Dec. 1928), 347-362.
48. "William Joseph Snelling and the Early North West." *Minnesota History,* 10 (Dec. 1929), 367-385.
49. *Le Roman de Bas-de-Cuir, Etude sur Fenimore Cooper et Son Influence en France* (Paris: Librarie Ancienne Honoré Champion, 1927), p. 198.
50. Masi, *Giacomo Costantino Beltrami . . .* , p. 49.
51. Giovanni Schiavo, *The Italians In America Before the Civil War* (New York-Chicago: The Vigo Press, 1934), p. 97.
52. Miceli, *The Man with the Red Umbrella,* p. 133.
53. Ernest Dick, *Plagiats de Chateaubriand, le Voyage en Amérique* (Berne, 1905), pp. 5-53.
54. Miceli, *The Man with the Red Umbrella,* pp. 134-135.
55. Miceli, *The Man with the Red Umbrella,* p. 136.
56. Ernest Dick, "Quelques Sources Ignorées du 'Voyage en Amérique' de Chateaubriand." *Revue d'Histoire Littéraire de la France,* XIII (1906), 228-245.
57. Masi, "Notizie di G.C. Beltrami . . . , " p. 692.
58. "The Wild-Rice Gatherers," p. 1090.
59. Robert L. Brunhouse, *In Search of the Maya* (New York: Ballantine Books, 1976), pp. 28, 127.
60. Victor W. Von Hagen, *The Aztec, Man and Tribe* (New York: Mentor Books, 1961), p. 207, note 48.
61. *Pilgrimage,* pp. 258-259.
62. *Costantino Beltrami da Bergamo . . .* , pp. 34-35.

1827 MAP OF BELTRAMI'S EXPLORATION AREA

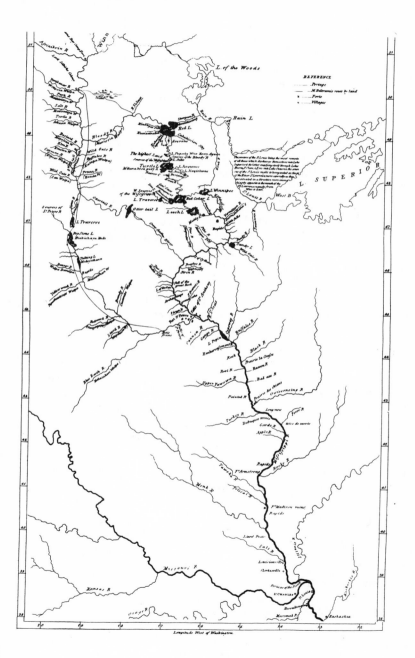

Chapter 2

FRANCIS BARRETTO SPINOLA, NINETEENTH CENTURY PATRIOT AND POLITICIAN

Salvatore John LaGumina
Nassau Community College

Francis Barretto Spinola stands in a dominant position in the history of Italian-American politics. The first of his heritage to be elected to Congress and possibly the first to be elected to the New York Assembly and the New York State Senate, he was also one of the very few generals of Italian descent to serve in the Civil War.

Although born in the United States, Spinola may well serve as an exemplar of the nineteenth century Italian expatriate in America — one driven into exile because of the vicissitudes of political and social currents of the post-Napoleonic Italy of the early nineteenth century. His mother was American-born and of Irish descent, while on his father's side the background was resolutely Italian. It was said that his grandfather was a descendent of a venerable Genoese family who removed from that city to the island of Madera where Francis' father was born.[1] Sometime early in the nineteenth century and probably because he chose to go into exile in the wake of the Napoleonic upheavals impacting the Italian peninsula, Francis' father migrated to the United States, settling in Stony Brook, Long Island.[2] The motivation for that location is unknown but it is recorded that he married the daughter of an officer who had fought as a captain under George Washington during the American Revolution.

Clearly this is not the background of the typical Italian immigrant. Indeed there were hardly any Italians in the United States at the time. When the first United States Census was taken in 1820 only 30 Italians were listed as immigrants in the entire nation. Furthermore, there could be only very few Italians living on Long Island outside of the descendants of Pietro Cesare Alberti who had emigrated to the island in 1639. Finally the Spinola story is different from that of other exiles who tended to settle in the larger cities.

Given the paucity of Italians in the region it is not surprising to learn that Francis' father married a non-Italian. This provided for Francis a grandfather who served in the cause of the American Revolution, a heritage which made a lifelong impression on Francis, who never forgot the sacrifices made by his grandfather's generation and never tired of calling for appropriate monuments in their behalf.

22

Although precise verification is lacking it appears that Francis' father settled down to a life of farming in Stony Brook, Long Island, a village in the town of Brookhaven, in Suffolk County. That part of Long Island was predominantly rural and agriculture was the major pursuit of the day. It was in that community that Francis was born in 1821. His elementary education consisted of attendance in the public school system of the village until he was ten years old. He then was sent to the Quaker Academy located near Poughkeepsie, New York where he remained until he was fifteen. Although his formal education was not extensive, he possessed sufficient knowledge for a variety of business and political undertakings which lay ahead. The period away from home apparently caused him to conclude that he would not return to his Long Island home, preferring instead to try his luck in the burgeoning city of Broklyn to the west thereby joining a growing exodus of young people who were leaving the farms of mid-nineteenth century America for the big cities.[3]

As a young man of sixteen he tried his hand at a number of occupations, being apprenticed for a few years as a jeweler, then taking up blacksmithing, and working also as a grocer and a carpenter. He also received an appointment as a clerk to the Brooklyn Common Council, that city's governing body.

By his early twenties Spinola had become strongly attracted to the political whirligig of his day — a trait which would mark the rest of his life. Appropriately he became a lawyer and was admitted to the bar in 1844. At the age of twenty-two he was elected alderman and served in Brooklyn's Common Council for five years. Later he was elected to the Board of Supervisors for Kings County, a post he held for a few years. He also received appointment as harbor master.

At the outset of his career Spinola was a Whig, the political party which emerged to challenge the Democratic Party in the 1830's. In part it stood in opposition to the influence of "King Andrew" (Andrew Jackson, the powerful Democratic president) and in part it wrapped itself in a name that was bound up with the triumph of the Revolution and therefore synonomous with "patriotism".[4] Spinola's party affiliation was in sharp contrast to that of his Brooklyn political birthplace which was a Democratic stronghold. Nevertheless, his popularity was such that it sufficed for him to win his first election, but was not quite strong enough for him to succeed in his second political contest which he lost by one vote. At this juncture in his career Spinola became a Democrat and remained a staunch, loyal regular party member to the end. Indeed he acquired a reputation as a dedicated supporter of Tammany Hall, a posture which earned him frequent reprobation from "good government" advocates such as the New York *Press* which highlighted this attachment in his obituary, "General Spinola has for many years been a devotee at the shrine of Tammany Hall."[5] Likewise the New

York *Times* repeatedly lashed out at him as one growing "gray in the practice of political corruption of the smallest and meanest kind..."[6] because of this coziness with the Tammany organization.

Firehouse politics was a unique phenomenon of nineteenth century urban America. To obtain a position in the municipal fire department was the driving ambition of many a newly-arrived resident who harbored aspirations for political activity. The firehouse political model established in New York City provided many examples of upward mobility from the ranks of the fire department to the arena of larger political life. In the 1890's for example, Alfred E. Smith, Tammany stalwarth and future Governor of New York as well as Democratic presidential candidate, became deeply involved in matters within the local firehouse. This was to serve him as an important backdrop to the business of government. As one of his biographers put it:

> Like many other lads too, Al loved to lounge about the firehouse on John Street, where politics was the staple of conversation. The members of the company talked endlessly of the exploits of the leaders. The question of who controlled the government was vital to the welfare of men whose very jobs depended upon the answer.[7]

Spinola likewise became active in Brooklyn firehouse activities as a young man and it is interesting to note that Hugh McLoughlin, legendary Brooklyn political leader of the era, was a leader in the local firehouse. Spinola became so attached to these activities that he adopted the shirt worn by the firemen as his own trademark, changing only the color from red to white. Almost as an eccentric, he wore this type of high shirt collar for the rest of his career, and became widely known as "Shirt collar Spinola."

Having enjoyed a number of years of political success in local level government in 1855 Spinola strove for success on a state level gaining election as assemblyman and a few years later a state senator. In 1860 he was designated a delegate to the Democratic National Convention in Charleston which selected Stephen Douglas as its presidential candidate for 1860, but which also split as Southern Democrats broke off and nominated their own candidate. At the time he represented a number of wards located in the Brooklyn towns of Flatbush, Flatlands, Gravesend, New Lots and New Utrecht, inhabited primarily by poor German and Irish immigrants.[8]

Like all Americans Francis Spinola was affected by the firing at Fort Sumpter in April 1861, an action which marked the outbreak of the Civil War, the cataclysm which was to last for four long years. Few leaders from either the North or the South possessed a clear inkling as to what lay ahead. That the North did not expect a protracted conflict is evident in Lincoln's call for 75,000 troops for a three month duration. During the early part of the conflict when there was total dependence on voluntarism, the role of the large states, especially New York, would be critical to the success of the Union's mobilization plan. The alacrity with which Italians in America, along with citizens of foreign birth from other countries, responded, was indeed remarkable. From the outset of the call for volunteers, their zeal for the northern cause was manifest. *L'Eco d' Italia,* the Italian paper in New York City, issued a call for the organization of an Italian Legion. In addition, a military outfit called the Garibaldi Guard was organized.[9]

There is no evidence that Spinola was involved with either of these ventures, nor that he was a collaborator among the Italians in New York City then issuing calls for induction into these units. Perhaps his absence from these ventures was due to his immersion in Brooklyn events, and it must be remembered that at that time Brooklyn was a separate city from New York. In any event Spinola was not wanting in loyalty. He may, in fact, be credited with a principle role in convincing New York to endorse the Union cause. A member of the state Senate and a dedicated Democrat who was instrumental in nominating Douglas against Lincoln, and highly critical of Lincoln, Spinola, nevertheless, put aside partisan considerations and demonstrated a patriotism which served as estimable example to others.

New York Governor Morgan, heeding Lincoln's April 15 call for men, sent a message to the New York State Legislature asking for immediate enactment of measures to enable the state to fill her quota of the call for troops. The bill enrolling such enlistees passed the Assembly and was sent to the Senate which met in an extraordinary evening session. Because New York was expected to supply more than one-sixth of all the Union troops great interest was felt in the chamber when the bill reached the floor and Senator Spinola rose to speak. What was in the offering was the first act of the Legislature which would express the sentiments of the Empire State respecting vigorous prosecution of the war. Known as a strong party leader stubbornly opposed to the Republican administration, Spinola's refusal to support the enlistment measure could well reflect the sentiment of the masses in the great cities. Although still critical of the Republicans, the Brooklyn senator steadfastly upheld the Union cause, casting aside party labels.

> War in any shape is a calamity, but more so when it assumes the shape of arraying brother against brother; this is not a time for bandying words. War is upon us. The American flag for the first time has been torn down, and it remains for us to say whether it shall be allowed to trail or again wave in triumph. The Republicans, by failing to agree upon a fair compromise, have brought this war upon us, but now that it is here the

> Democrats are ready to fight the battles and fight as long as necessary. I believe that unless the request that has come from Washington is promptly responded to, the President and his cabinet will not occupy their positions on the Fourth of July. From this time on you will not hear me say anything about "my party" but hereafter it will be "my country."[10]

Spinola then dramatically took the Stars and Stripes from his desk and waved it in the chamber. "This is my flag which I will follow and defend."

Senator Spinola's words and action became the catalyst for a rallying of the masses in support of the Federal Administration. Although some allowance must be made for exaggeration and hyperbole given at eulogies, it is still of some merit to weigh the words of a Spinola colleague with respect to his actions in the New York Senate.

> These words of Senator Spinola, more than the utterances of any other man in the Senate, gave assurance that the masses in the great cities were devoted to the Union and ready to enlist for its defense. With a wisdom and foresight possessed by few he urged the raising of large levies and the making of prompt vigorous preparations for active hostilities.[11]

Spinola's contribution was not limited to exalted oratory as he took it as his function to acquaint the citizens of the growing community of Brooklyn of the grave situation. Informing Brooklyn residents that he ceased being a legislator in this crisis, he was, as were other Americans, asking for support for the cause of the Union and proceeded to raise levies of men in its behalf. By the summer of 1862, Spinola joined with other Brooklyn leaders to discuss quotas for enlistments which had been set by the government. He became active in rallies endorsing the war effort, becoming Grand Marshal of a major effort in February 1862.[12] Finally, with the permission of the New York Governor, in June 1862, he enlisted four regiments of troops from his city into what became known as the "Spinola Empire Brigade." He was assigned to the unit for a time and soon appointed Brigadier General. In making the appointment, President Lincoln honored Spinola "for meritorious conduct in recruiting and organizing a brigade of four regiments and accompanying them to the field."[13]

His early military career did not proceed without trouble, however. On August 24, 1862, the Empire Brigade, then stationed in the East New York Section of Brooklyn, became engaged in a riot over non-payment of bonuses promised them. Hundreds of men in a great state of excitement, broke away from their barracks, wrecked a hotel opposite them, and then scattered. When apprised of the situation, Spinola, who was at a public meeting at City Hall at the time, quickly set about corralling his forces.[14]

This incident served as the background for his appearance before a Court Martial in 1864. A superior general had submitted charges of "misconduct unbecoming an officer and a gentleman and of negligence of duty."[15] Specifically there were accusations of allowing persons to receive money from the recruits, unlawfully depriving them of their bonuses and enlisting men while under intoxication. Some sessions of the trial were held and Spinola prepared a vigorous defense of his conduct charging that the court's composition was improper and that he was being denied his constitutional rights in that he was being tried by his accusor. The military superiors, who apparently mis-judged their man, even tried to censor the proceedings, but eventually withdrew the charges.[16]

Spinola's military activity during the war was truly remarkable. A man of civil pursuits, without military education or experience in the field, he entered upon the duties pertaining to high military rank at the age of 42 and acquitted himself in active hostilities to win the respect of professional military officers, thereby furnishing strong evidence of his ability to command.

It was on July 23, 1863, at Wapping Heights, Virginia, that General Spinola showed his mettle while engaged in operations of the Third Army Corps. He was assigned to march his Excelsior Brigade across a ravine, a difficult undertaking since the heights were held by well-entrenched rebel troops. Unless the enemy could be extricated the advances of the Union Army would be hampered. Since continued fire-power failed to dislodge the enemy, Gen. Spinola, after studying the advanced maps of the position, hit upon a courageous policy of leading his brigade in a direct bayonet charge. Realizing that such a move would result in tremendous casualties, he, nevertheless, determined that it must be done to insure passage and movement of troops. With the launching of the attack there ensued one of the fiercest battles of the area. As one of his commanding officers described it:

> General Spinola, Commanding Second Brigade, Second Division, formed his troops in a ravine in front of the enemy position, and charged them in magnificent style, drove them from the field in confusion, the major-general commanding the corps, witnessing the whole operation. In this charge General Spinola was twice wounded.[17]

Indeed General French, Commander of the Third Army, was generous in his praise of Spinola.

> The brigade was at once deployed at the base of the knoll and advanced upon the enemy. Halting for a moment upon the crest of the hill, the line rushed upon the enemy with the bayonet

giving cheer after cheer and driving them back in confusion out of the gap. Nothing could be more brilliant than the conduct of the officers and men in this affair, evincing fighting qualities of the highest order.[18]

It should be pointed out that the rebels, which included brigades of Georgian and North Carolina sharpshooters, outnumbered Spinola's forces at least six to one. In addition, the enemy possesed numerous artillery pieces while the Union forces had none. The two wounds sustained by Spinola were very severe, one in the right foot tore open the heel, and the other passed through the fleshy part of the right side.[19] These wounds would cause him physical hardship for the rest of his life.

Following his discharge from the Army at the conclusion of the war in 1865, Spinola returned to New York where he became involved in a number of business enterprises which brought him considerable prosperity. Thus activities in insurance companies and banking firms together with real estate enabled him to amass a million dollar estate by the time of his death. He and his wife seemed to enjoy their position as part of the post-Civil War nouveau riche. They owned extensive property on Long Island in addition to their city residence, and even commissioned a well-known painter of the day, William S. Mount, to paint their portrait.[20]

The monetarily rewarding business undertakings, did not, however, satisfy the garrulous Spinola temperament which once again sought to move into the vortex of partisan politics. Having now re-located to New York City, he developed formidable and lasting ties with the Tammany political organization, becoming an important factor in the Democratic politics of the city and beyond. His oratorical abilities rendered him a popular figure who was in constant demand for party activities. In 1876 he became a candidate for elective office winning a seat as state assemblyman for the 16th A.D. He was re-elected to the position many times relinquishing it in 1886 when he ran for the United States Congress. During his assembly tenure he became conspicuous for his role in public issues. The heavily partisan nature of city politics earned him, however, an opprobrium usually reserved for rascals. Undoubtedly much of the criticism which was levelled against him was due to his close association with Tammany Hall Boss Tweed, who in the 1870's stood as the archetype of the worst kind of machine politician. Anyone with intimate links with Tweed was bound to share in the criticism and Spinola was conspicuous in this regard.

In March 1877 Spinola was the central figure in the excitement which swirled in Albany for several days after his caustic remarks in attacking a colleague. He was accused of harrassment for its own sake. "Spinola is the rough and ready jester of the House, with his mission to have fun with the boys."[21]

Two weeks later continued acrimonious debate in which he was the main figure, brought him to the brink of a political eclipse. His brutal tirade against the Assembly Speaker proved so intemperate and obnoxious that charges of citation for contempt were raised. Indeed a rumor that he was on the brink of contempt caused such a commotion that many people flocked to the Assembly to witness the outcome. The House galleries were jammed in anticipation; but the uproar was of such a volume that he was compelled to retract his statements and the contempt resolution was set aside.[22]

In 1878 Spinola once again became the object of censure because of a purported conflict of interest charge involving a business venture in which he joined other associates to form a company which put forth a proposal before the New York City Public Works Commission to lay pipes in the city streets for the purpose of supplying steam. Despite the general's assertion that adoption of his plan would save the city $50,000.00 per year, his critics remained unmoved. They saw the scheme as one designed to enrich him and his associates.[23] Accordingly they bewailed the failure to acknowledge any impropriety on his part. The criticism notwithstanding, Spinola and his associates were successful in obtaining the job from the Tammany-controlled city government.

Frustrated by its efforts to expose Spinola and thereby impede his steam-heating venture, the New York *Times,* unlike the rest of the city press, emphasized the legislator's problems with the Assembly. In February 1881, it devoted major front page coverage to his behavior in that body accusing him of being an obstructionist who savagely impugned the motives of his colleagues. At one point he attacked an assembly opponent in the following bullying tones: "The point of order comes from a good source—from my good friend from New York, who represents all the thieves and prostitutes of that city on the floor of this house." This display of injudicious language elicited the dismay of numerous colleagues and once again there surfaced the possibility of contempt citation, followed by his retraction of statements.[24]

By the mid 1880's the New York *Times* was predicting the demise of Spinola's political career. It highlighted a rumor that Tammany Hall was prepared to part with the old warrior. "In short, there is a combination against the old warrior, and a combination which bids fair to become strong enough to knock him out of his leadership...." It stated furthermore, that Spinola had lost his patronage power and consequently would be out of office. "The leaders are, however, after General Spinola's scalp."[25] The prediction that Spinola's political demise was imminent was premature, however. Although he did not return to the State Assembly he won a seat to the 10th Congressional District, better-known as the "Gas House" district, thus becoming the first man of Italian background to achieve such high honor. Anti-Tammany sources lamented the outcome, in one case assailing him for his anti-civil service reform position. Interestingly enough when he ran for re-election for the Congressional seat in 1888, even his critics were prepared grudgingly to concede that he was not altogether a negative force. "Spinola of the Tenth belongs to a low type of politician and is not above using corruption and indirect means to attain his ends, but he has made a decent record in Congress."[26]

The veteran politician did indeed make himself felt in the halls of Congress on a number of issues. One of the most creditable services he performed was in connection with legislation designed to revive the American Merchant marine. Accordingly he was one of the few Democratic congressmen who voted for the Farquhar bill which became law. He was also an important factor in preventing the passage of an inflationary measure, with one source going so far as to credit him with being the single most important opponent of the measure. He worked zealously to line up votes, including some that had originally been pledged to the bill, to vote against it. "Had it not been for him it is quite possible that the Bland Free Coinage rider to the Sundry Civil bill would have passed the House."[27] He also spoke out strongly in behalf of the rights of American free labor.

But the area of his most dedicated interest while in Congress was his repeated and spirited efforts to gain a memorial in recognition of veterans of the American Revolution who had been imprisoned in British prison ships and whose remains had been gathered for interment in Wallabout Bay, Brooklyn. Undoubtedly he was deeply impressed with the role of his forefather, his mother's father who had served as an officer under Washington. As a youngster he recalled the annual celebrations of the veterans of the Revolution. As one of his Congressional colleagues recalled it:

> Although very young at the time, he was one of the procession that marched with uncovered heads, bearing upon their shoulders the remains of the victims of the British prison ships from their temporary resting place to their final entombment at Ft. Greene, in Brooklyn.[28]

The great ambition of his life then, was to secure a fitting monument to the memory of these heroes of the hulk ships. He offered more bills in their behalf than any other congressman had ever presented. Although his efforts did not succeed, his activity in this regard is noteworthy because it above all demonstrates a patriotism which was acknowledged by friend and foe alike. Congressman Cummins expressed well this patriotism in the florid but picturesque language of nineteenth century orators. He did it moreover, by linking his patriotism to his Italian heritage.

> ...I know Francis B. Spinola for thirty years. He once told me of Italian lineage...It was an Italian who gave the Old World a

New World. It was an Italian who brought countless worlds within our view.

I know not from what particular family our friend sprang, but there were traces of Rienzi, Masaniello, Savanarola, and of the Montagues and Capulets in his composition. Even Macchiavelli had left his mark. One characteristic, however, was prominent. The Italian loved Italy as the land of his birth. Spinola loved America with an Italian devotion. Her flag was as precious to him as the *fleur de lis* to a Bourbon or the cloak of the Prophet to a Mohammedan. He drank from a perennial spring of Patriotism. It was the spirit of his fathers in the Revolution.[29]

Spinola's pride in his Italian roots, nevertheless, had its limitations. Throughout his political career Italian immigration was very modest and did not become a major phenomenon until the last years of his life, especially while he was in Congress. These were the beginning years of mass immigration which would bring millions of Italians to these shores. Despite his unabashed feeling for his Italian ancestry, he could not really be considered an Italian-American politician in the sense of reflecting the aspirations of a distinct minority striving to obtain a position of importance and prestige. While he did express sympathy with newcomers to this country, this was offset by his failure to attribute priority to the matter of alleviating problems besetting Italian immigrants. For example, although he was a member of a special House Committee on Immigration then conducting an investigation concerning immigration problems in New York City (undoubtely many of them were Italians), he declined to attend the committee sessions.[30] His explanation that he had even more important duties to attend to in Washington would be an unthinkable confession for one who would lay claim to championing the interests of Italians in America.

This limitation notwithstanding, the Italian-American press hailed him as an outstanding representative of the Italian people in the United States. *Cristoforo Colombo* cited him as "one of the most honored Italian names abroad."[31] *Il Progresso Italo-Americano,* stated:

> But one gift more serious and more noble attributed to us Italians, is that, during a valorous and distinguished career in the army and in politics, he did not repudiate nor deny that Italian heritage which he admitted in private and in public.[32]

Il Progresso Italo-Americano was not blinded in its evaluation of the man, thus even while it hailed him as an outstanding citizen of Italian roots, it also acknowledged that in his public career he was wont to do what he pleased regardless of the abrasiveness with which he affected others.

The English language newspapers duly noted his death — simultaneously remembering his foibles as well as his strengths. Perhaps the *Brooklyn Eagle* summarized it best.

> In the death of General Francis B. Spinola a familiar and picturesque figure is removed. General Spinola was neither scholar nor statesman, but he occupied, nevertheless, a conspicuous place in the sphere of public observation. Critical analysis of his character would show that he was not without the demagogic traits usually essential to success in what goes by the name of "practical politics".... Greatly to his credit was his service to the Union Army. No citizen of the republic responded more promptly to Mr. Lincoln's call for troops than General Spinola. If his speeches and general behavior were sometimes demagogic there remains throughout the compensating truth that he was faithful to the flag and courageous in its defense and vindication.[33]

Of Spinola's religious inclinations there is very little information regarding his early years except that there was no reference to the Catholic Church but that he was associated with a Quaker school. One of his close associates gave a glimpse of his religious interests by stressing a private inner self.

> Of his religious views he rarely spoke, and then only with his most intimate friends. He preferred to exhibit the principles of his creed in his practice instead of proclaiming his sentiments from the housetop. They were too sacred for the coarse ribaldry of the vulgar scoffer.
>
> But those who lived nearest to his heart and were permitted to look in upon the secret chamber of his inner life found there not only the pleasing longing after immortality which filled the soul of the ancient philosopher, but the most serious and childlike faith in the full realization that heaven sent hope through the priceless promises of the gospel.[34]

What is known for certain is that by the end of his life he had converted to Catholicism largely through his Catholic wife and the teaching of a New York City priest. His funeral service was held at the city's Immaculate Conception Church.

Francis B. Spinola was then, a man with a long and distinguished career. He was not without fault — indeed, depending on particular political persuasion, he might have been considered a negative force in the body politic. Undoubtedly he had his weaknesses which were deplorable. He was after all, human; but outbalancing them by far were his strong points: his commitment and dedication to government and especially his sense of patriotism. For the Italian-American public interested in gleaning insight into the generation of nineteenth century Italians in America who made a special impact on their adopted land, the Spinola story is truly remarkable. Although technically not an expatriate, although his father may have been, he, nevertheless, identified strongly with his ethnic roots and made a memorable contribution on the American scene. His lasting work which should continue to be celebrated was his unqualified and unsullied patriotism. It was of such a nature that it should have served to negate any future notion regarding the loyalty of Italian-Americans. It was with that thought in mind the *Il Progresso Italo-Americano* devoted three articles to his life story over three separate weeks in 1940.[35] Spinola's career stands as a testimony to love and devotion to the United States which deserves the commendation of all Americans.

Notes

1. Cristoforo Colombo; April 15, 1891.
2. For purposes of clarification it should be noted that nineteenth century Long Island was located east of New York City and encompassed the counties of Brooklyn, Queens and Suffolk. Brooklyn was a separate municipality which, along with Queens, was merged into New York City in 1899. Currently the designation Long Island is usually a reference to Nassau and Suffolk Counties.
    It is not known for certain the year that Francis' father emigrated to New York, however, there is a reference to a John Spenola in the *New York 1810 Census,* p. 297.
3. New York *Times,* April 14, 1891.
4. Dixon Ryan Fox, *The Decline of Aristocracy in the Politics of New York, 1801-1840,* (Harper & Row, New York, 1965), p. 367.
5. *The Weekly Press,* (New York) April 15, 1891.
6. New York *Times,* November 6, 1876.
7. Oscar Handlin, *Al Smith and His America,* (Little, Brown & Co., Boston, 1958), p. 18.
8. New York Legislative Manual, 1859, 1860. See also Richard DeMayo, *Hugh McLoughlin, Political Leader of Brooklyn 1870-1903,* (Master's Thesis, St. John's University, 1976), p. 43.
9. Howard R. Marraro, "Lincoln's Italian Volunteers From New York," *New York History,* (Vol. XXIV, January 1963, No. 1), pp. 56-7.
10. *Congressional Record,* 52nd Cong., 1st sess. Vol. 23, p. 2588.
11. *Congressional Record,* 52nd Cong., 1st sess. Vol. 23, p. 2588.
12. Henry R. Stiles, *History of the City of Brooklyn,* (Brooklyn, 1869), Vol. 2, p. 449.

13. Frederick Phisterer, *New York in the War of the Rebellion, 1861 to 1865,* (J.B. Lyon, Co., Albany, 1912), p. 726.
14. New York *Times,* April 14, 1891.
15. New York *Times,* August 2, 1864.
16. New York *Times,* August 20, 1864.
17. *Congressional Record,* 52nd Cong., 1st sess., Vol. 23, p. 2589.
18. *Congressional Record,* 52nd Cong., 1st sess., Vol. 23, p. 2589.
19. New York *Times,* July 28, 1863.
20. For information on Spinola's business activity see, *The Evening Post,* April 14, 1891. For his land-holdings on Long Island see *Suffolk County Deeds,* Liber 119, p. 416 and Liber 242, p. 204. See *Receipt* from William S. Mount, to the Spinolas, dated May 27, 1867, for a portrait of the husband and wife. Housed in the New York Historical Society.
21. New York *Times*, March 1, 1877.
22. New York *Times*, March 16, 1877.
23. New York *Times*, July 24, 1878, August 1, 1878, August 4, 1878, September 18, 1878 and June 18, 1878.
24. New York *Times,* February 11, 1881.
25. New York *Times,* July 25, 1886.
26. New York *Times,* October 9, 1888.
27. *The Weekly Press,* April 15, 1891.
28. *Congressional Record,* 52nd Cong., 1st sess., Vol. 23, p. 2593.
29. *Congressional Record,* 52nd Cong., 1st sess., Vol. 23, p. 2590.
30. *Congressional Record,* 50th Cong., 2nd sess., Vol. 20, pp. 999-1000.
31. *Cristoforo Colombo,* April 15, 1891.
32. *Il Progresso Italo-Americano,* April 15, 1891.
33. *Brooklyn Eagle,* April 15, 1891.
34. *Congressional Record,* 52nd Cong., 1st sess., Vol. 23, p. 2591.
35. *Il Progresso Italo-Americano,* June 23, 1940, June 30, 1940, July 7, 1940, for coverage of Spinola's career, highlighted by this Italian American newspaper. It must be remembered that Generoso Pope, the publisher, was trying to overcome allegations that his paper was pro-fascist.

Chapter 3 ITALIAN EXPATRIATES AND
THE AMERICAN CIVIL WAR

Remigio U. Pane
Rutgers University

The Italian *Risorgimento,* which began in the early 1800's and culminated with the Unification of Italy in 1870, forced many patriots to become expatriates or exiles in many European countries and America.

We know very little about the first group who arrived in New York between the years 1811 and 1819 in addition to what Lorenzo Da Ponte tells us "a swarm of exiles arrived at New York without means or profession and, unfortunately for themselves, without abilities. They exchanged their rifles and bayonets for dictionaries and grammars and set about teaching languages."[1]

As the revolutionary movements spread throughout the peninsula the number of expatriates arriving in the United States grew to reach over two hundred in the twenty-year period 1836-1856.[2]

Some of these exiles, like Garibaldi, returned to Italy as soon as conditions permitted it. Others became American citizens and remained here permanently. Both groups were respectable people with university degrees and experience in politics, military affairs and business and were welcomed with sincere admiration and goodwill by the public and private sectors in America, and it is to the credit of both the exiles and Americans that an atmosphere favorable to Italian Independence was created which resulted in American moral and financial support of the movement.

The *Risorgimento* fighters admired America for having led the way in achieving independence and appreciated its Democracy and its welcome to all exiles.

Garibaldi himself expressed best this Italian feeling toward America in a letter he wrote President Lincoln, shortly after his Emancipation Delcaration, where he states in part "If in the middle of your titanic struggle our voice may still reach you, oh Lincoln, allow us, free sons of Columbus, to send you a word of good wishes and admiration for the great work begun by you, the heir of Christ and Brown...America, the teacher of freedom to our fathers, opens once more the most solemn era of human progress." The letter, dated August 6, 1863 is signed by Giuseppe Garibaldi and his two sons Manlio and Ricciotti.[3]

Many veterans of the *Risorgimento,* since Italy had become united under the House of Savoy in 1861, came to enlist in the Union Army. In

35

this paper I will deal with the participation in the American Civil War by four of the Italians who remained in the United States and became citizens: Colonel Louis W. Tinelli, Doctors Tullio and Ciro Verdi, and General Luigi Palma di Cesnola.

Luigi Tinelli (1799-1873) was born of a noble Milanese family at Laveno, on the shore of Lake Maggiore in Lombardy. He had just received his university law degree when he joined the Piedmontese revolutionaires in their 1821 uprising. Their defeat resulted in Tinelli's exile first in Genoa and later in Switzerland, England and Spain for a total of seven years.

When conditions permitted it Tinelli returned to his home in Laveno and married Anna Zannini, whose father was a general in Napoleon's army and had died in the Russian campaign of 1912.

Tinelli now dedicated himself to industry, first in the manufacturing of silk and in 1830 he was one of the founders of GINRAD, a firm created for the manufacture of lombard porcelains. In 1833 he bought out his partners and became the sole owner and director of the firm. With his great artistic ability and vast energy he created the famous artistic ceramic and porcelain factory of San Cristoforo in Milan.[4]

Like a number of his contemporaries, Tinelli represented well the two leading initiatives of his time: politics and industry, for while he was designing his famous artistic ceramics he was also plotting for the liberation of Italy from the Austrians. He joined Mazzini's *Giovine Italia* and became its leader for his region, spending large sums of money for the purchase and distribution of revolutionary literature and arms among the people of the valleys and mountains around the lake to prepare them for the fight for independence. Both his house at Laveno and his factory at Milano were used for secret meetings to discuss the ideas of the *Giovine Italia* and the news which Tinelli received directly from Mazzini.[5] Tinelli's wife Nina was also an ardent patriot and a leader of the women conspirators who met regularly in her house.[6]

On August 3, 1833 Tinelli was arrested by the Austrian police for treason and imprisoned in Milan. In February 1835 Emperor Francis I signed Tinelli's death sentence three days before dying. His son Ferdinand, who succeeded him to the throne, issued an amnesty for the political prisoners changing the death sentence to twenty years of prison or perpetual exile in America. Tinelli chose the latter but was kept in prison until the summer of 1936 before he, together with a number of illustrious patriots from the infamous Spielberg prison, were deported to New York aboard the Austrian Imperial Brig *Ussero,* which had sailed from Trieste on August 6, 1836 and landed in New York on October 20.[7]

The New York Times commented on the arrival of the illustrious exiles and gave information concerning the background and abilities of each. In the case of Tinelli it mentioned his success as an agriculturist and a manufacturer who had contributed to the well-being of his region and *The Times* hoped that he would introduce the silk industry in a large scale in the United States.[8]

Tinelli lived up to his reputation and proceeded at once to plant mulberry groves in Weehauken, N.J. across the Hudson and then he built spinning mills and weaving plants so that he established a complete silk manufacturing complex in Weehauken. In 1837 he published a pamphlet with the title: *Hints on the Cultivation of the Mulberry with some General Observations on the Production of Silk*. He succeeded so well that in 1840 the Institute of American Industry awarded him its Gold Medal for his achievement in the manufacture of silk. Meanwhile he had also established an import-export business in New York with the title "Luigi Tinelli e C. Agents, Commissioners et Importeurs à New York".

Two other important recognitions came to Tinelli in 1840: the Governor of New York appointed him Lieutenant Colonel in the 43rd Regiment, and the Federal Government appointed him U.S. Consul General in Oporto, Portugal. He accepted the latter and by 1841 he was in Oporto where he was an effective and diligent American representative while he established a silk manufacturing industry there also and renewed with vigor his relations with the Italian liberation movement and its leaders. With the passing of time he, like Garibaldi, came to the conclusion that the unification of Italy could only be accomplished with the Royal House of Savoy and corresponded with the King, Charles Albert who, after the defeat of his armies at Novara abdicated in favor of his son Victor Emmanuel II, and went into exile at Oporto, Portugal on March 29, 1849. Tinelli was in the party that went to meet the king before entering the city, and later visited him daily. The king died four months later and Tinelli was one of the witnesses signing the death certificate. Is it possible that the king had chosen Oporto because Tinelli was there?

In spite of his political activities on behalf of the Italian Unification Tinelli did not neglect his duties as a U.S. consul as evidenced by a letter he wrote in 1849 to United States Senator D. L. Yuleb telling him of the latest Portuguese methods of protecting crops from insect damage and also of a new variety of olive tree "recently introduced in France, Spain and Portugal, which yields an abundant crop of fruit the second year after plant and suggests to the senator that his variety be introduced in the States, and volunteers to ship "well rooted plants which can be bo 18 to 22 cents each," and to emphasize the importance of reminds the senator "I am proud of being one of the first to United States the culture of Silk."[9]

In 1850 Tinelli resigned his position as Consul York to open a law office and continue his import active in politics first as a Free Soil Democrat and

1852 he started to publish a periodical which he called *European Mercury,* but it did not last long.

When Tinelli was exiled, his wife had gotten permission to follow her husband with their two sons, but she refused, then and later, to join her husband. After several years Tinelli remarried in New York and had five children.[10]

When the Civil War broke out Tinelli entered the Union Army with the rank of Lieutenant Colonel of the famous Garibaldi Guard Regiment. He saw action in Virginia, Caroline, Florida and Louisiana and was still in action at the final battles leading to Appomatox. Ill health caused Tinelli to leave the Army before the end of the war, but his two sons who had volunteered with him served until the end of the war. Giuseppe Tinelli had the rank of Acting Master and Franco Tinelli was a Second Lieutenant.

The elder Tinelli resumed his law practice in New York and participated in a number of important trials. He continued to follow Italy's vicissitudes with great interest and in 1870 was the main speaker at a New York celebration of the final unification of Italy with the taking of Rome. He died in 1873 and was buried in the Evergreen Cemetery in Brooklyn.

Tinelli was truly a remarkable citizen of two countries contributing a great deal to both and I hope that some research will be done to evaluate fully his many contributions to the United States, and also on his descendants. I discovered that his son Frank published a book of "Pointers" to commercial travellers,[11] which may be an indication that he followed in his father's footsteps in business.

The best known Italian exile involved in the Civil War was Luigi Palma di Cesnola (1832-1904) winner of the Congressional Medal of Honor, renown archeologist, and first Director (1879-1904) of the Metropolitan Museum of Art in New York.

Son of a noble Piedmontese army officer, he followed in his father's footsteps and at the age of 15 enlisted in the Sardinian Army. At the age of 17, fighting at the battle of Novara in 1849 as corporal, he distinguished himself and won a field commission as a Second Lieutenant and a silver medal for bravery.[12]

He later graduated from the Royal Military Academy and fought in the Crimean War (1853-56). After the war he travelled in the Middle East until 1858 when he sailed directly from Turkey to New York.[13]

Little is known of Cesnola's life in New York during the years 1858 and 59 except that he tried to earn a living unsuccessfully as a translator and a composer. He was so discouraged that he attempted suicide by ingesting a large quantity of laudanum.[14] He survived, however, and things improved.

Cesnola began to give Italian and French lessons to well-to-do women. A year later one of his students, the thirty-year old

Mary Reid, daughter of a U.S. Navy captain recently deceased, fell in love with Cesnola and in June 1861 they were married against the wishes of the socialite family of the bride who considered the poor immigrant Cesnola below their social status.

As the Civil War had broken out two months before his wedding Cesnola now opened a private military academy in the Hotel St. Germaine on the then fashionable corner of Broadway and 22nd street.[15] A sign stretched across the facade of the building announced the school to the public in cubic letters SCUOLA DI GUERRA DEL CONTE LUIGI PALMA DI CESNOLA, CAPITANO NELL'ESERCITO ITALIANO (WAR SCHOOL OF COUNT LUIGI PALMA DI CESNOLA, CAP-TAIN IN THE ITALIAN ARMY).[16] Veteran Cesnola taught his students the rudiments of infantry, artillery, and cavalry warfare. The latter mounted on barrels fastened on wooden frames in the absence of real horses.[17] Within six months Cesnola graduated 700 future officers and his success gained him the commission of Lieutenant Colonel in the 11th New York Cavalry Regiment when he volunteered in the Union Army.

Cesnola became a hero to his soldiers and a problem to his superiors and within four months he resigned and, accused of insubordination, was put in jail. Shortly thereafter as the result of letters by Cesnola's soldiers to the Union Commander and Cesnola's own letter to General George B. Mc-Clellan, Cesnola was released from prison and appointed commander of the Fourth Regiment of New York State's Voluntary Cavalry, which he eventually made one of the finest regiments of cavalry in the Civil War.[18] But he first had to recruit his men and he opened two offices in New York: one paid for by the State and one at his own expenses.

By November 1862 Cesnola had gained a very good reputation as a cavalry officer and had been given three other cavalry regiments to command. Later he was put in command of a brigade of five regiments and was on his way to become a brigadier general, but on February 2, 1863 Cesnola was dishonorably discharged from the Union Army by Secretary of War Stanton because he had shipped six Remington pistols to his wife in New York and this was considered a theft of Union property. Cesnola maintained the guns were property of the State of New York and he had sent them for use by the guards at his induction center in Staten Island. He even possessed a receipt for the pistols from the New York State Arsenal, as he stated in a letter to Stanton.[19] Since his ability as a cavalry commander was never disputed it seems that the discharge was perhaps caused by Cesnola's lack of tact with some of his superiors.

True to his family crest motto *Oppressa Resurgit* (Oppressed, he rises again), on March 3, 1863, Cesnola was reinstated as a full colonel in command of his won Fourth New York Cavalry regiment and participated ' the Union victory over the Confederate Cavalry at Brandy Station in Virg'

Cesnola and his men fought with distinction at the battles of Chantilly, Berryville, and at Aldie, where on June 17, angered by the promotion over him of a junior officer, Cesnola complained so vehemently that he was placed under arrest and his sword was removed from him.[20]

His regiment galloped to its first charge without him but was repulsed and his men refused to return to the attack without him. Cesnola, rather than see the regiment dishonored, disregarding his arrest, jumped, unarmed, on his horse and led his men in four valiant, bloody but unsuccessful assaults against the Confederate cannon fire. The Union cavalry commander, Brigadier General L. G. Estes, who was present, was so impressed by Cesnola's gallant action that, when the regiment returned to camp, Estes gave Cesnola his own sword, released him from arrest and urged him to try again. Cesnola led his fifth charge during which his horse was shot dead under him and he himself received a bullet wound in his left arm and a saber cut in his head. He lay pinned under his horse in the battle field until the victorious Confederate troops picked him up and transferred him to Libby Prison in Richmond where 1200 Union officers were crowded into six rooms.[21]

Cesnola was no docile prisoner. He complained constantly about the treatment of the Union enlisted men and according to an Italian newspaperman in New York, Alfredo Bosi, in November 1863 Cesnola, although still remaining prisoner, was appointed by Confederate General Dowe to oversee the distribution of food to his fellow prisoners and as a keeper of the commissary at Belle Isle, where there were kept 18,000 Union prisoners. This position gave Cesnola the opportunity to observe conditions at the prison camp and at Libby and as a result of his inside information he was able to hatch a plan of escape for the entire officers contingent from Libby. He tried to communicate this plan to President Lincoln and Secretary of War Stanton through his friend and fellow Italian expatriate Tullio Verdi, an M.D. who was Secretary of State Seward's private physician.[22]

Meanwhile Mary Reid Cesnola pulled strings in Washington and the men of his New York Regiment made a special petition and on May 21, 1864 Cesnola was freed in a prisoners' exchange and returned to fight in the war until the term of his regiment was up. He returned to civilian life on September 4, 1864 a thirty-two-year-old cavalry veteran whose lack of political skill and humility had cost him a general's star and a lot of heartaches.

With nothing to do, and worried about the future, he joined the thousands of office seekers swarming around the White House after Lincoln's reelection.

Cesnola was received by President Lincoln on April 12, 1865, two days before his assassination, and according to Cesnola, the President, in the presence of New York Senator Ira Harris, awarded him the brevet rank of

Brigadier General and approved Cesnola's request to be appointed U.S. Consul somewhere in Europe.[23]

Some twenty days later Cesnola was received by Secretary of State Seward who appointed him Consul to Cyprus. Accordingly on August 16, 1865 Cesnola became a United States citizen in New York and on September 25 he sailed together with his wife and infant daughter, arriving in Cyprus on Christmas day of 1865,[24] unsuspecting that his eleven-year residence in Larnaca was to make him one of the most successful archeologists of his time.

Cyprus was a primitive island ruled by the Turks with little to do for diplomatic representatives except in moments of tension between the Turks and the Greeks. But this was the time of the archeological fever and the chief of the British mission to Cyprus was the leading archeologist on the island. With time on his hands, Cesnola began at once to devote his prodigious energies to the study of the ancient history of Cyprus and, learning the then current methods of excavating antiquities, soon he began to dig seriously with native workmen. His results were gratifying and the numbers of his diggers grew like an army. The archeological objects he collected attracted interest in Europe and in America and in 1873 the New York Metropolitan Museum of Art bought for $60,000 its first Cesnola collection consisting of over 6000 pieces. They were mainly sculptures, terra cottas, glass, and other ancient objects and the museum to house them had to move to larger quarters on West 14th Street.

General Cesnola came from Cyprus to supervise the installation and returned to Cyprus with a contract from the Metropolitan to continue his excavations at the Museum's expenses, but the panic of 1873 and the lowered income of the Museum caused it to cancel the contract and Cesnola continued the excavations at his own expense.

In 1876 the Metropolitan acquired a second Cesnola collection of over ten thousand items of antiquity and again he came in 1877 to supervise the unpacking, cataloguing and displaying.

The trustees were so impressed by Cesnola's efficiency that they offered him the job of secretary of the Board of Directors. A job he accepted happily because Mrs. Cesnola was anxious to return to New York.

During his eleven years in Cyprus the General had identified the sites of 16 ancient cities, 65 necropolises and other sites, and had excavated 15 temples and 60,932 tombs and collected a total of 35,373 objects.[25]

His work as secretary was so efficient that in 1879 when the Metropolitan Museum of Art moved to its present site on Fifth Avenue at 82nd Street he was appointed Director with an annual salary of a little less than $1000 per year!

The Cesnolas bought a four-story brownstone on 57th Street and the General began a tenure at the Metropolitan which lasted a quarter of a century, during which four wings were added to the museum and it became a world-class institution.

In 1879 Princeton University awarded Cesnola a Doctor of Laws degree *Honoris Causa* and Columbia University awarded him another. He also received 13 medals and knightly orders from various governments.

One of Cesnola's best deeds for the Museum was his cultivation of the New Jersey locomotives manufacturer Jacob S. Rogers from Patterson who became a yearly member of the Museum and each year delivered his ten-dollar annual dues check personally to Cesnola asking him many questions about the Museum. In 1901 Rogers died and left the Metropolitan Museum his estate which brought the Museum five million dollars net. This was a tremendous endowment fund. J. Edwards Clark, U.S. Secretary of the Interior wrote to Cesnola: "It is an event of which the whole United States are to be congratulated for it gives pecuniary independence to the chief art power of the country."[26]

While the General's professional life was often the center of controversy, his personal life was tranquil and warm. Mrs. Cesnola or the Countess Cesnola, as she was called (her husband had given up his title but she liked it) delighted in entertaining her friends and the Museum's wealthy sponsors at their elegant brownstone. In later years she spent much of her time at the family's 76-acre estate at Mount Kisco, which, with the help of eight servants, she made the center of family life and devoted herself to Catholic Charities, helping Mother Cabrini to found *Cristoforo Colombo Hospital* and the Italian orphan asylum, *West Park* at Peekskill, N.Y.

In 1897 the Congress of the United States awarded General Cesnola the Congressional Medal of Honor for his heroism at Aldie and at Malvern Hill 34 years earlier. As we say in Italian *è meglio tardi che mai* (it is better late than never).

On December 3, 1904 at the age of 72 Cesnola died and his funeral at St. Patrick's Cathedral brought together for a rare hour the leaders of the Italian community and such mighty figures as the Morgans and the Vanderbilts. Archbishop Farley officiated and J.P. Morgan led the honorary pallbearers. A chorus of little Italian orphans from *West Park* sang during the Requiem Mass.

And thus the career of this most remarkable Italian expatriate immigrant who had started so inauspiciously with an attempted suicide and progressed through three brilliant phases: military, diplomatic-archeological, and cultural-administrative ended in a blaze of glory, more brilliantly shining because it had triumphed over myriads of impediments both natural and artificial. Just three months before he died the *Arena* magazine for September 1904 speaking of the Metropolitan Museum had stated: "New York, therefore, had its solid rise in the founding of the noble institution, and in the determined character and genius of General L.P. di Cesnola almost from the beginning. Not until the Cyprus collection arrived was there any strong artistic impulse in the greatest city in America. They formed the nucleus around which one of the greatest art institutions of the civilized world has been formed".[27] Cesnola himself had published a three-volume catalogue of the entire Cesnola Collection at the Museum.[28] The *Union Catalog* of the Library of Congress lists some 25 publications under Cesnola's name.

Cesnola's brother, Alessandro also served as U.S. Vice Consul in Cyprus and conducted archeological excavations for the British Government in Paphos and Salamis in Cyprus.

An unwritten but important chapter in the history of Italy and the United States in the 19th century is one dealing with the Italian expatriates who had spent their early lives fighting for the liberation of their country from Austrian domination and, as the Unification of Italy was finally achieved in 1861, the American Civil War broke out and they volunteered in Lincoln's army to fight for the liberation of the slaves and the preservation of the Union.

I have already mentioned two outstanding examples of these citizen-soldiers of the two countries and will conclude with a brief summary of the vicissitudes of three brothers: Tullio, Ciro, and Teodoro de Suzzara-Verdi.

The ancient and noble family of Carlo de Suzzara-Verdi lived in Mantua, Lombardy, which was under Austrian domination, but Carlo and his five sons were strong supporters of the House of Savoy and his country estate became the headquarters for anti-Austrian activities. Two of his sons, Tullio and Teodoro enrolled in the Sardinian Army and fought in the first war of liberation with Carlo Alberto in 1848-49. The defeat of the Sardinian army placed the young Verdi brothers in danger of imprisonment by the Austrians as traitors and they avoided this by escaping just as the Austrian police was encircling their palace. Both were condemned to exile, but they had arrived in New York in 1850.

All we know of Teodoro Verdi is that he remained in the United States eight years, returned to Italy, was married, and named his first child America.

A third and younger brother, Ciro (1834-1887) preferred exile to serving in the Austrian army and joined his brothers in New York in 1852. He studied medicine and graduated as an M.D. in 1860 from the New York Fourteenth Street College. During the Civil War he served as assistant surgeon, second lieutenant in the 101st New York Volunteers Infantry and afterwards as surgeon at the Norfolk Hospital under General Butler. "After the War he was Professor and Dean of the Faculty of the Cleveland College and Hospital for Women. He was author of *Progressive Medicine* and a regular contributor to the several medical magazines."[29]

The *City Directory* of New Brunswick, N.J. from 1874 through 1880 lists Dr. Ciro Verdi as practicing surgery there, and the U.S. Census for 1880 confirms his residence at the corner of George and Oliver Streets there.

In 1879 he married Caroline Minturn, daughter of William H. Minturn, one of New York's leading families. In 1881 the Verdis went to Italy and their daughter Bina was born there on February 6, 1881. Shortly after they returned to the United States and resided in Washington, D.C. until 1886 when they again went to Italy. They bought a residence in Florence and on August 2, 1887 their son was born and they named him Ciro Luigi. But later that year Dr. Ciro Verdi died and his widow returned to America the following spring and lived in New York at 142 East 37th Street, where she was still living on July 1, 1918.

Ciro Luigi, with his name changed to Minturn de Suzzara Verdi, became a lawyer and practiced law until 1957 in New York City.[30] His son, John Minturn Verdi born in New York City in 1928 retired from the USMC in 1970 after a brilliant career having reached the rank of Colonel. He now lives in California.

Tullio de Suzzara Verdi (1829-1902) simplified his name to Tullio Suzzara Verdi. He arrived in New York in 1850 with one *lira* and 75 *centesimi* and letters from Mazzini to Felice Foresti and Garibaldi, who promptly got him a job with a painter who was decorating the Bowery Theatre and Verdi's job was to paint walls and ceilings perched on a stepladder. Shortly his feet became swollen and he could no longer paint and he was sorry to lose his five dollars a week salary, but Foresti and Garibaldi got him another job with a store that sold pumps. The owner did not speak Italian and Verdi did not speak English so there was no communication and Verdi spent his time studying English grammar. But soon Foresti called with the wonderful news that he had gotten him a job as teaching assistant for French and Italian at Brown University where George Washington Greene was teaching Italian.[31]

After one happy year at Brown Verdi went to Philadelphia where he enrolled at Hannemann Medical College and received the M.D. degree in 1856. He was the first Italian immigrant to do so. In 1857 he moved to Washington, D.C. and practiced medicine there. In 1860 he married the daughter of a prominent Pittsburgh family and this introduced him to Washington Society and Verdi became the physician of many social and political leaders. His most famous patient was William H. Seward, the Secretary of State in Lincoln's cabinet.

Dr. Verdi became one of the best known physicians of his time. In 1871 President Ulysses S. Grant appointed him a member of the Board of Health of the District of Columbia, of which in 1876 he was elected president.[32] In 1873 he was sent to Europe as Sanitary Commissioner to inspect hospitals in the principal cities.[33] In 1879 he was appointed by President Rutherford B. Hayes as a member of the National Board of Health. He was the founder of the National Homeopathic Hospital of Washington.

Dr. Verdi wrote a number of medical books that had a very wide circulation. His *Maternity: A Popular Treatise for Young Wives and Mothers* went through seven editions between 1870 and 1880.[34] This was followed by *Mothers and Daughters: Practical Studies for the Conservation of the Health of Girls* in 1876.[35] He also published a witty satire on the prevalent way of raising children entitled *The Infant Philosopher; Stray Leaves from a Baby's Journal.*[36] His last medical book was *Verdi's Special Diagnosis and Homeopathic Treatment of Disease for Popular Use.*[37]

Dr. Verdi's last book *Vita Americana* (Life in America) is the most interesting for our purpose because it is a 300-page essay on American life and manners of the second half of the nineteenth century, which he wrote in English, but was translated in Italian and published in Italy in 1894.[38] The first three chapters are a brief account of his arrival in New York with only one *lira* and 75 *centesimi* and two letters from Mazzini to Felice Foresti and Giuseppe Garibaldi, and his experiences in New York City and Providence, R.I. The next 27 chapters deal with all phases of American life. Chapter 31 is dedicated to a brief account of the Civil War, and Chapter 32, the last, is a firsthand account of the attempted assassination of Secretary of State William H. Seward by Lewis Payne while John Wilkes Booth was assassinating Lincoln.

At the time of the assassination Secretary Seward was confined to bed, recovering, under Dr. Verdi's care, from a carriage accident. The assassin, in order to gain entrance in Seward's house, claimed that he was a messenger sent by Dr. Verdi with a special medicine to administer to the Secretary. Once inside Payne wounded seriously not only Seward, but two of his sons, his secretary, and a military guard stationed there. Dr. Verdi was called immediately to minister to the wounded and his narrative of that infamous night is very gripping. Another version of the events was written by Seward's daughter Fanny in her *diary* and it corroborates Dr. Verdi's story.[39] The story of the use of Dr. Verdi's name by the assassin to gain entrance to the Seward's home is told by Jim Bishop in his *The Day Lincoln Was Shot.*[40]

While Dr. Verdi became completely americanized and participated fully in American life and politics, he did not lose his *Italianità,* and kept in touch with events in Italy and with his fellow exiles in America. I suspect he may have been responsible for Palma di Cesnola's appointment as consul to Cyprus by Secretary Seward. And when *Il Progresso Italo Americano* and *L'Eco d'Italia* decided to exhume Maroncelli's remains and send them to his native town, it was Dr. Verdi who at his own expenses took them to Italy, sailing on July 24, 1886 on the *S.S. Archimede* of the Italian Line and delivering them personally to Forlì.[41]

King Umbert I of Italy awarded Verdi the title of Cavaliere with the citation "As an American citizen who on countless occasions has shown zeal, activity and disinterested interest in the highest degree to the advantage and glory of the Italian name in America."[42]

Tullio Suzzara Verdi died on November 26, 1902 in Milan, Italy, where he had gone hoping to restore his health.[43]

Notes

1. *Memoirs of Lorenzo Da Ponte. Translated by Elisabeth Abbott from the Italian. Edited and Annotated by Arthur Livingston.* Philadelphia: Lippincott, 1929, pp. 420-21.
2. Schiavo, Giovanni. *The Italians in America Before the Civil War.* New York-Chicago: The Vigo Press, 1934, p. 212.
3. Quoted by Schiavo in his *Four Centuries of Italian American History.* 5th Ed., New York: The Vigo Press, 1958, p. 317.
4. Castelli, Giuseppe. *Figure del Rinascimento Lombardo: Luigi Tinelli. Da Mazzini a Carlo Alberto.* Milano: Ceschina, 1949, p. 48.
5. *Ibid.,* p. 49.
6. *Ibid.,* p. 51.
7. *Atti del I Congresso Internazionale di Storia Americana.* Genova: Tilgher, 1978, p. 285.
8. Castelli, *op. cit.,* p. 88.
9. "Reports and Letters Relating to Crops" in *Report of the Commissioner of Patents for the Year 1849. Part II Agriculture.* Washington: Office of Printers of the Senate, 1850, pp. 461-62. I am indebted to my colleague Dr. Peter Wacker of the Geography Department of Rutgers University in New Brunswick, N.J. for finding this letter.
10. Castelli, *op. cit.,* p. 170.
11. Tinelli, Frank B. *Pointers to Commercial Travellers: or, How to Become a Successful Salesman; Interspersed With a Few Reminiscences, Experiences and Witticisms.* South Norwalk, Conn.: The Schumann Art Print, 1906.
12. McFadden, Elizabeth. *The Glitter and the Gold: A Spirited Account of the Metropolitan Museum of Art's First Director, the Audacious and High-Handed Luigi Palma di Cesnola.* New York: Dial Press, 1971, p. 7.
13. Amfitheatrof, Eric. *The Children of Columbus.* Boston: Little Brown, 1973, p. 110.
14. McFadden, *op. cit.,* p. 14.
15. Tomkins, Calvin. *Merchants and Masterpieces. The Story of the Metropolitan Museum of Art.* New York: Dutton, 1970; Paperback 1973, p. 50.
16. Bosi, Alfredo. *Cinquant'anni di vita italiana in America.* New York: Bagnasco Press, 1921, p. 90.
17. Tomkins, *op. cit.,* p. 50.
18. Amfitheatrof, *op. cit.,* p. 112.
19. McFadden, *op. cit.,* p. 43.
20. Tomkins, *op. cit.,* p. 50.
21. *Ibid.,* p. 49.

22. Bosi, *op. cit.*, pp. 92-93. I have not been able to find any reference to this story in any other source.

23. McFadden, *op. cit.*, p. 76.

24. On the way, General Cesnola, as he now called himself, had stopped for a triumphal visit to his native Rivarolo Canavese, Province of Turin, and a reception by King Victor Emmanuel II at the Royal Palace in Turin which included the presentation of a gold medal.

25. For a full account of his activities in Cyprus see: *Cyprus: Its Ancient Cities, Tombs, and Temples. A Narrative of Researches and Excavations during Ten Years' Residence in That Island.* By General Louis Palma di Cesnola. New York: Harpers and Brothers, 1878.

26. Tomkins, *op. cit.*, p. 90.

27. Quoted by Schiavo in his *Four Centuries of Italian American History,* p. 236.

28. *A Descriptive Atlas of the Cesnola Collection of Cypriote Antiquities in the Metropolitan Museum of Art, New York.* By Louis P. di Cesnola. Boston: J.R. Osgood and Company, 1885-1903. 3 volumes.

29. *[In Memoriam] Ciro Virgilio Giovanni de Suzzara Verdi.* Privately printed pamphlet kindly furnished to the author by Ciro Verdi's grandson, Colonel John Minturn Verdi.

30. About the name change, his son told me in a letter of 8-13-82 that his grandmother had changed the name from Ciro Luigi to her maiden name Minturn because "this camouflage was thought useful by the good lady during that time of our national history when all Italians of whatever degree were called 'Wops' and other similar epithets".

31. G.W. Greene had been U.S. Consul in Rome from 1837 to 1845 and had married an Italian. He taught Italian at Brown from 1848 to 1852.

32. Upon his appointment to the Board he wrote its *Code of the Board of Health of the District of Columbia, 1871.* Washington: Chronicle Publishing Co., 1872.

33. *Dr. T.S. Verdi's Report as Special Sanitary Commissioner to European Cities.* Washington: Gibson Brothers Printers, 1873.

34. New York: J.B. Ford, 1870; Fifth edition, New York: Ford, 1873; New York: Boericke & Tafel, 1879; New York: Ford, Howard & Hulbert, 1880.

35. New York: J.B. Ford, 1876; reprint 1877; new edition 1878.

36. New York: Ford, Howard & Hulbert, 1886.

37. Philadelphia: Boericke & Tafel, 1893; reprint 1895.

38. Verdi, Tullio Suzzara. *Vita americana; versione dall'inglese di Edoardo Arbib.* Milano: Hoepli, 1894.

39. "I Have Supped Full Horrors" *American Heritage,* October 1959, pp. 60-65; 96-101.

40. New York: Harper and Bros., 1955, p. 193.

41. Bosi, *op. cit.,* p. 68.

42. Cambridge *Tribune,* March 31, 1894.

43. Schiavo, *Four Centuries Of Italian American History.* p. 293.

PART II

Giuseppe Garibaldi In America

Chapter **4**   GIUSEPPE GARIBALDI:
ITALIAN PATRIOT WITH AN
INTERNATIONAL VISION
Frank J. Coppa
St. John's University, N.Y.

Giuseppe Garibaldi, along with Cavour and Mazzini, was one of the makers of modern Italy. Cavour has been described as the brains of unification, Mazzini the soul, and Garibaldi the sword. Of these three, Garibaldi was always the most popular and remains so on the centenary of his death. He alone, among the *Risorgimento* figures who brought about the resurection of Italy, had a wide personal following and attracted almost fanatical devotion not only in Italy but abroad. Alessandro Manzoni in Italy and Alexandre Dumas in France sang his praises, President Lincoln offered him a command in the Civil War against the South, and Kossuth of Hungary looked to Garibaldi for inspiration. Streets and squares have been named in his honor from Boston to Bologna.

One of the foremost guerrilla fighters of all times, Garibaldi championed protest movements all over Europe and the Americas. Convinced that tyranny led to the corruption of humanity he lent his support to the cause of liberty worldwide.[1] Small wonder that kings and rulers feared him, politicians sought to discredit or use him, while the lower classes hailed him as one of their own. Although dedicated to his country whose cause he championed with valor, he was at the same time a convinced internationalist and among the first to call for a united Europe. Garibaldi's part in the liberation and the unification of Italy has been studied and restudied, his role as an internationalist is less well known. It is upon the latter that I shall focus here.

From the first Garibaldi was open to outside influences and forces. Born in Nice on July 4, 1807, when the city was controlled by France, he came into the world a French citizen and would remain one until the city was returned to the Kingdom of Sardinia following the Congress of Vienna. As a child he spoke the provencal of Nice, with French his second language. Like Cavour his Italian accent was less than perfect.[2] During the twelve years he lived in South America as an exile he learned Spanish. Born in a humble home near the harbor wall in Nice, he was early drawn to the sea and longed to join his father Domenico, a sailor whose merchant ship traded along the Ligurian coast. Finally in 1824 he was allowed to sail to Odessa on the Costanza, which flew the Russian flag.[3]

49

Before he acquired his certificate as a merchant captain in 1832, Garibaldi served as a sailor in the Mediterranean and Black Seas. He relates that during a journey to Taganrog in the Black Sea he was initiated into the national movement by another Ligurian sailor, Giovanni Battista Cuneo.[4] On another crossing he encountered a group of Saint Simonians who were on their way to Constantinople. These men introduced Garibaldi to the thought of this utopian socialist about whom he had known nothing before. "The essentially cosmopolitan outlook of such people," he later confessed in his memoirs, "showed me the one sidedness of my national feeling and lifted my eyes beyond mere patriotism and toward the larger cause of humanity."[5] The words of one of these utopian travelers haunted Garibaldi. "A man who defends his own country or attacks another's is no more than a soldier...," he had been told, "But he, who adopts some other country as his own and makes offer of his sword and his blood, is more than a soldier. He is a hero."[6]

In 1833 Garibaldi ventured to Marseilles where he met Mazzini and enrolled in his Young Italy. The impact of this patriot and philosopher upon the young sailor was tremendous and Garibaldi would always acknowledge Mazzini as his master. It was Mazzini who taught Garibaldi about the unity of the human race and convinced him that the Italians were a Messianic people destined to initiate a new epoch of the human race. A prophet of a new order and religion, Mazzini truly believed that the destiny of Italy was intertwined with that of the entire world.[7] These ideas were imbibed by Garibaldi who was taught to champion every just cause and to seek a political, social, and religious transformation of humanity.

In February 1834 Garibaldi participated in an abortive Mazzinian insurrection in Piedmont, was sentenced to death in absentia by a Genoese court, and fled to Marseilles. The prospect of exile now loomed before him. He sailed to Tunisia with the intention of enrolling in the fleet of the bey Hussein but then left for Brazil. He remained in South America from January 1836 until the outbreak of the revolutions of 1848 in Italy. The years he spent there influenced his personality, private life, and career.

In Brazil Garibaldi encountered Anna Maria Ribeiro da Silva, whom he called Anita, a woman of mixed Portuguese and Indian descent, who became his lover, companion in arms, and wife. With other Italian exiles he fought on behalf of the separatists of the Rio Grande do Sul. "My followers," he wrote, "were truly a cosmopolitan crew, made up of all colours and nations."[8] After a series of victories by the Brazilians in 1839 and 1840, Garibaldi and Anita left for Montevideo.

His arrival coincided with a national emergency. The Republic of Uruguay was endangered by the Argentinians led by Jan Manual Rosas, their president. Calling upon the Italians of Montevideo, Garibaldi formed the Italian Legion in 1843 and shaped it into a skilled and dedicated fighting force. The Legion's flag was black for Italy which was in mourning, with a volcano at its center, symbolizing the hidden power that lay dormant in the homeland. It was in Uruguay that the Legion first sported the Red Shirt, obtained from a factory in Montevideo which had intended to export them to the slaughter houses of Argentina. Subsequently it became the symbol of Garibaldi and his followers.

In April 1848, before his forty-first birthday, Garibaldi led some sixty members of his Legion back to Italy. At home he offered his services to Carlo Alberto of Sardinia who had declared war against Austria, but was turned down. Rebuffed, he and his followers crossed into Lombardy where they offered assistance to the provisional government of Milan.[9] Subsequently they marched south to Rome and played a major role in the defense of the Republic against the armies of France, Austria, Spain, and the Kingdom of the Two Sicilies. Garibaldi's heroic defense of the Roman Republic coupled to his exploits in South America earned him the title of "hero of two Worlds."

Following the fall of the Roman Republic and the Papal Restoration, Garibaldi resumed the sea-faring life of his youth, traveling first to Tangier where he remained half a year and in June 1850 sailed for New York. He eventually settled in the house of Antonio Meucci on Staten Island and worked in his candle factory which employed a number of Italian exiles.[10] Although he had filed his intention of becoming an American citizen, he never did so but instead returned to South America. Garibaldi reached Lima in October 1851, where he assumed command of the Carmen, a sailing ship bound for China.[11]

For two years he sailed around the world on the Carmen taking her to such places as China, Australia, and Peru. In 1854 he was offered command of the Commonwealth which took him back to Europe: to England first and then to Genoa. The sad condition of his homeland continued to trouble him.[12] With the formation of the Italian National Society, in which Garibaldi accepted the honorary post of vice president, he drifted from Young Italy to support the foreign policy of Cavour and accepted the leadership of Victor Emmanuel's Kingdom of Sardinia. Following the Plombieres agreement of Cavour and Napoleon III of France, in the Franco-Piedmontese war of 1859 against Austria Garibaldi coordinated the activities of the volunteer troops. Once again he was disappointed by the conduct of the Piedmontese. "General Lamarmora, minister of war, who had always been averse to the enrollment of volunteers, refused to recognize the rank of my officers," Garibaldi complained.[13] He was even more distressed by the Villafranca armistice and the news that Cavour had decided to turn over Nice and Savoy to France in return for the right to annex north central Italy.

Spurred on by Mazzini and Francesco Crispi, Garibaldi now began to plan for the *Spedizione dei Mille* (1860) which overthrew Bourbon rule first in Sicily and then in Naples and led to the inclusion of the *Mezzogiorno* in the Kingdom of Italy that Cavour was in the process of creating. Garibaldi wished to include Rome as well, but Cavour feared this would create problems with his French ally whose forces preserved Rome and the surrounding area for the Papacy. Consequently Cavour had Victor Emmanuel and the army march south to prevent the volunteers from crossing into what was left of the Papal State. Frustrated in 1860, Italy's most popular revolutionary figure did not abandon the dream of acquiring Rome and sought to lead his forces into the Pope's territory in 1862 and again in 1867. Both expeditions ended in disastrous failure.

While contributing to the creation of the Italian Kingdom, Garibaldi continued to call for international peace and harmony. Even before the proclamation of the Italian State, he had advocated the formation of a united Europe and deplored the fact that Europeans spent their lives in perpetual threats and mutual hostility. "But if only Europe formed a single state," he wrote in 1860, "who would there be to disturb us, and who in the outside world would threaten the peace of such a sovereign power?" In his view European union was not a utopian dream.

> The basis of such a federation would have to be France and England. If these two states could frankly and honestly agree, then Italy, Spain, Portugal, Hungary, Belgium, Switzerland, Greece and Macedonia would instinctively group round them. At the same time the divided and oppressed nationalities — for example the Slavs, the Celts, the Germans, Scandinavians, and that colossus Russia — none of these could afford to remain outside such a process of political regeneration. [14]

At the same time Garibaldi was convinced that the United States had a bright future and hoped that it would act as a counterpoise to the aristocratic and tyrannic powers of Europe. He was therefore disturbed by the prospect of its disruption. In 1861 following the outbreak of the Civil War, an appeal was made to Garibaldi that the fall of the American Union would be a disastrous blow to the cause of human freedom in America, Europe, and the world. To counter such a consequence, he was offered a Major-General's commission in the Army of the United States. Garibaldi responded that he would only render service as Commander in Chief of the American forces with the additional power of declaring the abolition of slavery. [15] His terms were refused, but he watched events across the Atlantic with interest. He was delighted that Lincoln eventually did liberate the slaves. He wrote the American President:

> In the midst of your titanic struggle, permit me, as another among the free children of Columbus, to send you a word of

greeting and admiration for the great work you have begun. Posterity will call you the great emancipator, a more enviable title than any crown could be, and greater than any merely mundane treasure.[16]

In 1864 Garibaldi visited England and was given a raptuous reception and hero's welcome. Although a private trip, he sought to secure English support for Poland, Greece, and Denmark. At Portsmouth he inspected the British fleet, on the Isle of Wight he met Mazzini and visited Tennyson, and in London more than half a million turned out to see him according him a reception given to no king or Emperor. While dining with the Russian revolutionary Herzen outside of London he revealed his international outlook in his toast. Raising a glass of Marsala he said:

> To Poland, the land of martyrs, to Poland facing death for independence and setting a grand example to the peoples!
> Now let us drink to young Russia, which is suffering and struggling as we are, and like us will be victorious....
> And finally to England, the land of freedom and independence, the land which for its hospitality and sympathy with the persecuted deserves our fullest gratitude....[17]

When the third war of national liberation erupted against Austria in 1866, Garibaldi and some twenty thousand volunteers aimed to capture Trent and to close the valley of the Adige. While the regular army had been checked by the Austrians at Custozza and the navy defeated at the island of Lissa, Garibaldi was in a position to capture Trent when he was ordered to withdraw from the area by the terms of the armistice agreed upon by the government. Despite inferior equipment and second class treatment, he and his forces won battles while the regular army lost them.[18] A disappointed Garibaldi returned home. Nonetheless he continued to interest himself in all sorts of issues including racial equality, religious freedom, woman's emancipation, the abolition of capital punishment and above all the completion of Italian unification.

In September 1867, Garibaldi departed for Geneva to take part in a Congress of the International League of Peace and Liberty over which he had been appointed honorary president. Alongside such figures as Bakunin, Garibaldi gave one of the principal speeches urging the delegates to destroy despotism and to outlaw war, with the exception of that waged by the oppressed against the tyrant.[19] Among other things he suggested:

1. All nations should be regarded as sisters.
2. War between them should be thought of as impossible.

3. All international quarrels ought to be decided by a Congress.
4. The members of this Congress should be democratically elected.
5. All peoples, however small, should have the right to representation in this Congress.[20]

Garibaldi's commitment to what he considered the just, regardless of frontiers, was manifest in his decision to fight for the Republic in the Franco-Prussian War, once the Emperor had been captured and his Empire collapsed. He declared that he was going to uphold the sole system that could assure peace and prosperity for all nations and to safeguard the principles of the revolution which were in danger.[21] "The Government of National Defense," complained Garibaldi, "received me, because forced to do so by the course of events, but coldly enough, and with the manifest intention of...making use of my name, but nothing more."[22]

At first offered only a token force by Leon Gambetta, he soon assumed command of an international force composed of Italians, Americans, Englishmen, Spaniards, Irishmen as well as Frenchmen. They fought well but could not alter the course of the war.[23] For his efforts on behalf of France, Garibaldi was elected a member of the Bordeau Assembly. However that body refused to seat him on the ground that he was not a Frenchman.[24] One of the delegates who supported his inclusion pleaded:

Garibaldi is a French citizen by the adoption of many of our principal cities – Paris, Lyons, Marseilles, Algiers; and above all, by the devotion which led him, with all his family, to the defense of France.[25]

This plea was to no avail for the vision of the Assembly was considerably narrower than that of the man who fought on their behalf.

By the time Garibaldi returned home, France was troubled by the Civil War brought about by the Commune. Garibaldi did not join Mazzini in condemning the Commune and the International. In 1871 he declared, "The International wants all men to be brothers and seeks the end of privilege; naturally I sympathize with their view."[26] In fact Garibaldi claimed to be a socialist as well as an internationalist. However he was certainly not a Marxist and his socialism reflected his sympathy for the poor and downtrodden. Indeed there was little difference between his socialism and the humanitarian radicalism of the Left.[26] Thus the attempt of Marx and his followers to capitalize on his enormous popularity by having him sponsor their revolutionary societies was doomed to failure.

There were those who considered Garibaldi's socialism romantic and idealistic and as utopian as his belief that once nationalist aspirations had been realized, there would be a federal union in Europe. Others did not consider his views so unrealistic and noted he always attracted followers to his cause. Cesare Cantù wrote:

> So confident was he in himself, that he assumed others must think as he did. And since he was sincere, his words carried great weight; and sometimes indeed he was in the right however impractical or fantastic his beliefs may have seemed. He was not the kind of person who urges others to act so that he can then step in and take all the winnings, but tilted straight at his goal, ready to stand down and disappear as soon as it was reached.[28]

Garibaldi's words and actions were of one piece and they showed that he transcended a narrow nationalism and aimed at human liberation rather than political aggrandizement.

Notes

1. Giuseppe Garibaldi, *Memorie,* ed. Ugoberto Alfassio Grimaldi (Verona: Bertani Editore, 1972), p. 25.
2. Giuseppe Garibaldi, *Autobiography,* trans. A. Werner (New York: Howard Fertig, 1971), I, 7-12.
3. Ibid., I, 15.
4. Denis Mack Smith (ed.) *Garibaldi* (Englewood Cliffs, N.J.: Prentice-Hall, 1969), p. 3.
5. Ibid., p. 14.
6. Christopher Hibbert, *Garibaldi and his Enemies* (New York: Plume Books, 1965), p. 17.
7. Gaetano Salvemini, *Mazzini,* trans. I.M. Rawson (New York: Collier Books, 1962), p. 70.
8. Garibaldi, *Autobiography,* I, 54.
9. Ibid., I, 267.
10. Ibid., II, 54.
11. Ibid., II, 64; Hibbert, pp. 121-122.
12. Hibbert, p. 123.
13. Mack Smith, p. 33.
14. Ibid., pp. 68-69.
15. Ibid., p. 70.
16. Ibid., p. 72.
17. Ibid., p. 75.
18. George Martin, *The Red Shirt and the Cross of Savoy* (New York: Dodd, Mead and Co., 1969), p. 693.
19. Pietro Nenni, *Garibaldi* (Milan: Edizioni *Avanti!*, 1961), p. 89.
20. Mack Smith, pp. 79-80.
21. Frederico Chabod, *Storia della politica estera italiana dal 1870 al 1896: I: Le Premesse* (Bari: Laterza, 1951), pp. 28-29.

22. Garibaldi, *Autobiography,* II, 317.
23. Hibbert, p. 363.
24. Nenni, p. 96.
25. Garibaldi, *Autobiography,* III, 420.
26. Nenni, p. 97.
27. Mack Smith, p. 118.
28. Ibid., p. 154.

Chapter **5**   GARIBALDI IN THE
UNITED STATES: HAVEN FOR
THE HERO OF TWO WORLDS
Joanne Pellegrino

The struggle for Italian independence produced many exiles to foreign lands—and none so well known as Giuseppe Garibaldi. The United States, and particularly Staten Island, N.Y., was his home in 1850-51 and 1853-54. America was his respite from the rigors of war and political struggle.

This was not the first American exile for Garibaldi. From 1835 thru 1847 he had been in South America, fighting first with the forces of the Rio Grande do Sud province which had asserted its independence from Brazil, later for Uruguay against her neighbor Argentina. Here he led the Italian Legion, made up of fellow Italian exiles, and developed the principles of guerrilla warfare which he later employed in Italy. Born in Nice, July 4, 1807 and a sailor by profession, Garibaldi became a member of the *Giovine Italia* and it was for his Mazzinian activities in 1834 that he was condemned to death and forced into exile.

With the outbreak of revolution in Italy in 1848 together with the First War of Independence, Garibaldi returned home to offer his sword to Carlo Alberto. He was curtly refused, but he led a band of volunteers which won several brilliant, but short-lived, victories and which continued to fight briefly after the armistice. Garibaldi intended to reach the Republic of Venice, but political events drew him to Rome. The Republic was proclaimed on February 7, 1849 and soon had to defend itself, as the French landed to restore the temporal power of the Pope. Garibaldi directed the desperate, heroic effort which won him the admiration of the world. It was crowned by his daring retreat across Italy, during which his beloved Anita died. Garibaldi finally reached Piedmont in September 1848, only to be arrested and deported by the Sardinian government.

Garibaldi was first taken to Tunis, where the Bey refused him permission to land, possibly due to the counsel of Louis Napoleon. Similar permission was denied at Gibraltar and this action by an English representative deeply wounded Garibaldi. The American consul there offered him passage to the United States, but he was not yet ready for such a long separation from Italy. In November 1849 Garibaldi arrived at Tangiers where he was warmly received by the Sardinian consul Giovanni Battista Carpenetti and remained for six months.

Although he describes his life among the Turks as tranquil, Garibaldi was anxious to end his idleness and sail again. A friend, Francesco Carpanetto, was engaged in shipping and promised to help him. For commercial reasons it was thought best to travel to the United States, build a ship there and sail under the American flag, and it was under these circumstances that Garibaldi came to America. Jesse White Mario suggests, however, that Garibaldi was dissatisfied with Vittorio Emanuele's strong-arm Proclamation of Moncalieri and for this reason decided to become a seaman.[1] But Garibaldi's correspondence does not mention politics and in a letter from Gibraltar of June 13, 1850 Garibaldi says:

> Today I leave for England, from where I will proceed to New York. My friends in Italy were so kind as to acquire a ship for my command — for this reason I am going to America. I will sail commercially as long as it pleases God...I can, therefore, perhaps under the mighty flag of the United States, see again the dear shores where all the hope of this poor life lies.[2]

Garibaldi's approaching visit was hailed in the American press. The *New York Herald* praised him:

> Few men have achieved so much for the cause of freedom, and no one has accomplished so many heroic acts for the independence of a fatherland as General Garibaldi has for Italy.[3]

When he landed at the Quarantine Station on Staten Island on July 30, 1850, the port physician, Dr. A. Sidney Doane, ordered the Italian tricolor hoisted in Garibaldi's honor to fly with the flags of the other nations at the Station. As he was suffering from severe arthritis and could hardly walk, Garibaldi remained on Staten Island several days at the Pavilion Hotel as its guest.

Meanwhile preparations for a gala reception were progressing. An Italian Committee of welcome had as its members Felice Foresti, Giuseppe Avezzana, Quirico Filopanti, Antonio Meucci, Domenico Minnelli, G. F. Secchi de Casali, Luigi Chitti, Michele Pastacaldi, Gugliemo Gajani, and Luciani—all themselves political refugees. Mayor Woodhull and his administration were planning to receive Garibaldi at City Hall and to offer the Governor's Room for a reception. At the *Café de la République* at 307 Broadway a register had been set up where participants in a parade could sign for the order of march. Noted Americans joined with the Italian Committee in preparing a banquet at the Astor House scheduled for August 10.

However, on August 8 Garibaldi addressed a letter to the Committee from Hastings, where he was visiting, declining the invitation because of his poor health. He expressed his deep thanks and his wish to live quietly in America, become a citizen and sail under the United States flag to earn his livelihood until a time more favorable to the Italian cause presented itself. He added:

> Such a public demonstration is not necessary to prove to me the sympathy of my compatriots, of the American people and of all true republicans for the misfortune I have suffered and for the cause that gave rise to it...
>
> Next to the cause to which I have dedicated myself, there is nothing closer to my heart than the approval of this great nation, and I am certain that I will obtain it when it has been convinced that I have honestly and faithfully served the cause of liberty, of which it has itself given the world such a noble example.[4]

Another very real reason behind his decline of a reception, however, was the opposition of Catholics, particularly the Irish, to the man who had fought so vigorously against the Pope's temporal power.[5]

Garibaldi remained with his friend Bagioli at Hastings and then with the Ferrero family in Yonkers for about two weeks. For the next six weeks he lived with Michele Pastacaldi in Manhattan at Irving Place, also the home of Felice Foresti. In the first days of October he moved to Staten Island, to the home of the Florentine expatriot Antonio Meucci "to enjoy rest, full liberty and economy."[6]

Garibaldi's life on Staten Island was simple and he spent his time hunting, fishing and helping Meucci in a candle works the latter had set up. He joined the local volunteer fire department and became a third-degree Mason in the Tompkins Lodge No. 401. Garibaldi describes his life and hopes to a friend in Cuba, Elidore Specchi:

> I write you with cold hands for this is no oven...There is little game on this Island and then there is a veto for rabbits and quails and many other animals which certainly do not exist. One of the incontestable prerogatives of mankind is to frustrate each other. Fortunately Meucci has had the idea of making candles and we are producing some really fine ones. I therefore spend my time making wick and mixing wax. Near the cauldron the temperature is almost Cuban...
>
> In Italy there is no sign for the moment of what we want, but our people are progressing. We cannot fail to attain our regeneration.[7]

His *Memoirs* added:

> There was no luxury at the home (Meucci's), however, nothing
> was lacking of the primary necessities of life, both in lodging
> and food.[8]

On Staten Island Garibaldi enjoyed the company of Col. Bovi-
Campeggi, a companion in arms who also lived there, and such exiles as
Foresti, Avezzana and Pastacaldi often visited. Foresti also wrote to Maz-
zini that Garibaldi received...

> ...frequent visits from distinguished Americans and foreigners,
> letters of love and esteem from many parts of the Union...[9]

Senator Lewis Cass wrote:

> General, you possess the regard and the sympathy of the
> American people and you well merit this distinction...Your
> glorious exertions, followed by misfortunes borne with equa-
> nimity, are a passport to the hearts and homes of my country-
> men.[10]

Requests to honor him still came, but Garibaldi refused. In one instance he
declined the offer of the Societá Nazionale Italiana of New Orleans, asking
that the money for a reception be used instead to help his fellow exiles and
to buy supplies for a new effort to win freedom for Italy.

In accordance with his original plans to sail under the American flag,
Garibaldi filed initial papers for citizenship, but never completed the final
application, although on occasion in later years he claimed to be a United
States citizen. There were complications regarding his plans with Carpanetto
for building the merchant ship, and Felice Foresti and several friends tried
to obtain a government position for him, preferably in the Post Office, but
the effort failed. He and Meucci continued their work on Staten Island,
although Garibaldi records how one day he became tired of making candles
and went down to the docks to seek work as a simple sailor. No one would
hire him.

> I repressed the mortification, and returned to working with
> wax.[11]

At this time Garibaldi also began to write his *Memoirs* for Theodore
Dwight, and his first sketch was of Anita, "my constant companion in good
and bad fortune,"[12] but he requested that publication be suspended while
he remained in the United States.

Garibaldi was generous in his help to his fellow exiles — even distributing to them $500 given him by an American admirer. He worked with interested Americans as Henry Theodore Tuckerman to further their cause and was a member of the Committee of Italian Political Refugees which organized a benefit concert for the exiles at which Teresa Parodi and Adelina Patti performed. But his concern was always with the future of Italy as his correspondence indicates. H. Nelson Gay suggests this had long-range results:

> And of special interest is the fact that at that time in his conversations with his most intimate companions and with American friends of Italy he proposed that same expedition which nine years later he was fated to accomplish with his Mille.[13]

Giuseppe Garibaldi was an ardent admirer of the United States and regarded her "as the only intrepid bulwark against despotism in Europe."[14] He spoke proudly of sailing under her flag and wrote:

> This nation lives certainly by her traditions and will soon become the first among the great nations.[15]

In April 1851 he obtained an American passport, but did not realize his hope to command an American ship and left the United States soon after, again for commercial reasons.

Garibaldi's merchant friend Francesco Carpanetto had arrived from Europe and on April 29, 1851 he and Garibaldi sailed from New York for Central America where Garibaldi traded under the assumed name of Giuseppe Pane. The friends proceeded to Lima where a wealthy Italian gave Garibaldi command of the *Carmen*. In January 1852 he sailed for China, spending about a year in the Orient. He then traded cargoes of wood and copper between Chile and Peru for several months, returning to America, to the port of Boston in September 1853. Garibaldi visited his friends in New York and contemplated returning to South America, but was swayed by news from Italy to end his exile. On January 12, 1854 he sailed from Baltimore for Genoa via London.

This briefer stay of Garibaldi in America may be more significant historically than that of 1850-1851. Sometime during his American exile, Garibaldi's political ideas underwent a change, which was manifested in 1853. He noted with distress the discord among the expatriates, especially in New York and usually along monarchical versus republican lines, and he wanted to effect a reconciliation. On September 19, 1853 he wrote from Boston to Felice Foresti:

I have decided to work actively (as much as possible) toward the conciliation of Italians of whatever opinion, and I sincerely wish to see you guide the plan, in New York especially, where above all you are esteemed and loved. I would like you to see Valerio, to whom I am writing on this matter, and to speak with him on this undertaking. I will write to Avezzana, Forbes, Gavazzi, and if it is possible I will also return to New York.[16]

Valerio was the Sardinian Consul General in New York, and the following letter Garibaldi wrote him from Boston September 22, 1853 shows the direction of the understanding Garibaldi sought to achieve:

Concerning the idea manifested to you of reconciliation among the Italians, I have written to various of the most influential men proposing as a program: To muster around the Italian flag of Piedmont whatever may have been their conviction of a system for the past and (to do this) decisively; not having any other means than this, to reunite Italy to that Government, fighting all the foreigners that oppress her.[17]

This realization of the leadership role of Piedmont in the struggle for Italian unification, manifest during Garibaldi's American exile, was later raised by him during the expedition of the Thousand as "Italia e Vittorio Emanuele." It contributed immeasurably to making Italian independence a reality.

Notes

1. Jesse White Mario, *Garibaldi e i suoi tempi.* (Milano: 1884) p. 400.
   Vittorio Emanuele had dissolved Piedmont's Chamber when it refused to ratify the peace treaty with Austria following the War of 1848-49. In the Proclamation of Moncalieri of November 1849, he appealed directly to the electors for a Parliament amenable to the treaty, stating he would not be responsible for the future if such a Parliament were not elected — a hint at possible extraconstitutional measures.
2. Quoted in H. Nelson Gay, "Il secondo esilio di Garibaldi (1849-54)" p. 648.
3. Quoted in Howard Marraro, *American Opinion on the Unification of Italy 1846-1861.* (New York: 1969), p. 166.
4. Quoted in H. Nelson Gay, *op. cit.,* p. 650.
5. Howard Marraro, *op. cit.,* p. 168.
6. Quoted in H. Nelson Gay, *op. cit.,* p. 650.
7. Giuseppe Garibaldi to Elidore Specchi. Letter of February 10, 1851 from New York. Garibaldi-Meucci Memorial Museum, Staten Island, New York.

8. Giuseppe Garibaldi, *Le memorie di Garibaldi.* A cura della Reale Commissione. (Bologna: 1932) Vol. I., p. 221.
9. Quoted in H. Nelson Gay, *op. cit.,* p. 654.
10. Quoted in Howard Marraro, *op. cit.,* p. 168.

Lewis Cass (1782-1866) was a Senator from Michigan and a member of the Foreign Affairs Committee. From 1836 to 1842 he had been minister to Paris and in 1858 he served as Buchanan's Secretary of State. He approved of the French revolution of 1848 and lauded the liberal reforms of Pius IX. Cass championed the cause of oppressed nationalities, including the Italians, and in January 1850 introduced a resolution in Congress to suspend diplomatic relations with Austria for her treatment of Hungary and Venice.

Lewis Cass, Jr., his son, became Chargé d'Affaires to the Papal States in 1849 where he was a friend of the Italian cause and aided liberals after the fall of the Roman Republic.

11. Giuseppe Garibaldi, *op. cit.,* Vol. I, p. 220.
12. Giuseppe Garibaldi, *The Life of General Garibaldi.* Edited by Theodore Dwight. (New York: 1861) p. 3.
13. H. Nelson Gay, *op. cit.,* p. 657
14. Giuseppe Garibaldi, *Epistolario di Giuseppe Garibaldi.* Edito da Enrico Emilio Ximenes. (Milano: 1885) Vol. I, p. 45.
15. Quoted in Vincent A. Caso, *Il centenario dello sbarco di Giuseppe Garibaldi a New York in esilio dal 1850-1853.* (New York: 1950) p. 14.
16. Quoted in H. Nelson Gay, *op. cit.,* p. 659
17. Unedited letter of Giuseppe Garibaldi to N. Valerio, Consul General of Piedmont, mailed from Boston on September 22, 1853. The original is displayed in the Garibaldi-Meucci Memorial Museum, Staten Island, New York, and is reproduced here with permission of the Museum.

Boston 22 settembre 1853

Caro Valerio,

Le tante gentilezze vostre verso di me mi hanno ardito a chiedervi l'incamminamento delle acchiuse, e pregarvi di comandarmi alcuna volta a mio torno.

Circa all'idea manifestarvi di conciliazioni tra gl'Italiani ho scritto a vari di più influenti proponendo per programma: Rannodarsi intorno alla bandiera Italiana del Piemonte qualunque sia stata la convinzione di sistema per il passato e francamente non avendo altra meta che quella di riunir l'Italia a quel Governo; combattendo tutti gli stranieri che l'opprimano.

Io propagherò la stessa idea altrove a tutta possa, convinto di far bene. Se vi pare, scrivete a Gavazzi acciò si trove in New York, dove io penso essere tra 7 od 8 giorni e se troverele bene, sanzioneremo in una riunione quanto si è detto.

(Vostro)

G. Garibaldi

Chapter 6

GARIBALDI
IN AMERICAN POETRY

Joseph Tusiani
Herbert H. Lehman College, CUNY

Italy was the first European nation to acclaim in poetry the American independence. Vittorio Alfieri's *America the Free*[1] is the first literary recognition of the United States of America on the part of a country that was soon to imitate the same revolution for the achievement of her own independence and freedom, and no one was more amply qualified than Alfieri to salute the new free land in the name of all Italians.

In the first of his five Odes the great tragedian did not fail to remind America of the plight of his country. With a sudden, passionate outburst of patriotism he cried out:

> O Truthful Goddess, who the sunlit shores
> Of the Ausonian sea
> Made long ago far more than others blest;
> You, ever since not seen in Italy,
> Who now no more abhors
> Her fetters (thus well earned) and lives oppressed,
> Dormant in deadly rest;
> You, whom our guilt has kept so many a year
> Far from this globe, concealed within some star
> Less sorrowful by far
> Whence, loudly called by discord, bloodshed, tears
> Of men in grief, and sneers
> Of vile oppressors still,
> Into the midst of Albion's infamy
> Last you alighted: with such harshness fill
> My song, it may be hailed both true and free.

Now this is our question: If Italy was the first to acknowledge with a song the independence of the American people, was America also the first to celebrate Italy's fight for freedom? The answer is "yes," at least with regard to Giuseppe Garibaldi. Incidentally, Cavour, the great statesman without whose genius the Italian Risorgimento would not have come to fruition, did not fire the poet's fancy. Mazzini, instead, conquered England through Charles Algernon Swinburne's *Songs Before Sunrise,* a book completely inspired by and dedicated to Mazzini's dream of an Italian Republic.

Thus we come to the American apotheosis of Garibaldi as champion of liberty and deliverer of Italy.

Much has already been written on Garibaldi's brief sojourn in the United States of America.[2] Frances Winwar's *Meucci, Garibaldi and the Telephone,* reprinted in the Bicentennial issue of *La Parola del Popolo* (1976), captures by dint of memorable episodes the Italian spirit of the hero in his stay at the Meucci residence in Staten Island, New York.

It was exactly during that year, 1850, that the first poem in honor of the General appeared in a New York magazine. Its inconspicuous title was "Lines," somewhat clarified by the subtitle "Written after reading General Garibaldi's sketch of the life of his wife, Anna Garibaldi"—a subtitle that needs an explanation: "When Garibaldi came to New York in 1850, he wrote, at the request of Theodore Dwight, several sketches of his companions in arms which were later translated and published with his *Autobiography* in 1859. In an accompanying note in Italian to Mr. Dwight, dated Staten Island, October 30, 1850, Garibaldi wrote: 'I send the first of my biographical sketches, which I promised you; do not be surprised to find that it is that of my wife. She was my constant companion in good and evil fortune, sharing, as you will see, my greatest dangers, and overcoming every difficulty by her fortitude...' Yours, G. Garibaldi."[3]

The poem, signed Anonymous, is possibly by Theodore Dwight himself. The seven quatrains are rather pedestrian as far as elegance of diction and poetic inspiration are concerned, but, to be sure, they contain the first of the several remarks against the Church of Rome that we shall encounter in the course of our analysis of the Garibaldian saga in American poetry:

> Oh, now shall no longer the rack or the flame
> Of the fell Inquisition demand her its prey,
> Or the Jesuit plot, in revenge of my name,
> The noblest of women to lure or to slay.

It is, indeed, baffling that most of the American poems written for Garibaldi were not proudly signed by their authors. I am tempted to venture a theory wholly my own: that the anonymity of these poems was meant to shield their respective creators — possibly Roman Catholic — against the censure of the American Church, for, in those days, especially in the sixth decade of the century, to praise Garibaldi, eager to conquer Rome, was tantamount to dethroning Pius IX. But, in all fairness, such a theory cannot be successfully defended, for there are at least five poems with no reference whatsoever to the Church and still unsigned by their authors.

For a better appreciation of the poems inspired by Garibaldi in 1860, the most glorious year of his military life, we must remember, in Howard R. Marraro's words, that "the attachment of Americans to Garibaldi grew out of their Italian sympathies; it grew also out of his personality peculiarly captivating to the American, who saw in him the rover of great spaces on land and sea, the fighter against desperate odds, the hero who had defended the Roman Republic against the French legion, the champion of the oppressed, the patriot, the humane and generous man, all in one. He touched a chord of poetry and romance; his name combined the attributes accorded to Rienzi and Murat—the patriotism of the Roman tribune with the chivalry of the illustrious soldier. Not only that, but his conduct was so analogous to that of the father of their country, that Americans could not but refer to Garibaldi as the Washington of Italy....[4] "During 1859 and 1860, sympathy meetings for Garibaldi were held in many American cities. It was estimated that during these two years contributions of arms, money, and provisions, amounting in value to $100,000, had been sent to Italy from New York City.[5]" The Garibaldi fever swept over America. Here are the minutes, fortunately preserved, of the meeting held in the Cooper Institute on December 18, 1860:

"Mr. Eli P. Norton, after reading an address of sympathy and encouragement to the people of Italy, submitted the following resolutions:

Resolved, That we hail in the resurrection of Italy one of those grand events which mark an era, and command forever the admiration and wonder of mankind.

Resolved, That in the heroic assertion of their rights, and the orderly reconstruction of their government, the Italian people have been true to the civilization of this age, and loyal to the memories of their ancient history.

Resolved, That with a reverent faith in the Providence of the Ruler of the Universe, we believe that Garibaldi, by his simplicity and purity of character, his lofty elevation above the selfishness of a conqueror, his marvelous successes and his great wisdom, stands near our Washington, as a divine instrument in the cause of free government.

Resolved, That we, the citizens of the United States, who saw the daily toil and manly honor of Garibaldi, once an exile on our soil, will not limit ourselves to mere words; and that therefore we pledge ourselves to give such aid to struggling and gallant people as should become a free and generous nation (applause).

Resolved, That our fellow citizen, John Anderson, Esq., shall be the treasurer of our Garibaldi fund, and make such arrangements for its collection and transmission to Garibaldi as may be deemed proper.

Resolved, That the chairman and secretary of the Committee on arrangements be requested to transmit to the Italian people, through General Garibaldi, the proceedings of this meeting.

The Hon. Luther R. Marsh delivered an address extolling Garibaldi and the cause of liberty the world over. Following this, Dr. Guilmette sang the following ode, entitled "The Triumph of Italian Freedom," which had

been composed by William Rose Wallace at the request of the Committee
for the Grand American Mass Meeting in Favor of Italian Freedom and
Nationality.

The ode, I assure you, does not have the immortality of its subject but
I will nonetheless quote its first stanza not to demonstrate what needs no
demonstration but only to stress the detail of a paean officially "requested"
for that meeting:

> Ye sons of freedom, wake to glory!
>   See Italy at last arise!
> The dungeon bolt and fetter hoary
>   Are burst beneath her azure skies!
>   Beneath her broad, rejoicing skies!
> No more her tyrants, ruin breeding,
>   With hireling hosts, a demon band,
>   Shake horror o'er earth's loveliest land,
> While sacred Liberty is bleeding!
>   Shout, shout aloud, ye brave!
>   All climes breathe freer now!
>   And Washington's own country wreathes
>   Italia's beaming brow![6]

The first American poem that celebrates Garibaldi's sailing for Sicily
with his one thousand Volunteers from Quarto, near Genoa, on May 5,
1860, to free the Kingdom of the Two Sicilies — is entitled "A Cheer for
Garibaldi." The poem was published in *The Living Age* of Boston on July
20th of that year.

The author was not even sure that Garibaldi would succeed in his
audacious enterprise. He only knew what he felt — that the General's daring
was already sacred to history. So he compared him with Dante's — rather
than Lucan's — Cato, thus transforming an impulsive, military man into an
old, invulnerable guardian of the vast purgatory that is the world:

> Honor to Garibaldi! Win or lose
> A hero to all time that Chief goes down.
> Whatever issue his emprise ensues,
> He, certain of unquenchable renown,
> Fights for a victor's or a martyr's crown,
> Another side than Cato's Heaven may please:
> Forbid it, Heaven!

Hiding behind the protection of anonymity, the author of the good but not
spectacular Petrarchan sonnet goes on to say that, even if Garibaldi falls

victim to a bullet of the Pope's mercenary troops, nothing will ever mar the splendid record of his life:

> .... the devotees
> Of Priestly tyranny shall never drown
> His name in his true blood; their hireling balls
> May gore his noble bosom; but he falls
> The champion of united Italy
> Against brute force with monkery allied.
> Staunch wrestler, as a man, for liberty,
> 'Twill be on record how he fought and died.

Obviously our author, perilously anticipating history, mistook the Bourbon King for poor, apprehensive Pius IX.

Two months and two days later, on September 22, 1860, also in *The Living Age* of Boston, appeared a more ambitious poem, an "Ode to Garibaldi" with a rather intricate and intriguing rhyme pattern binding its trimeters, pentameters, and hexameters, *aaBccBdd*.

The new Anonymous, a far better craftsman, does not mention Garibaldi in the first five stanzas of his ode, so that, were it not for its title, we would fail until then to recognize its author's idol. But this is possibly the reason why the poem succeeds in striking a true patriotic chord in spite of its rhetorical excesses. Our Anonymous describes Garibaldi by describing Italy's need of him:

> Louder and louder still,
> From valley and from hill,
> Rings the glad shout, delighting Nature's ear;
> For long, with bitter smart,
> The mother's tender heart
> Has bled with anguish for her children dear,
> Who, crushed and helpless in their living tomb,
> Struggle for second birth within her laboring womb.
>
> Again, and still again,
> O'er the exulting main,
> Meeting the half-stifled cry of misery
> From tyranny's dark cells,
> The sacred anthem swells,
> To that wild summons making glad reply —
> "We come, the sons of Freedom come to save,
> To bind the tyrant, and let loose the slave!"

This tyrant of Italy does not even deserve the human dignity of a name. Our poet calls him a "thing, misnamed by men a King." The readers of *The Living Age* knew, of course, who that "thing" or rather that "King" was, just as they knew who the "monsters" around him were. It was not necessary to mention either the Bourbon "Franceschiello" or the monks and priests of Pope Mastai-Ferretti.

> Upon his throne a thing,
> Misnamed by men a King,
> Heard the lamentings with inhuman glee;
> While round about him stood,
> Disguised in stole and hood,
> Monsters in human shape more vile than he,
> A hellish crew in sacred vesture drest,
> The vermin of the State, the Church's pest.

The ode should have ended with a line that clearly compares Garibaldi to Moses, "At the loud shout of God-led Israel." Instead, not knowing that his inspiration had left him, our poet writes three more stanzas, so embarrassingly mediocre as to provoke a shudder in Alexander Pope's distant sepulcher:

> For Garibaldi led them to the fight,
> The generous champion of the people's right...

Another poem appeared in *The Liberator* of Boston (November 23, 1860), by one Jane Ashby. It was entitled "Brown and Garibaldi." Since we know about John Brown, the American abolitionist who led the attack upon Harper's Ferry in October 1859, and was, alas, overpowered by the United States Marines, taken prisoner, and hung on December 2nd of the same year at Charlestown, we easily comprehend the Brown-Garibaldi parallel of the title. What one fails to fathom is that *The Liberator's* editor felt it necessary to append this statement: "We copy the following 'incendiary' and 'murderous' lines from the Boston *Courier,* which affect such horror of mind in regard to the nobly disinterested efforts of Capt. John Brown to liberate the slaves of Virginia."

The poem is far from "incendiary" and "murderous." It simply says that mankind is sure of Garibaldi's place in history — at least in European history:

> We praise thee, Garibaldi!
> And in the roll of fame,
> Among her noblest heroes,
> Shall Europe place thy name.

It also praises Garibaldi's selfless nobility of character and patriotic love:

> Among them — far above them —
> Thou dost not fight for gain,
> For crown, or lands, or titles,
> Or empty glory vain.

Then, with a foreseeable plunge into history, the poet compares the object of her hero-worship with the Greek and Latin heroes of Plutarch's fame, and tells him that America watches his flight, hour by hour:

> We watch your progress, eager,
> As victory marks your way;
> And read how town, fort, city,
> Yield to you day by day.

Was it wrong to compare Garibaldi to Lincoln in the year 1860? Of course not. And so, truly inspired by her own knowledge of American history, our poet did not hesitate to say:

> For the hand that helps one people
> Their freedom to regain,
> Will aid to break those fetters
> That the poor slave detain.

With Garibaldi and Brown as champions of the century, can slavery endure? The answer is obvious:

> For sure as sin is mortal,
> Must wicked slavery die,
> And Freedom smile for ever
> On the earth of the Most High.

The following day, on November 24, *The Living Age* replied with a sonorous encomium of Garibaldi by another or the same Anonymous — a very clever, tongue-in-cheek, ebullient poem entitled "Exit Bombalino."

The poem celebrates Garibaldi's tumultuous entrance into Naples on September 7, 1860, the day after King Francis II, better known as "Franceschiello," had made his hasty, ignominious "exit." The poet's coinage of the word "Bombalino" for the twenty-four-year-old son of King "Bomba," Ferdinand II, is a felicitous one. It allows him to expose to universal execration the Nero of the nineteenth century by dismissing Ferdinand's inane and ignorant son. It is "Bombalino" that *exit,* but through

"Bombalino" *exit* "Bomba"; *exit,* in other words, that Kingdom of the Two Sicilies that had appalled William E. Gladstone, whose famous "Two Letters to the Earl of Aberdeen on the State Prosecution of the Neapolitan Government," in turn, appalled the entire world.

The poem consists of five three-quatrain stanzas of tetrameters, each ending with "Et exit Bombalino," skillfully and facetiously rhyming with the antipenultimate line.

The action is as rapid as the earthquake growling under the feet of the frightened young King. We see bewildered *Sbirri* slink through the streets and terrified priests holding up their hands before the statue of their deaf San Gennaro. In the meantime the "hireling bands" (a reference to the fifteen thousand Swiss soldiers who guarded the Bourbon's throne) feel most uncomfortable as they muse on their last pay.

> Armed retribution pours its force
> From Spartivent to Porto Fino,
> Resistance melts before its course —
> Et exit Bombalino.

In his hour of need, poor "Franceschiello" has no friend but his own despair. What he has until now thought to be a scepter of steel proves to be a broken reed; each safeguard, a trap. His troops, his ministers, till yesterday so swift to serve him, today are even swifter to betray him. Franceschiello is alone and trembling, and Garibaldi is galloping faster and faster toward the city.

> What faith is bought by fear or gold
> 'Tis time, at length, that even *he* know —
> His soldiers false, his courtiers cold,
> Et exit Bombalino.

Has Garibaldi entered? Has he already freed the many thousands of political prisoners who have lain for years in the darkness of the most inhuman dungeons? At least, unafraid of stick or sword, Goddess Truth can lift her "sorely-scarred yet stately brow."

> Amid such greeting and good will,
> As subjects unto King or Queen owe,
> Who've ruled but by the powers of ill —
> Sic exit Bombalino!

Pictures of Garibaldi are seen all over, on every window, on every door. "Garibaldi! Garibaldi!" should the Neapolitans, finally free, and the sound of the Liberator's name "on wings of blessing" reaches and ripples the Tyrrhenian waves. People kiss and hug one another in great jubilation. Life is new and radiant now. Italy is being made. Garibaldi has come, has looked, has conquered.

> But now alone against a host
> And now a host, as land and sea know,
> Unboasting he caps Caesar's boast —
> Et Exit Bombalino!

The final stanza lays bare the moral of the story: the "powers" of God triumph over the "power" of Ill; there is an Armageddon for every despot on earth. The didactic note neither mars the poem nor makes its reader uneasy, for, soon afterwards, the return of that infectious *ee-no* rhyme re-establishes the equilibrium by recapturing the vividness of the entire scene:

> With jubilee and joyous din,
> From Sicily to San Marino,
> Lo! Garibaldi enters in,
> Et exit Bombalino!

Notice the supple meaning in the sound: *He, No!* (The King, No!)

The news of Garibaldi's retirement to private life in Caprera, a small island off the northeast coast of Sardinia, aroused the admiration of all Americans but, strangely enough, failed to ignite the poet's wonder. Only one poem, by still another Anonymous, was published in *The Living Age* of Boston on January 19, 1861. But here is the poem, simply entitled "Garibaldi's Retirement," which, in spite of its archaic ring, I would not hesitate to place among the best and most successful sonnets written in America.

> Not that three armies thou didst overthrow,
> Not that three cities oped their gates to thee,
> I praise thee, Chief; not for this royalty,
> Decked with new crowns, that utterly lay low;
> For nothing at all thou didst forsake to go
> And tend thy vines amid the Etrurian Sea;
> Not even that thou didst *this* — though History
> Retread two thousand selfish years to show
> Another Cincinnatus! Rather for this —
> The having lived such life that even this deed
> Of stress heroic natural seem as is

Calm night, when glorious day it doth succeed,
And we, forewarned by surest auguries,
The amazing act with no amazement read.

As we know, Garibaldi's retirement did not last long. In the summer of 1862, America was shocked by the news that came from Aspromonte: Garibaldi wounded and arrested!

Soon an Anonymous, one of our many Anonymi, wept in a poem which he called "Aspromonte: Garibaldi," thus making for all future generations the mountain peak of Calabria synonymous with the General. The lines reveal a rather unskilled hand, but succeed nonetheless in telling a story — the sadness of the American people.

O the pity and the passion of that morrow,
When, all lost, all ended, he the invincible
Lay there stricken in his ruin and his sorrow,
Prisoner in the hands of those he loved too well.[7]

Another poem, entitled "Garibaldi Imprisoned," was written at Pontresina, Switzerland, soon after the surrender of Aspromonte, but was published in *The Times* of San Francisco five years later, in 1867, when the circumstances that had inspired it were the same, as the author himself, then living in California, wrote to the editor of that newspaper. Fortunately, then, we are not dealing this time with an Anonymous. On the contrary, we even know that our poet, E. De Meulen, was at the Volturno and Sant'Angelo in command of the "Bersaglieri Lombardi," and that, as soon as he came to this country, he proudly joined the American Army. On November 16, 1867, thirteen days after Garibaldi's defeat at Mentana, to the General once more arrested by the Italian Government and sent once more to his home in Caprera, from his Headquarters, District of Beaufort in Alcatraz Island, California, he sent a letter from which I will quote the beginning and the end: "Dear General, One of your most faithful soldiers and most sincere admirers who fought with you from the Stelvio to the Volturno, I cannot help, in this your hour of Golgotha, come and weep with you over the misfortune of Italy. Oh! the stones, if they could talk; the dead if they could rise, how they would curse those who brought such a misery upon the head of the father of Italy! Here, too, are some of those cowardly slaves of the French Despot and it is not without pain that we can silence them. Lately one of them, Derbec, the editor of a French paper, published a series of injurious articles and he was challenged but refused to fight. An Italian, a man of the people, served the coward right by publicly throwing mud upon him. I replied to him in a few lines which were published in the San Francisco *Times*...Hoping, dear General, that your great soul shall not give up under the weight of ungratefulness and sorrow, I remain, Your most devoted servant, (signed) E. De Meulen, Lieutenant 2nd U.S. Artillery."[8]

The "few lines", published in the San Francisco *Times*—those written after Aspromonte—served, then, a new purpose after the recent disaster of Mentana: to express America's indignation and dejection.

E. De Meulen's "Garibaldi Imprisoned" is a truly, deeply felt poem. It starts:

> Garibaldi imprisoned! and yet the hills
>   Are as free as they were at morn;
> And a mountain soul in fetters?—God!
>   The Alps grow pale with scorn!

From such an impassioned beginning the poet proceeds to describe the first luminous dawn of creation,

> When the wakening world was young,
>   When the little hills lay down to dream,
> And the stars of the morning sung.

There was then only Freedom—Freedom and God, Freedom that was Goddess. And, that very morning, Goddess Freedom, who took her dwelling-place "upon the mountain fair," saw on the snowy breast of a glacier the picture of her child—Garibaldi! But why is the Goddess weeping now? The last two quatrains provide the answer: No, she is not weeping.

> At Garibaldi's prison bars
>   The wounded goddess SINGS!
> She lifts the blood-stained "Stripes and Stars"
>   OVER THE THRONES OF KINGS!

> She sees her glorious flag unfurled
>   To every nation's breath—
> Her clarion war-cry for the world
>   is "LIBERTY, OR DEATH!"[9]

In Envelope No. 360 of the Archivio del Risorgimento in Milan, Italy, is the original of another poem, in French, which bilingual De Meulen sent to his General, whom he called *nouveau Jésus,* inviting the new Messiah to leave his Caprera and redeem the world even if he is destined to die on a cross. *"Ton Sang sera fécond,"* he concluded with an echo of Prudentius' ardent exaltation of the Christian martyrs.

I will, in turn, conclude with a poem that, though not the best, was written by one of the best-known American poets in October 1869, less than a year before the conquest of Rome. John Greenleaf Whittier's "Garibaldi" summarizes for us the entire Garibaldian epos in American poetry. It ends with these lines, worthy of the fervent abolitionist who had earned for himself the title of "poet of human freedom":

> God's providence is not blind, but, full of eyes,
> It searches all the refuges of lies;
> And in His time and way, the accursed things
> Before whose evil feet thy battle-gage
> Has clashed defiance from hot youth to age
> Shall perish. All men shall be priests and kings,
> One royal brotherhood, one church made free
> By love, which is the law of liberty!

Notes

1. *America the Free,* Five Odes by Vittorio Alfieri. Translated into verse by Joseph Tusiani. New York: Italian-American Center for Urban Affairs, Inc. 1976.
2. I must at this point salute a man who devoted his entire life to a search of any link, great and small, official and unofficial, in verse and in prose, between America and Italy during the Risorgimento. His many articles and, above all, his monumental volume entitled *American Opinion on all the Unification of Italy* (1846-1861), endear him to all of us, especially in this Garibaldi centennial, made easier and more luminous by the acumen of his scholarship. His name is Howard R. Marraro.
3. All the poems studied in this article were diligently collected by Howard R. Marraro as an appendix to his major opus. The inscription on the pamphlet that he gave me in 1953 reads: "To Professor Tusiani these Garibaldi poems, so that he may study them." This is what I have done, availing myself of the texts that he collected and also of the notes that accompany them.
4. Howard R. Marraro, *American Opinion on the Unification of Italy* (1846-1861), New York: Columbia University Press, 1932, p. 306.
5. *Ibid.,* p. 292-3.
6. *Ibid.,* p. 296.
7. It is not clear to me if this poem, which Henry W. Longfellow included in his anthology, *Poems of Places,* published in Boston in 1877, originally appeared in a magazine called *Italy,* on pages 70-71. Professor Marraro's note does not provide other details.
8. This unpublished letter was found by Marraro in the Archivio del Risorgimento, Milan, Italy, in Busta No. 360.
9. The capital letters appear in the original.

PART III

Unions, Politics, and Social Mobility: Four Case Studies

Chapter 7   UNIONISM AND THE ITALIAN
AMERICAN WORKER: THE
POLITICS OF ANTI-COMMUNISM
IN THE INTERNATIONAL LADIES'
GARMENT WORKERS' UNION IN
NEW YORK CITY, 1900-1925

Charles A. Zappia
University of California, Berkeley

The history of the International Ladies' Garment Workers' Union (ILGWU) is a very important piece in the whole cloth of Italian-American history. The shapers of the union were men and women of the immigrant generation who struggled to make a place for themselves in the industrial America built by their labor. Not only were the ladies' garment workers pioneers in both industrial unionism and labor-management cooperation; they also molded an organization with broad social aims and important political connections. In fact, the ILGWU was part of the foundation upon which the New Deal was constructed.

Politics, then, was of great significance within the ILGWU. This paper is intended as a preliminary investigation into the emerging political activism of the Italian members of the International Ladies' Garment Workers' Union in New York City prior to the economic collapse of 1929. I will pay particular attention to the role which the Italians played in the ILG's "civil war," a period of factional struggle which dominated the International's political life during the 1920's. I will sketch briefly the organization of Italian garment workers into two important language locals and then examine the ways in which these locals participated in the intra-union struggle between the communists and the "right-wing" socialists, focusing most directly on the Special Convention of 1925, an important battleground in the contest for power in the ILGWU.

In the years between 1880 and 1920, millions of Italians, mostly southerners, immigrated to the United States. Though a small number of craftsmen and shopkeepers left southern Italy for the U.S., most of those who emigrated were landless agricultural workers and *giornalieri,* or hired days laborers. Most of these Italians were among the seventeen million immigrants who, between 1880 and 1919, sailed through America's "golden door" into New York City.[1]

New York City supported a small Italian community throughout the nineteenth century. By 1881, there were more than 20,000 Italians in

Manhattan. The recent arrivals clustered together in colonies, the most sizeable of which was located around Baxter and Mott streets, some dozen or so blocks from the "sweater's district" of the Lower East Side.[2] At first, few Italians found employment in the needle trades. But as both the garment district and the Italian population expanded, the industry opened its doors to many Italians. By the time the ILGWU was chartered in 1900, thousands of Italians, including many women, worked in the needle trades. Among all Italian women working in the United States in the period between 1900 and 1910, 34.7% were employed in the needle trades.[3] In New York City, Italians comprised 15.0% of the work force in the clothing industry as early as 1900.[4]

During the first decade of the twentieth century, 14.0% of all southern Italian immigrants who worked in the garment industry were organized.[5] Despite the fact that this figure exceeded the national average percentage of worker organization, Italians still carry the reputation of having been obstacles to needle trades organization prior to World War One.[6] Much of this reputation is based on accounts of the Italian response to the shirtwaist strike of 1909-1910. Nearly twenty thousand young women struck for almost three months. Most of these women were recent Jewish immigrants; but they were joined on the picket lines by their Irish-American sister workers and smaller numbers of women from other ethnic backgrounds. The walkout received sympathetic coverage in the news media, particularly since the New York City police were resolutely non-sexist in their beating and arresting of strikers.[7] But the media's sympathies were rarely extended to the Italian workers. In fact, it was widely reported that Italian women had refused to strike and were thus prolonging the conflict. A journalist writing in *Colliers* concluded that the Italian women, "brown, ignorant [and] silent," were immune to abstract arguments for unionization: they would not listen and would not, or could not, understand.[8]

It is true that Italian women were reluctant strikers and sometime strikebreakers during the shirtwaist walkout. There were a variety of factors which may explain the Italian response. Italian women worked only with the permission of the male head of the family. Thus when strikers approached Italian women and requested that they join the walkout, this could not be done without consulting with the family head. Since so many men seem to have been reluctant to allow "their" women to strike, the entire affair may have been viewed by the men as a challenge to their prerogatives of absolute control over female family members.[9]

Another problem that hindered organization among the Italian women was the fact that the strike was directed by Jewish women who often spoke only in Yiddish.[10] This language barrier was so formidable that the Jewish workers had virtually ignored attempting to organize the Italians prior to 1909.[11]

There is even more confusion over the role of the Italian men in the far more successful cloakmakers' strike that followed on the heels of the "Uprising of the Twenty Thousand." By 1910, the Cloak Joint Board in New York City had organized 10,000 workers, about one-third of whom were Italians. Again the strike was directed by Jewish leaders, some of whom claimed that the Italians were hapless strikers *(Jesoimim)* who selfishly raided strike benefit committees.[12] The Italian cloakmakers, once they got around to writing their own history, bitterly denied the charge that they were or had been poor strikers. Quite to the contrary, the Italians insisted that they supported wholeheartedly the 1910 strike and were always in the vanguard, demonstrating *"sempre una dedizione completa alla causa per la quale si lottava."*[13] The Italian cloakmakers' version of their strike participation, written thirty-one years after the events of 1910, explained that the Italians were dedicated strikers but could not speak or understand the Yiddish spoken at union meetings: Thus their role in the strike was ignored or distorted.[14]

The success of the cloakmakers' strike of 1910, the important educational activities of Italian radicals, the public outcry following the Triangle Fire of 1911 and the impressive display of immigrant solidarity that arose during the Lawrence Strike of 1912 transformed the consciousness of the Italian garment workers and won them increasing support within the broader Italian community in New York City.[15] As Italians continued to flow into the needle trades, many of them began to join the various locals of the ILGWU, further belying the belief that Italians rejected unions. By 1912, there were Italian minorities in Locals 1, 9, 17 and 35 — organizations of operators, finishers, children's cloakmakers, and pressers.[16] These trades were so constituted that most of their practitioners were male. Many Italian women were working as shirtwaist- and dressmakers by this time as well; and in 1913, a committee was formed by Luigi Antonini, an executive board member of Local 25, expressly to recruit Italian women workers into the ranks of the Dressmakers.[17] These efforts proved to be successful as the Italians of Local 25 were active in the strike of 200,000 garment workers later that year.[18] By the time the post-World War One strike wave rippled through the garment trades, there was very little scabbing by Italians. Thus the role of the Italian workers in 1919 was dramatically different from the one they played only 10 years earlier. Julius Hochman, manager of the New York Dressmakers Joint Board, wrote that the Italian women were not only good strikers but also proved to be loyal unionists once peace had returned to the industry.[19]

The Italians, growing ever more numerous, were aware of their potential power within the Union well before 1919. This potential was unfulfilled largely because the Italians were scattered in several locals, all of which were dominated by those who spoke languages other than Italian. Not surprisingly, then, the main demand of the Italian delegates to national Union conventions was the creation of Italian language locals. This demand first arose during the convention of 1910 and was rejected for five successive years.[20] The Italians argued that they were virtually excluded from union business because the locals to which they belonged transacted their affairs in "Jewish." The convention majorities—in 1910 and 1912— rejected the Italian resolutions on the grounds that many locals already had Italian sub-branches.[21] Finally, in 1916, the International organized Local 48 consisting of all the Italian workers in New York City's cloak trade.[22] In 1919, Local 89—the Italian Dressmakers, the second and eventually more important of the New York City locals, was formed.[23] Thus by the dawn of the 1920's and the beginnings of the ILGWU's "civil war" of that decade, the Italians constituted a major force within the International.

The International Ladies' Garment Workers' Union had a well-deserved reputation for radicalism. Many of the Jewish immigrants who poured into Manhattan's Lower East Side after 1880 and found employment in the readymade clothing industry that dominated the area, were veterans of the eastern Europe socialist labor movement.[24] The fact that nearly all of the leaders and most of the members of the early union were inclined toward socialism did not prevent frequent and acrimonious disputes within the organization concerning ideology and tactics. In fact, ideological arguments raged among the garment workers throughout the first decade of the twentieth century while the union itself stood on shaky ground.[25]

The bargaining position of the ILGWU improved considerably after the dramatic 1910 strikes of the shirtwaist makers and cloakmakers temporarily united the warring factions within the union.[26] The tragic fire at the Triangle Waist Company, occurring one year after the waistmakers' strike ended, focused public attention on the deplorable conditions in the New York "women's trades" and moved many middle-class Progressives, including a number of socially prominent women, to support the trade union demands of the garment workers.[27] Thus a union of no more than 10,000 members before 1910 grew to include 90,000 workers by June of 1913.[28] Eighty percent of these members worked in shops covered by union-management agreements under the "Protocol of Peace" which ended the cloakmakers strike of 1910.[29] The Protocol period ushered in an era of decreased factional activity within the ILGWU as the more moderate socialists succeeded in electing Benjamin Schlesinger to the presidency of the International in 1914.[30]

Developments across the globe soon split the ILGWU socialists into hostile camps. Lenin's rise to power in Russia caused particular excitement in Local 25, the organization of waist and dressmakers. Many of the dressmakers were young women of Russian-Jewish ancestry; some had even participated in the Russian revolution of 1905. The dressmakers had provided much of the idealism and fighting spirit that was indispensable to union growth in 1910.[31] During the years of wartime prosperity and concomitant union security, however, the International leadership under the socialist Schlesinger seemed to emphasize stability and purely trade union issues. Many of the women of Local 25 considered this approach to be sterile and soulless: to them, the union was the agency that could create a better way of life, not simply a vehicle for winning higher wages.[32] By 1919, insurgents were organizing "workers councils" along the Soviet line within most of the locals of New York City. These councils attempted to form shop delegates' leagues which would then elect a Council of Delegates which was to replace the General Executive Board (GEB) of the International. Clearly, this movement was a threat to the power of the union leaders.[33]

The leadership, after a period of vacillation, finally struck at the growing insurgency. The GEB, in 1921, declared the shop delegates leagues unconstitutional. As a tactical move, Local 25 was divided — the shirtwaist makers remained in the old local and the dressmakers, greater in number but supposedly cooler in revolutionary fervor, were organized into Local 22.[34] But this attack on the insurgents backfired in several ways: first of all, the unilateral action of the GEB only served to make the International leaders appear dictatorial; secondly, the left opposition did not weaken but rather grew in strength; and, thirdly, the "lefts" were pushed toward the newly-emerging Communist Party.[35]

By the end of 1922, a mixture of Communist agitation and stiffening non-Communist resistance had so polarized the Union that only two "sides" existed. President Schlesinger could not handle the explosive situation and finally resigned at a GEB meeting in January of 1923. Schlesinger was succeeded by Morris Sigman, an implacable foe of the Union's Communist insurgents.[36] In fact, Sigman was the first to issue a virtual declaration of war when, in August of 1923, he instructed the GEB to order the disbanding of all Communist groups within the locals.[37] Sigman's policies only incited fiercer opposition and did not reduce the Communist influence within the International. In early 1925, the Communists after signing Sigman-mandated "loyalty oaths", were elected *en masse* to the executive boards of Locals 2, 9, and 22.[38] This meant that the Communists controlled the vast majority of the cloak and dressmakers in New York City.

On June 11, 1925, Sigman suspended the Communist members of the executive boards of Locals 2, 9, and 22. He charged them with anti-union activity and instructed them to stand trial on such charges. Communists responded to Sigman's attack by refusing to recognize their suspensions and by forming a Joint Action Committee which functioned independent of the International. When new elections were held, the Communists gained control of the New York Joint Board and with it the representation of 70-75% of the ILGWU membership.[39]

The International was thus in chaos. A special convention, to meet in Philadelphia in November of 1925, was arranged in an attempt to iron out the political differences between the "lefts" and "rights". It is to the role which the Italians played at that convention that I now turn.

Institutional and organizational matters were of great importance to the convention assembled in Philadelphia. The very way in which the International was structured would determine which faction would become dominant. The main convention battles between the Communists and the Italian locals were fought over organizational resolutions, particularly those concerning business agents, representation, and amalgamation. The principal conflict centered around selection of business agents: The Communists insisted that all business agents under the authority of the New York Joint Board should be elected by the membership at large whereas the Italian dressmakers demanded that business agents be elected or appointed only by the various locals they represented.[40] The stakes in this particular conflict were high as they involved questions of the autonomy of the locals and the distribution of power within the International. From the wording of Local 89's resolution it is obvious that the Italians were concerned that only Italian business agents represent the Italian workers and that the local must have the exclusive right of agent selection.[41]

Though the number of Italian workers was constantly increasing, the New York City needle trades were still dominated by non-Italian and largely Jewish workers. Furthermore, in 1925, the majority of the membership affiliated with the New York Joint Board were members of locals dominated by Communists. The situation was simple: At-large election of business agents favored the selection of non-Italians and Communists; election or apointment by the locals protected local autonomy and, in the cases of Locals 48 and 89, insured that Italian workers would be represented by Italian agents. It seems that the Italians feared that Communist business agents would be more concerned with the needs of the Party rather than the needs of the workers; but at least as important was the feeling that non-Italian business agents simply could not understand the particular priorities of Italian workers. The fight for the creation of autonomous Italian locals had been a long one. The Italians were convinced that this autonomy could be preserved only if business agents were selected on the local and not the Joint Board level.[42]

The attack on the Italian resolution was vigorous and, interestingly, spoken partly in Yiddish.[43] Both Antonini and Salvatore Ninfo of Local 48 defended the resolution by labelling the Communists as opportunists and by reiterating the position that business agents were paid to represent *specific* groups of workers. When the resolution was brought to a vote, it was carried by a 145 to 105 tally, a vote distribution which closely approximated the non-Communist to Communist delegate strength.[44]

Proportional representation was also a major issue at the 1925 convention. The Communist delegates advanced several proposals which attempted to gain Joint Board and "Central Bodies" representation in proportion to the actual membership of each of the locals.[45] The Italian dressmakers presented a counter-proposal suggesting that a *graduated* system of proportional representation be adopted. The proposed system was complex, but its intended result was not: The Communists, entrenched in the huge New York City locals, would gain more equitable representation but the very small though numerous conservative out-of-town locals would still be over-represented. The new result would be that the International administration, through its control of the out-of-town locals, would maintain its direction of union policy while making a show of initiating a more democratic system of representation.[46] The fact that the Italians presented the "graduated" resolution serves to underscore the growing alliance betwen the Italian locals and the Local 10 machine directed by David Dubinsky. Dubinsky had been one of the strongest supporters of the Italians in the fight for local selection of business agents.[47] The Italians, in turn, supported Dubinsky's views on representation even to the extent of finally withdrawing their own resolution and supporting instead a substitute suggested by Dubinsky. The substitute measure was even more effective in securing the over-representation of the smaller locals.[48] The communists objected strenuously, but eventually had no choice other than to accept the Dubinsky proposal.[49]

The most interesting organizational resolution suggested by Local 89 was that which dealt with the question of amalgamation. The convention's Resolutions Committee reviewed four separate proposals, each suggesting the formation of some particular type of alliance that would include all of the needle trades' unions in one joint organization. The communist resolution advocated "the amalgamation of all the needle trades unions into one powerful international of needle trades workers." It further urged that the GEB immediately join with the Fur Workers in calling a conference of all needle trades unions which would result in the chartering of a new organization.[50] The communist resolution was partly an attempt to build a union that would more effectively protect the workers and could better organize the unorganized; but it was also an attempt to consolidate communist strength and insure party hegemony over the proposed industry-wide organization. The new international would be constructed by the Fur Workers, the most thoroughly communist of all needle trades unions, and the ILGWU with its powerful bloc of communists. The existing internationals would be dissolved, thus destroying the power of the anti-communists in both the ILGWU and the Amalgamated Clothing Workers. The new organization would be centrally directed, that is, directed from New York, and the existing autonomy of the locals, particularly those from out of town, would be seriously reduced. Thus the communist proposal for amalgamation was also a draft for the seizure of industry-wide control of labor organizing.

Local 89's resolution concerning amalgamation also demanded the formation of one "centralized organization" of all the unions in the needle trades; however, it differed sharply from the communist proposal in that it specified that delegates to a founding convention must be elected from each existing *Local* and not from the at-large membership of the Internationals.[51] Obviously, this method of delegate selection would make it unlikely that the communists would come to dominate the executive positions of a new international. Thus the Italian dressmakers sought to build one big union in the needle trades without sacrificing local autonomy and without yielding complete political power to the communists.

The convention did not act upon the amalgamation proposals as the Resolutions Committee referred these proposals to the General Executive Board. The Committee did report that it was indisposed to accept the need for amalgamation, claiming that such a program was not practical and not really desired by the majority of the workers.[52] The Resolutions Committee, chaired by David Dubinsky, was a staunch defender of the power of the Sigman administration. It is clear from the Committee's extensive defense of the organizational *status quo* that the administration recognized that amalgamation would result in a loss of power for present International leaders. Antonini and the other delegates from Local 89 must have recognized this as well; still, they took a stand close to that of the Communists on the issue of amalgamation.

The Italian delegates to the ILGWU convention of 1925 stood near center stage in the struggle for the control and future direction of that important labor organization. It is certain that the Italian delegates supported and voted with the Sigman administration at the convention. The fact that the Italians voted against the communists, however, has been misinterpreted by some labor historians as proof of the basic peasant "conservatism" of the members of the Italian locals.[53] It may be that the politics of the Italian garment workers have been misunderstood or ignored for two reasons: The highly visible and articulate socialism of the Jewish workers has tended to overshadow the contributions of the Italians; and, many historians have assumed that the roots of Italian-American politics are buried in the ancient sands of Catholicism and peasant indifference.[54] Benjamin Stolberg, a close observer of the events of the 1920's (and a strong defender of the ILGWU hierarchy), wrote of the membership of Locals 48 and 89:

> The rank and file of these two Italian unions were never radical. Many of them had been Sicilian peasants a few years back, Catholic and tradition-bound.... During the early stages of the

civil war these Italian workers remained fairly tranquil. It was only when the struggle got desperate that they became involved. And then they sided with the Sigman administration and stuck to it through thick and thin.[55]

Even this brief examination of the role of the Italian unionists at the 1925 convention calls into question Stolberg's often-repeated assumption that anti-communism was the natural heritage of Italian nativity. Italian opposition to the communists at the Philadelphia convention was not primarily the product of peasant conservatism, Catholicism, or belief in "pure and simple" trade unionism; rather, the Italian position vis-a-vis the Communists was more likely based on several considerations. The first of these was a realistic conception of power politics within the ILGWU. The communists, very few of whom were Italians, clearly intended to capture the leadership of the International. Furthermore, these communists advanced a program for union amalgamation that would have destroyed the autonomy of the Italian locals. Thus Italian support for the Sigman administration was basically a pragmatic move to protect the growing power of Locals 48 and 89 against *any* challenges, regardless of the ideologies of the challengers. When the GEB postponed local elections in the Dress Division, which included Local 89, in February of 1925, ostensibly because of "inflammatory" electioneering by the communists, Luigi Antonini demanded not only that the elections be held immediately but that the International never again interfere in the election affairs of the locals.[56]

The Italians did object to certain tactics and political positions of the communists; however, the basis for objection was not a comprehensively anti-communist world view. During the early convention wrangling over delegate seatings, the case of Elias Marks came before the Credentials Committee.[57] Marks, along with many other radicals, had been arrested in the government witch hunts of 1919. When Marks was brought to trial, he denied participating in radical activity or even holding radical beliefs. He did so on the instructions of the Communist Party to which he belonged. The Communists felt that the very existence of their organization was threatened by the government attacks; therefore, the Party theorized that it would gain them nothing to hold to principle in a capitalist court of law—survival was more important than martyrdom. Then Marks denied and even denounced his beliefs, did not suffer imprisonment, and was free to continue clandestine activity as a Communist. But his public recantation had stigmatized him among the Italians as an unprincipled weakling. Shortly after Marks' release, Nicola Sacco and Bartolomeo Vanzetti were arrested for a murder charge and tried instead for their outspoken anarchism. Sacco and Vanzetti had never denied their beliefs, even in the capitalist courts that they too despised. It seemed to at least some of the Italian unionists that the Communist tactic of denying one's beliefs was far more reprehensible than those beliefs themselves. As a matter of fact, when Luigi Antonini stood to comment on the Marks matter, he expressed his sympathy for all the Communists who had suffered persecution without retracting their principles; but he had nothing but scorn for Elias Marks. Still, Antonini, voicing the position of the Italian locals that no duly elected delegate should be refused a seat at the convention, argued that Marks should be admitted.[58]

There was another important dimension to the Italian-Communist confrontation of 1925; the broader interaction between Italians and Jews in the garment trades. Arturo Giovannitti, speaking at an ILGWU function in 1924, pointed out the "remarkable solidarity" between Jewish and Italian workers. He went on to praise the readiness among the Jews to help the less organized Italians and to condemn the anti-Semitism being expressed in the New York fascist press.[59] There does seem to have been far less tension among Jews and Italians in the garment trades than among Italians and Irish on the docks, for example. But this, sadly, does not tell the entire tale: The Italians did express some animosity toward the Jewish workers, and, at times, even some anti-Semitism. I have already mentioned the Italian dislike for the use of Yiddish as the semi-official union language and the Italian feelings of rejection by Jewish unionists during the cloak strike of 1910. The feeling persisted until as late as 1941 that the Italians never received the credit they deserved as good unionists and strikers and that, in the early days of the trade, the Jewish workers had an easier time of things since many of the employers were also Jewish.[60] Local 48's "Libro Ricordo" claimed that the Jewish workers got a better deal from the bosses since they had certain things in common, like a similar attitude of stinginess (*pitoc-cheria)*![61] Clearly, the Italians resented Jewish domination of the ILGWU. At least under the Schlesinger and Sigman administrations, the Italians had won the right to build their own locals. These organizations were threatened by the Communists, a number of whom spoke only in Yiddish at the convention of 1925. This fact serves as the basis for Italian "anti-communism" during the "civil war" of the 1920's.

Last of all, the Italian delegates possessed a strong sense of loyalty to their two major leaders, Salvatore Ninfo and Luigi Antonini, both of whom opposed the Communists, though for different reasons. Ninfo, a Gompers-style trade unionist, believed that the Communists were disloyal unionists; Antonini, sensitive and egotistical, had resigned from the Communist Party when that group had attempted to censure him for paying a compliment to the socialist newspaper *The Call*.[62] It was not simply that Antonini and Ninfo were union leaders, they were also community leaders —*uomi rispettati*. The relationship between these leaders and the Italian unionists was charged with some of the Old World feelings of honor, respect, and deference. For example, many union functionaries were given gifts in appreciation for services rendered; most of these gifts were small and non-personal. However, when Salvatore Ninfo was presented with a gift, it was an expensive ring, a symbol of authority and power in the Italian Church and community.[63]

Discovering the workplace and union histories of Italian-Americans is central to understanding the entire Italian-American experience. After all, Italian immigrants and second-generation Italian-Americans were found most often among the traditional industrial proletariat in the United States prior to 1945. Participation in strikes and union activities helped to mold an Italian-American working-class culture. This culture was strongly influenced by Italian family arrangements and value systems. These must be studied in depth if a comprehensive picture of Italian-American history is to be painted.

Italian-Americans, as this paper indicates, were also capable of self-conscious political activity that was not merely the product of a mythical peasant conservatism. This political activity needs to be examined more closely, despite the fact "political history" is somewhat out of vogue at present. Old world political activity must be studied, particularly that taking place in the south of Italy. This is of great importance since too many assume that Southern Italians were all cut of the same cloth and emigrated from "pre-political" societies. The leaders of the Italian locals in the ILGWU, men like Antonini and Ninfo, deserve full-scale and impartial biographies. The history of the rank-and-file can be and should be reconstructed. There are still many "old-timers" alive who are willing and even eager to talk about their experiences in the needle trades. The radical communities in New York City and other garment centers like Rochester and Chicago should be focuses of serious studies. Interviews, like those conducted by the investigators of the "Italians in Chicago" project, show that the influence of the radicals was widespread, even among those workers generally regarded as "Catholic and tradition-bound."

This paper is meant to show only that Italian-American unionists thought and acted in political terms. The ILGWU Italian locals were just emerging as political and social institutions in the 1920's. By the 1930's, they had become part of the center around which Italian-American life in New York City revolved. Certainly, the history of these locals is an important part of the history of all Italian-Americans.

Notes

1. Humbert Nelli, *The Italians in Chicago, 1880-1930* (New York: Oxford University Press, 1970), p. 4; Andrew Rolle, *The Immigrant Upraised*

(Norman: University of Oklahoma Press, 1968), p. 95; Joseph LoPreato, *Italian Americans* (New York: Random House, 1970), pp. 21-35; Thomas Kessner, *The Golden Door* (New York: Oxford University Press, 1977), pp. 4-5.

2. Federal Writers' Project, *The Italians of New York* (New York: Random House, 1938), pp. 3-22; John H. Mariano, *The Second Generation of Italians in New York City* (Boston: The Christopher Publishing House, 1921), p. 13.

3. This figure compares favorably to statistics concerning unionization among Polish workers (0.0%) but is much smaller than the percentage of unionization achieved by "Hebrews" (23.9%). These statistics are somewhat difficult to interpret. First of all, they are representative of all branches of the clothing industry. Secondly, the statistics are drawn from a tiny sample of only 200. In New York City alone, there were more than 82,000 womens' garment workers in just the dress and cloakmaking trades in 1910. The *entire* ILGWU had fewer than 10,000 members prior to September of that year. Thus it is probable that fewer than 13% of all workers in the needle trades were organized prior to 1910. If this was indeed the case, then southern Italian unionization exceeded the national average for the garment industry. *Report of the United States Immigration Commission,* by William Dillingham, Chairman (Washington, D.C.: Government Printing Office, 1911), 42 vols., 2: 297-313; 11: 660. (hereafter referred to as USIC); Louis Levine, *The Women's Garment Workers* (New York: B.W. Heubsch, Inc., 1924), p. 145, 169; John H. M. Laslett, *Labor and the Left* (New York: Basic Books, Inc., 1970), 110.

4. Edwin Fenton, "Immigrants and Unions, A Case Study: Italians and American Labor, 1870-1920," (PhD, Harvard University, 1957), p. 482.

5. USIC, 2: 298.

6. Levine, *Garment Workers,* 156; Rudolf Glanz, *Jew and Italian* (New York: Shulsinger Bros., Inc., 1970), p. 45.

7. *New York Tribune,* 4 December 1909, p. 1; 11 December 1909, p. 1.

8. Adriana Spadoni, "The Italian Working Women of New York," *Colliers,* March 23, 1912, p. 5.

9. "Report of the Committee on Organization" in Womens Trade Union League (WTUL), *Proceedings of the Fourth Biennial Convention* (St. Louis, 1913), p. 24.

10. Sarah Comstock, "The Uprising of the Girls: Some Circumstances of the Strike of over Thirty Thousand Garment Makers," *Colliers,* December 25, 1909, p. 17.

11. WTUL, *Annual Report* (1908/1909), p. 7.

12. Benzion Hofman, *Fifty Years Cloakmakers Union, 1886-1936* quoted in Glanz, *Italian and Jew,* 43.

13. Locale 48 — ILGWU, *"48"; Libro Ricordo del XXV Anniversario della Unione dei Cloakmakers Italiani* (New York: International Newspaper Printing Co., 1941), p. 75.

14. *Libro Ricordo,* 78.
15. Serafino Romualdi, "Storia della Locale 89" in *Local 89 Fifteenth Anniversary Commemoration Pamphlet,* (1934), pp. 36-39, Immigration History Research Center, University of Minnesota, St. Paul, Minnesota.
16. Benjamin Stolberg, *Tailor's Progress* (New York: Doubleday, Doran and Company, Inc., 1944), p. 111.
17. Romualdi, "Locale 89," 38.
18. Columba M. Furio, "The Cultural Background of the Italian Immigrant Woman and Its Impact on Her Unionization in the New York City Garment Industry, 1880-1919," in George E. Pozzetta, ed., *Pane e Lavoro* (Toronto: Multicultural Historical Society of Ontario, 1980), p. 94.
19. Julius Hochman, "Hail Local 89!" in *Local 89 Fifteenth Anniversary Pamphlet, 19.*
20. Glanz, *Jew and Italian,* 50-51.
21. ILGWU, *Tenth Convention Report* (Boston, 1910), p. 83.
22. *Libro Ricordo,* 25-30.
23. John S. Crawford, *Luigi Antonini* (New York: Educational Dept. of the Italian Dressmakers Union, 1950), p. 22; Luigi Antonini in *Libro Ricordo,* 12-15.
24. Laslett, *Labor,* 99; Abraham Menes, "The East Side and the Jewish Labor Movement," in *Many Pasts,* eds., Herbert G. Gutman and Gregory S. Kealy (Englewood Clfifs, N.J.: Prentice-Hall, Inc. 1973), pp. 227-237.
25. Levine, *Garment Workers,* 114-119.
26. Stolberg, *Progress,* 59-67; ILGWU, *ILGWU History-News, 1900-1950* (Atlantic City: 1950), pp. 25-30.
27. Melvyn Dubofsky, *When Workers Organize* (Amherst: University of Massachusetts Press, 1968), pp. 50-58.
28. Laslett, *Labor,* 110.
29. The Protocol was the brainchild of Louis D. Brandeis who believed that perpetual economic peace would come to the industry once all disputes were settled by an impartial board of arbitration, of which he agreed to act as Chairman. Specifically, the Protocol granted a six day, fifty-four hour week along with ten paid holidays, the limiting of overtime to two and one-half hours per day during busy seasons, and the institution of a joint board of sanitary control. The Protocol also established the "preferential union shop" and set up the permanent machinery for the arbitration of disputes and grievances. Thus the Union was recognized as the bargaining agent of the workers. Still the Protocol was never fully accepted by either employers or workers. Employers were reluctant to establish the preferential union shop as this excluded the manufacturers' hiring of non-union persons unless they could prove that no qualified union members were available for the particular jobs. The union had not won any specific rights concern-

ing the important matter of worker discharge; thus this tactic could still be used by an employer to stall union activity in a shop. Most importantly, the union promised not to strike for the duration of the agreement. But despite its limitations, the Protocol did minimize conflict within the industry for nearly six years. For the complete text of the agreement see Appendix A in Julius Henry Cohen, *Law and Order in Industry* (New York: The MacMillan Company, 1916), p. 243; Stolberg, *Progress,* 69-70, 91; Max Danish, *The World of David Dubinsky* (New York: The World Publishing Company, 1957), p. 29; Dwight Edwards Robinson, *Collective Bargaining and Market Control in the New York Suit and Coat Industry* (New York: Columbia University Press, 1949), pp. 34-35; ILGWU, *News-History,* 41.

30. For a brief discussion of "moderate" socialism, like that advanced by the *Jewish Daily Forward* under the editorship of Abraham Cahan, see Daniel Bell, *Marxian Socialism in the United States* (Princeton: Princeton University Press, 1967), pp. 98-99. Cahan's socialism was folk-oriented, undogmatic, and eventually very anti-communist. See also Foster Rhea Dulles, *Labor in America* (New York: Thomas Y. Crowell Company, 1966), p. 206.

31. Stolberg, *Progress,* 109. Stolberg's history of the ILGWU is an invaluable source of information; however, his prejudices are strong and are often given free reign. In dealing with the "romantic" immigrant dressmakers, he suggests that since there were no czars here, the women put their revolutionary fervor into a variety of "fad" movements.

32. *Ibid.*

33. See Theodore Draper, *The Roots of American Communism* (New York: The Viking Press, 1963), pp. 315-320, concerning the issue of "workers' control."

34. Levine, *Garment Workers,* 350-351.

35. Draper, *Roots,* 388-389; Stolberg, *Progress,* 115.

36. David Dubinsky, *A Life With Labor* (New York: Simon and Schuster, 1977), pp. 61-64.

37. *Justice,* 16 August 1923, p. 1.

38. Dubinsky, *Life,* 63.

39. ILGWU, *Proceedings* (Philadelphia, 1925), 18.

40. *Ibid.,* 83.

41. The "Honor Role" of Local 89, printed in *Justice* 16 January 1925 lists four non-Italian business agents out of a total of nine. See also ILGWU, *Report, 1928,* 175-176.

42. ILGWU, *Proceedings* (Philadelphia, 1925), 302-305.

43. *Ibid.,* 304.

44. *Ibid.*

45. *Ibid.,* 318.

46. *Ibid.,* 327.

47. *Ibid.,* 328-329.

48. *Ibid.*

49. According to Benjamin Stolberg, the communists, who had walked out of the convention, were ordered back by the Party which did not want to split the International at the time. *Progress,* 134.
50. ILGWU, *Proceedings* (Philadelphia, 1925), 357.
51. *Ibid.,* 356.
52. *Ibid.,* 357-358.
53. One good example of this interpretation advanced by a prominent labor historian can be found in Irving Bernstein, *The Lean Years: A History of the American Worker, 1920-1933* (Baltimore: Penguin Books, 1970), p. 138.
54. Rudolph J. Vecoli, "Italian American Workers, 1880-1920: Padrone Slaves or Primitive Rebels?" in S.M. Tomasi, ed., *Perspectives in Italian Immigration and Ethnicity* (New York: Center for Migration Studies, 1977), pp. 26-27.
55. Stolberg, *Progress,* 111-112.
56. *Justice,* 13 March 1925, p. 2.
57. ILGWU, *Proceedings* (Philadelphia, 1925), 93-103.
58. *Ibid.,* 96.
59. *Justice,* 11 July 1924, p. 2.
60. *Libro Ricordo,* 74-76.
61. *Ibid.,* 79. "(The Jewish Workers) *avevano poca attitudine alla pitoccheria, caratteristica principale dei* cloakmakers *ebrei."*
62. *Justice,* 7 November 1924, p. 4.
63. *Justice,* 16 May 1924, p. 9.

Chapter **8** PIGTOWN, THE JAMES MADISON
CLUB AND POWER
Charles Lacerra
College of Staten Island

This paper is the result of efforts by Dr. Jerome Krase of Brooklyn
College, City University of New York, and me to write a history of the
James Madison Democratic Club of Brooklyn. From this perspective,
"Pigtown" is significant in that the leaders of the Madison Club and
Brooklyn's Democratic Party made deliberate efforts to enjoin ethnic
neighborhoods such as Pigtown and its Italians into their political base.
From another perspective, the significance of studying Pigtown is to docu-
ment the history of Italians and to see their experiences within the
framework of society-at-large. This author will combine these perspectives
and document through oral and written history how the Italian community
of Pigtown made its earliest entry into the political mainstream through the
Madison Club.

The James Madison Democratic Club of Brooklyn was founded in 1905
by John H. McCooey along with four other men.[1] McCooey was an ambitious man who was eventually to become Democratic Boss of Brooklyn, a
position equal to Charles Murphy, Tammany Hall leader who was head of
New York County, Manhattan. In the first three decades of this century,
Brooklyn grew enormously as immigrants migrated from Manhattan to
Brooklyn as a step upward and a way to leave the crowded tenements
behind. Immigrants also were entering Brooklyn in large numbers from
surrounding states and Europe. *The Brooklyn Citizen* commented on the
large growth of the borough in an editorial in 1905 pointing out that the
population of Brooklyn had grown 350,000 since 1900 to a total of
1,500,000.[2] By 1930, the population of Kings County was larger than that
of Manhattan.[3] With a 27% growth rate during the 1920's, Brooklyn
became the most populated county in the state.

This growth in population, of course, broadened the power of Democratic Boss John H. McCooey. Although he was not considered Tammany
Hall leader in New York City, McCooey had in Kings County the largest
voting constituency of all the borough leaders. Through his organizational
machine, the Madison Club, he was able to deliver the Brooklyn vote for
the Party. The open door that McCooey kept at the Madison Club was the
key to his success.[4] McCooey once stated in one of his rare interviews:
"Man is a gregarious animal and he can't expect to live by himself and get

on. He must help others and others in turn will help him."[5] Residents from Pigtown lined up to see McCooey for help and he did not disappoint them.

McCooey reigned as Democratic Boss of Brooklyn for almost thirty years and spun a web of control over the borough and Party members. In addition to the Madison Club, satellite clubs were established around the borough to support his control.[6] The arm of the Madison Club that reached into Pigtown was the Three Leaf Club, later changed to the Three Leaf Democratic Group.[7] It was through this Club that Italians touched base with the Madison Club, and the power of the machine.

That area of what is now called Crown Heights in Brooklyn, that was known as Pigtown, had as its northern border Lefferts Avenue. To the south, Pigtown extended to Rutland Road. Its western border was Brooklyn Avenue and its eastern extremity went to Troy Avenue.[8] It roughly took in about 12 square blocks when it was finally paved.

The name Pigtown apparently was a misnomer as former residents and the *Brooklyn Eagle* recall that there were more goats than pigs in the area.[9] Perhaps the name Pigtown seemed more accurate because of health conditions in the area. In 1906, a riot broke out between the Italian community and the authorities. A Patrolman, Charles Orr, tried to apprehend an Italian who was dumping "a cartload of dirt on a public highway."[10] Other Italians came to their countryman's aid including Antonio Pope who was acknowledged as "mayor" of a large portion of the neighborhood.[11] Pope, who had "for years been employed as a special officer for that section," worked with authorities, as did dozens of other ethnic mayors throughout the New York City, to keep order in his ghetto.[12] However, he was not very successful in keeping sanitary conditions acceptable to the authorities of the City. The residents were content to let conditions go as they were.

Two months later, Superintendent Clarke, of the Brooklyn Street Cleaning Department, stated that he was not responsible for the filthy conditions of the streets in Pigtown. Clarke noted: "We have no control whatever over in that section. We haven't money enough to clean the streets, much less to tackle the filthy roads in 'Pigtown.'" He said the Health Department should clean it up.[13] One resident that still lives in this Crown Heights area recalls that many of the Italians had small farms in the area and kept chickens and other fowl that roamed about freely along with the goats and pigs. It was unpaved with many vacant lots and after a heavy rain or snow he would have to use hip boots to laboriously move from one place to the other.[14] It was to take a generation before Pigtown improved its image.

This occurred when the community attempted to overcome the pejorative name Pigtown with the name "Crown Slope" (the southern most part of Crown Heights). In 1921, James Fenimore and Gabriel Damato, two influential business leaders, met in the Republican Club and organized the Crown Slope Community Center to upgrade the area.[15] The area had a stigma to it because in addition to its unsanitary conditions, there was a penitentiary there. But by 1921, it was gone along with the goats, and a rash of homes and rear garages appeared, indicating prosperity had come to the ghetto. The first phase of Pigtown had come to an end.

Pigtown gained further respectability in 1924 when an article appeared in the *Eagle* by reporter John H. McCandless titled "Modern Homes Surround Old Pigtown Settlement." McCandless noted that mostly Italians lived in the area and were truck gardeners and junk dealers. Some owned their own homes and the area was spared the crowding of the tenements. But in 1916, he noted, the Brooklyn Housing Committee made a study of the area. The result was that some streets and sidewalks were paved and main streets were cut to allow passage.[16]

Later, building took place on a large scale in and around the area as Brooklyn's population soared. McCandless noted: "It is only a question of time." The area was beginning to be absorbed. McCandless further stated: "It looks as if the Pigtown of 1916 is doomed in a few years to merge itself into the surrounding middle class neighborhood and be transformed into what perhaps may be described as a more tidy and respectable, if less interesting Flatbush home section."[17] Pigtown was ripe for political absorption.

The Jordan family (originally Giordano) tells the story of how Pigtown became tied to the Madison Club. It seems that one Sunday around 1925 John H. McCooey needed a plumber urgently and couldn't get the Irish plumber that usually serviced him. He called upon Anthony Jordan, Sr., who had established a plumbing business in Pigtown, to do the job. McCooey was very impressed with Jordan and asked him to act as liaison to the Italians in Pigtown.[18]

Judge Jordan, Anthony Jr., has stated that the Madison Club was a corporate structure that had social, political and financial ties to its satellite clubs. These subdivisions were controlled by lieutenants and captains. Anthony Jordan Sr. became captain of Pigtown and helped people get jobs. This was a big community service in the days when civil service was limited.[19]

Anthony Jordan's daughter Rose recalls her father helped fix traffic violations and aided in other legal problems that the residents had. Jordan was bi-lingual and this was a big plus for him since friendship and communication with his constituents was so important for his effectiveness. Jordan had connections and personally knew all the commissioners of the City. For Jordan, his role in the Madison Club made him feel part of the whole political machine. He was able to rub elbows with those politically prominent and get a sense of power.

Later, in 1930, Jordan opened a Bar and Grill at 525 East New York Avenue. Parties were frequently held there before and after elections. Besides McCooey, many prominent-to-be came such as Abe Beame, Judge Leon Healy, Judge Nathan Sobel, and Judge Murray Feiden. Candidates would come also to get Jordan's advice. It was a common sight to see Cadillacs arrive in front of the Bar. The establishment was also a frequent haunt for players of the Brooklyn Dodgers. The Bar was a social and political center for the area.

Anthony Jordan also served as President of the Madison Club for a number of years. He was close friends to the Steinguts after McCooey died in 1934. The children recall how McCooey, and later the Steinguts, frequently were on the phone with Jordan to keep politically updated.[20] Jordan would engage people in the neighborhood to go from door to door, as he did, to get the vote out. The Captain and his helpers were most crucial. One helper noted that they would tell the people which Democratic candidate to vote for. They would also encourage people to get out on election day. This was no small task in light of the fact that Italians were not likely to freely run to the polls. If anyone needed help or transportation to the polls Jordan would supply car service.[21] It was with these methods that the Steinguts, Irwin and Stanley, had an unbroken string of successes at the polls from 1921 to 1978.

Pigtown today has some residents who have lived there more than half a century. It still has the same lovely houses and courts where the remaining Italian-Americans live in harmony with the newly arrived Haitians. The Italian character in the area began to diminish after 1960. Up to that time feasts were held on Mount Carmel, St. John's and St. Rocco's days in the streets of Rutland Road and East New York Avenue. The Italian Church in the area was St. Blaise, where the Italians would go to be Baptized and attend Mass. Less than three blocks away still stands the Irish parish of St. Francis. Anthony Jordan frequently coordinated his efforts to aid Italians in the area by cooperating with St. Blaise. It was also known that the pastors over the years sometimes attended meetings of the Madison Club. In 1979, the remaining Italians lost their Church when the dioceses sold it to Seventh Day Adventists.[22] St. Francis is now called St. Francis of Assisi and St. Blaise. The Church has an Irish pastor.

The Boss system that was Irish style politics was raised to a paradigm by John H. McCooey. Tammany and its machine served a great purpose not only to the Irish but extended a warm and friendly hand to other immigrants coming into Brooklyn. Native Americans thought of those newcomers as "riff-raff." The regular political channels could not serve their needs.[23] McCooey always had a line of people at his desk in the Madison Club waiting to gain a favor. He made social services, naturalization and access to authority reachable to the so-called "riff-raff" of the big congested City. Many of these numbers were Italians entering the country and receiving no help from the system. Mr. McCooey sometimes saw as many as 200 people in a day.

Italians and their later descendants were not great advocates of participation in the political process. The efforts of men like Anthony Jordan Sr. and John McCooey sped up the process of assimilation of Italians into the mainstream. The former did it because he realized he was helping people and his own ancestors. McCooey helped people out of instinct. It was the way the machine worked. It was the way to engage the bewildered who needed help, but were unattended. In this way McCooey and his followers sustained a political base. In a modest way, Italians of Pigtown, in the first half of this century were discovering the value of McCooey's dictum about people helping each other.

Notes

1. Other charter members were Henry J. Dougherty, Ernest Eggert, Andrew T. Sullivan, and William L. Collins. *New York Times,* June 19, 1925, p. 14.
2. The *Brooklyn Citizen,* Oct. 2, 1905.
3. Francis T. White. *County Government A View Point from the Second Most Populous County in the U.S.A. The County Kings.* Copyright 1934 by Francis T. White. White was a member of the Supreme Court of the United States and Bar Association.
4. *New York Times,* Mar. 23, 1930. V, p. 10.
5. *Ibid.*
6. Abe Beame confirmed this in an interview on May 19, 1981. Beame formed the Haddington Democratic Club in Crown Heights, one of six satellite clubs of the Madison Club. Also see the *New York Post,* Oct. 20, 1965.
7. Brochure, Crown Slope Democratic Club, 19th Assembly District: Annual Entertainment and Ball. April 1, 1932. Many ads appear for the Three Leaf Club. Salvatore Jordan and Rose (Jordan) and Nicholas Micoletti confirmed this in interviews.
8. Dr. Jerome Krase. *Self and Community in the City.* University Press of America, 1982, pp. 102-3.
9. Interview, Joseph Di Giovanni, July 14, 1982. Also see the *Brooklyn Eagle,* April 6, 1921.
10. *Brooklyn Eagle,* June 14, 1906.
11. *Ibid.*
12. *New York Times,* Mar. 5, 1905. III, p. 6:1. Max Hahn was spokesman for The East Side Mayors Association. He makes some general observations about New York City's ethnic mayors.
13. *Brooklyn Eagle,* Aug. 17, 1906.
14. Interview, Joseph Di Giovanni.
15. *Brooklyn Eagle,* April 6, 1921.
16. *Brooklyn Eagle,* Sept. 14, 1924.
17. *Ibid.*

18. All three children of Jordan Sr. confirm this story.
19. Interview, Judge Anthony Jordan Jr., May 23, 1980.
20. Interview, Rose Nicoletti, July 7, 1982.
21. Interview, Joseph Di Giovanni.
22. Interview, Reverend John Regan, July 14, 1982. Father Regan is pastor of St. Francis.
23. Richard Hofstadter, *The Age of Reform,* Vintage Book: New York 1960, p. 178. Also see Robert K. Merton, *Social Theory and Social Structure.* Glencoe: Free Press, New York, 1957, p. 126.

Chapter **9**   STEELWORKERS AND
STOREKEEPERS: SOCIAL
MOBILITY AMONG ITALIAN
IMMIGRANTS IN BIRMINGHAM
Robert J. Norrell
Birmingham-Southern College, Alabama

The great tide of European immigrants to America in the late nineteenth and early twentieth centuries deposited relatively few newcomers in
the southern United States. Despite efforts by many southern state governments to attract immigrants as agricultural laborers, the foreign-born
population in the South always remained very low. The South offered few
of the industrial jobs that the new immigrants preferred. For the poor
Italian or Slovak just arrived at Ellis Island, the South was a long and expensive train ride away. The presence of millions of blacks kept away some
Europeans who feared labor competition with poor Negroes. Moreover,
many immigrants knew of the South's mistreatment of blacks and reasoned,
quite rationally, that they too might be mistreated there.[1]

This chapter examines the experience of a few European immigrants
who did try their luck in the South — Italians in Birmingham. Although the
Birmingham Italians are almost insignificant numerically — the Italian community there was less than one percent the size of New York's Italian community — they are important for revealing something about the Italian
immigrant experience outside the large northern cities of the United States.
Furthermore, the occupational mobility among Italian immigrants in Birmingham has implications for larger questions about social mobility in
America.

The Italian community in Birmingham was originally an outpost of an
Italian group in Louisiana. Sicilians following the path of the citrus trade
between their home and the southern United States settled in New Orleans
in the 1850s. In the 1870s Sicilian immigrants began to work on sugar plan-
tations in Louisiana. Sugar planters, dissatisfied with black labor, en-
thusiastically sought Italians to replace Negroes in their cane fields. By
1910, twenty thousand Italian immigrants lived in Louisiana. But by then
many of them had left the cane fields for better-paying work as truck
farmers, fruit and fish peddlers, and grocers.[2]

In the 1880s a few of the Louisiana Italians came to Birmingham, lured by
the promise of higher wages in the developing iron industry. A trickle of Italian
families to Birmingham in the 1890s turned into a steady, if narrow stream

in 1900. Labor shortages in the coal mines and steel mills and dissatisfaction with both native white and black laborers led industrialists to recruit immigrant labor both in the United States and in Europe. A few Italian immigrants were brought to Birmingham as strike-breakers in 1904 and 1908, but most came during years of industrial peace and prosperity. By 1910 there were 1,846 Italians in the Birmingham area, but still they made up less than one percent of the local population.[3]

Migration chains connected several Sicilian villages to Birmingham. Bisacquino, a village in the western interior, sent enough of its sons to compose forty-five percent of the Birmingham Italian community in 1920. The sulphur-mining region of southcentral Sicily contributed about fifteen percent. Another twenty percent came from various villages in the coastal regions of Sicily. Only one in ten was from the Italian mainland.[4]

Italian immigrants usually settled first near one of the mills or mines in the Birmingham area. The first home for many of them was a "company" house, a woodframed row house adjoining the mine or mill and owned by the company. Because the small population was scattered among several industrial sites, most Italian immigrants in Birmingham did not have the ethnic neighborhood experience that their counterparts in New York and Chicago often had. There was, however, one twenty-block area near a large steel mill where about half the residents were Italian immigrants. Predictably known as "Little Italy," this area might have been more precisely called "Little Bisacquino," because most of its residents were *bisacquinari*.[5]

At least half of the Italian immigrant men in Birmingham started out as coal miners or as laborers in steel mills. Such jobs always meant hard work for low pay. In 1910, the yearly earnings of Italian coal miners averaged $286, or about a dollar a day, as compared with $665 for Scottish immigrants, $534 for native whites, and $461 for Negroes. The higher earnings of the Scots, the native whites, and the Negroes were due partly to their longer residence in Birmingham, and hence, their seniority in the mines. The earnings of the Italians were slightly higher than those of the Greeks and the Bulgarians, other recent arrivals. The wages of Italians who stayed in the mines and mills for an extended time rose gradually, though job discrimination prevented Italian steelworkers from achieving the wage levels of some other white workers.[6]

Most Italian immigrants left the mine or mill after several years of working and saving. Mining was dangerous and dirty work that, in the days before strong unions, provided little economic security. Lay-offs and wage reductions were commonplace; pensions were paltry or non-existent. A business, however small, promised more security and a larger income if it was at all successful. For men who had dared to venture into a strange land to better their lives, leaving the mine or mill for a fruit wagon or a corner grocery store was the next logical step in their personal advancement.

The proprietorship of a "Mom-and-Pop" store soon became a leading occupation and a symbol of progress among Italian immigrants. Such a business attracted the Italians because it required relatively little money to get started. Also, many of the stores were operated initially by the wife and children while the man continued working at the mine or mill. Usually, the family lived above or behind the store. Most Italian grocery stores were located in predominantly black neighborhoods. An Italian groceryman just starting out was attracted to those neighborhoods because they often did not already have stores. Italians did not have the anti-Negro prejudice that kept some native whites from establishing businesses in black areas. Moreover, blacks willingly traded with Italians, whereas some native whites refused to buy from an immigrant storekeeper. By the 1930s Italians owned more than three hundred grocery stores in the Birmingham area.[7]

The move out of the mines and mills and into the corner grocery stores represented a rapid climb up the economic ladder for Birmingham's Italians. Sixty-seven percent of them ended their careers in middle-class occupations (See Table 1.). They were twice as likely to reach the middle class as were their counterparts in Boston and almost three times more likely than Cleveland's Italians. They climbed out of blue-collar origins more often than Italians in Cleveland and Boston[8] and they skidded out of white-collar positions much less frequently. They were less likely to persist in manual occupations than were Cleveland's Italians (See Table 2.). The unskilled were more likely to leap all the way out of blue-collar employment into the middle class than they were to edge slowly up the economic ladder through the manual occupations. The skilled persisted at an unusually low rate, a result generally of taking the one step up into the middle class. The higher persistence among the semiskilled largely represents steelworkers who held on to higher-paying industrial jobs.[9]

The sons of Birmingham's immigrants continued and improved on their fathers' success. More than seven in ten ended in the middle class, as compared with about three in ten in Cleveland (See Table 3.). More than half started in the middle class, and just fewer than half who started in manual occupations ended in white-collar jobs. The second generation in Birmingham was almost three times as likely to climb out of the blue-collar world than was Cleveland's second generation. As contrasted with the high skidding rates in Cleveland, Birmingham sons fell infrequently and usually only to a high manual position. The continuity in manual occupations among Birmingham's second generation was even weaker than it had been for their fathers (See Table 4.). Although blue-collar fathers in Birmingham were no more likely to start their sons off in white-collar jobs than were blue-collar fathers in Cleveland, about twice as many sons of blue-collar fathers in Birmingham ended in the middle class (See Table 5.). The correlation between the last job of Birmingham fathers and their sons' last job was

TABLE 1.

Interclass career mobility rates of first-generation Italian immigrants in Birmingham, Boston, and Cleveland (percent).

	Birmingham, born 1870-1895	Boston, born 1880-1890	Cleveland, born 1870-1890
Starting white-collar	48	10	16
Ending white-collar	67	33	24
Climbing blue-collar starters	41	28	15
Skidding white-collar starters	6	20	33
Number	(212)	(48)	(230)

Sources: The Cleveland data is drawn from Josef J. Barton, *Peasants and Strangers: Italians, Rumanians, and Slovaks in an American City, 1890-1950* (Cambridge, 1975), table 14, p. 111. The Boston data is drawn from Stephan Thernstrom, "Immigrants and WASPs: Ethnic Differences in Occupational Mobility in Boston, 1890-1940," in Thernstrom and Richard Sennett, eds., *Nineteenth-Century Cities: Essays in the New Urban History* (New Haven, 1969), table 8, p. 156.

TABLE 2.

Occupational continuity rates of first-generation Italian immigrants in Birmingham and Cleveland (percent).

	Birmingham, born 1870-1895	Cleveland, born 1870-1890
Continuity rate by stratum of first job		
High white-collar	67	67
Low white-collar	89	40
Skilled	43	89
Semiskilled	60	67
Unskilled	30	60
All	62	60
Number	(212)	(122)

Source: Barton, *Peasants,* table 9, p. 98.

TABLE 3.

Interclass career mobility rates of second-generation Italians in Birmingham and Cleveland (percent).

	Birmingham b. 1900-1909	Cleveland b. 1900-1909	Birmingham b. 1910-1925	Cleveland b.1910-1919
Starting white-collar	58	29	50	27
Ending white-collar	71	28	74	28
Climbing blue-collar starters	47	16	48	19
Skidding white-collar starters	21	40	7	50
All changing class	38	23	27	28
Number	(97)	(78)	(201)	(92)

Source: The Cleveland data is drawn from Barton, *Peasants,* table 8, p. 96.

TABLE 4.

Occupational continuity rates of second-generation Italians in Birmingham and Cleveland (percent).

	Birmingham b. 1900-1909	Cleveland b. 1900-1909	Birmingham b. 1910-1925	Cleveland b. 1910-1919
Continuity by stratum of first job				
High white-collar	100	100	100	60
Low white-collar	69	100	89	60
Skilled	33	82	30	100
Semiskilled	17	50	34	100
Unskilled	20	63	36	44
All	51	66	64	41
Number	(97)	(53)	(201)	(46)

Source: The Cleveland data is drawn from Barton, *Peasants,* table 9, p. 98.

TABLE 5.

Interclass career mobility rates of second-generation Italians in Birmingham and Cleveland according to class origins (percent)

| | Sons of blue-collar fathers | | | | Sons of white-collar fathers in Birmingham | |
| | 1900-1909 | | 1910-1925 | | 1900-1909 | 1910-1925 |
	B'ham	Clev'd	B'ham	Clev'd[a]		
Starting white-collar	42	26	31	28	71	64
Ending white-collar	64	28	54	29	76	79
Climbing blue-collar starters	53	17	40	19	65	53
Skidding white-collar starters	0	36	14	50	20	6
Number	(25)	(69)	(72)	(79)	(70)	(131)

[a]These figures are for second-generation Italian men born between 1910 and 1919.

Source: The Cleveland data is drawn from Barton, *Peasants*, table 11, p. 106.

TABLE 6.

Intergenerational career mobility and occupational continuity rates of second-generation Italians in Birmingham and Cleveland[a].

	Sons born 1900-1909		Sons born 1910-1925	
	Birmingham	Cleveland	Birmingham	Cleveland[b]
Interclass career mobility rates (percent)				
Climbing sons of blue-collar fathers	64	28	54	29
Skidding sons of white-collar fathers	14	71	4	47
All leaving class origins	38	33	27	33
Occupational continuity rates by stratum of father's job (percent)[c]				
High white-collar	0	–	0	80
Low white-collar	64	17	77	10
Skilled	50	43	30	38
Semiskilled	25	–	11	–
Unskilled	0	21	18	32
All	49	30	57	34
Number	(97)	(54)	(201)	(53)

[a] The Cleveland study followed careers from 1930 to 1950, the Birmingham study from 1922 to 1956.
[b] Born 1910-1919.
[c] Father's job at time of son's first job.

Source: The Cleveland data is drawn from Barton, *Peasants*, table 13, p. 109.

stronger than the occupational continuity among Cleveland fathers and sons, because the larger number of white-collar fathers in Birmingham usually begot white-collar sons (see Table 6.). The movement among classes in the second generation was comparable for Birmingham and Cleveland, but the movement trends were going in opposite directions. Birmingham sons were moving up, Cleveland sons down.[10]

What accounts for such success in Birmingham? One possibility was that Birmingham's Italians were especially well prepared for entrepreneurship. In his study of immigrants in Cleveland, Josef Barton observes that Italian immigrants' occupational background in Italy strongly influenced their performance in America. Cleveland's Italians of agricultural background fared poorly in comparison with the sons of artisans and merchants, who frequently moved into skilled and white-collar jobs. Sicilian fishermen initially did well in Cleveland partly because, Barton suggests, "fishing in the Mediterranean was a business enterprise" — fishermen had to sell their catch. Hence, they arrived in America with entrepreneurial experience.[11]

The occupational background in Italy of the Birmingham immigrants analyzed above is not known, but sources indicate that most Birmingham Italians had been farmers or farm workers. The Immigration Commission reported in 1910 that fifty-two percent of the Italian steelworkers in Birmingham had been farmers or farm laborers in Italy and that another twenty-nine percent had been engaged in "general labor." Only nine percent had been in "hand trades." Almost seventy percent of Birmingham's Italians were born in the interior of central and western Sicily, areas where the organization of peasant socialists called Fasci, founded to protest agricultural poverty, had thrived beginning in the early 1890s. Bisacquino, whence came almost half of Birmingham's Italians, was a center of Fasci activity. That most of Birmingham's Italians came from regions of agricultural poverty did not mean *ipso facto* that they had been poor farmers, but the likelihood of their having an agricultural background seems high. Thus, the occupational background in Italy seems not to explain the success of Birmingham's Italians.[12]

The Louisiana background probably did contribute significantly to Italian success in Birmingham. About sixty percent of Birmingham's Italians entered at New Orleans, and many of those worked for several years in Louisiana. Their experience there was a kind of apprenticeship where they learned the ways of their new home and accumulated some savings. There they also observed an Italian pattern of movement out of menial work into petty entrepreneurship. They noted that Italian merchants in Louisiana had found significant business opportunity in selling goods to blacks. It appears that some Italians moved from the Louisiana cane fields directly into grocery stores in Birmingham. The first Italians in Birmingham brought from Louisiana this pattern of rapid movement into the petty merchant class and established it as the norm for Italian behavior in Birmingham. The immigrants who entered later at New York usually came directly to Birmingham, but because this norm was well established and because they were almost always following village migration chains which eased the way for them in Birmingham, they too tended to move up quickly.[13]

One hypothesis offered about the origins of Italian success in Birmingham has been that their small number aroused little prejudice or discrimination among native whites. Plausible as this seems, the historical record belies it. Most Italians arrived in Birmingham just as native whites unleashed intense and sustained ethnophobic passions. Insecurity about the place of the Negro in their society underlay the racial hostility and blacks received most of the resulting aggression. But a goodly portion was displaced onto southern European immigrants. Oscar W. Underwood, the congressman from Birmingham and a strong proponent of literacy tests for immigrants, told the Congress in 1905 that "it is a well known fact in history that the Spaniard, the Italian, the Greek, and the Assyrian have mixed their bloods with the races of Asia and of Africa for many generations past. They are not of the pure Aryan race."[14]

The beliefs Underwood espoused politely in Congress usually were expressed more crudely in everyday life. Italians commonly heard the slur "dago" and disparaging remarks about their cleanliness and their racial characteristics. Prohibitionists played on anti-Italian feelings to promote their cause. The local police harassed Italian grocers and the Italian baseball league over Sunday "blue laws." The Ku Klux Klan regularly terrorized Italians during the 1920s. As late as the mid-1950s, realtors in new suburban areas refused to sell homes to Italians. Indeed, Italian success in Birmingham is even more noteworthy because of the prejudice that was overcome.[15]

But in other ways the Birmingham environment invited Italians to succeed. The total population of Birmingham more than tripled between 1890 and 1920, creating sustained economic growth that offered great opportunity for new businesses. Many native whites were poor, under-educated immigrants from rural Alabama who provided less able business competition to Italians in Birmingham than did Yankee farm boys to the Italians of Cleveland and Boston. Blacks, who made up forty percent of the local population, faced so many obstacles to advancement that they rarely competed at all with Italians for economic status. Indeed, the Italians' keenest competition might have come from other European immigrants, but few of them chose to enter the grocery business.[16]

The Italian success is somewhat less impressive when compared with the performance of other white groups in Birmingham. Although the quantitative study of the other groups has not been completed, it appears that

Jewish, Lebanese, and Greek immigrants were even more successful than Italians. One study that tracked a sample of white manual workers in Birmingham from 1890 to 1909 found that slightly more than half of those who stayed in the community for the whole period climbed into the middle class. While Italians were significantly more successful than the white group as a whole, their status achievement was just one highlight of an overall successful performance by whites.[17]

The experience of Birmingham's Italians underscores the importance of environment to social mobility. In his study of mobility in Boston, Stephen Thernstrom suggests that the cultural values which immigrants brought with them from Europe exerted more influence on their career patterns than did any other single factor. Immigrants from Catholic peasant societies like Italy and Ireland tended to put less importance on occupational success than did Russian Jews or Protestant northern Europeans, and consequently the Italians and the Irish moved up the social ladder less often, Thernstrom observed. His conclusion is born out by many studies on other American cities. But in Birmingham, immigrants from a Catholic peasant society were very successful. Moreover, the Birmingham Italians seem to confound Josef Barton's point that the occupational background in Italy strongly influenced the social mobility of Italians in America. Peasant farmers from Sicily became middle-class businessmen in Birmingham.[18]

The Birmingham contradiction of these two important and no doubt valid observations means that the explanation for Italian success in Birmingham lies *in Birmingham.* The rapidly expanding local economy and the weak occupational competition from natives were major factors. A third element was the early establishment of a pattern of successful career development among Italians. Italian immigrants in Birmingham followed one another into the grocery business, in a manner perhaps similar to the way the Boston Irish became city employees and the New York Jews entered the clothing trade. In short, the experience of the Birmingham Italians suggests that particular circumstances in the new environment can greatly influence immigrant career patterns, and even reverse strong trends in group behavior.

Finally, the impact of blacks on the Italian experience in Birmingham differed from what studies on other communities suggested that it might be. High mobility rates among immigrants in Atlanta and San Antonio have been attributed in part to the presence of large numbers of blacks who, it is suggested, by their very presence lessened native-white sensitivity to immigrants and, thus, removed a potential major obstacle to immigrant success. But in Birmingham, the presence of many blacks exacerbated ethnophobic tensions and resulted indirectly in virulent anti-Italian prejudice among native whites. Blacks did further Italian success in a negative way: because of the racial caste system, they were largely unable to compete with Italians occupationally. In a more positive way, blacks boosted Italians up the economic ladder by shopping at their grocery stores and, thus, providing the basis for the business opportunity that largely accounts for Italian social mobility. Again, the Birmingham example encourages the social historian to be alert to the particular circumstances of the community under study. Birmingham Italians had an experience as unique as the community into which they journeyed.[19]

Notes

1. Rowland T. Berthoff, "Southern Attitudes Toward Immigration, 1865-1914," *Journal of Southern History* XVII (August, 1951), 328-360; Bert James Loewenberg, "Efforts of the South to Encourage Immigration, 1865-1900," *South Atlantic Quarterly,* XXXIII (October, 1934), 363-385; The Birmingham *Age-Herald,* November 18, 1906.

2. Jean Ann Scarpaci, *Italian Immigrants In Louisiana's Sugar Parishes: Recruitment, Labor Conditions, and Community Relations, 1880-1910* (New York: Arno Press, 1980), 32-57; A.V. Margavio and Jerome Salomone, "The Passage, Settlement, and Occupational Characteristics of Louisiana's Italian Immigrants," *Sociological Spectrum* (1918), 345-359. I am indebted to Professor Margavio for many helpful research suggestions on Italians in Louisiana.

3. *Census of the Population.* Tenth, Eleventh, and Twelfth Census of the United States; U.S. Congress. Senate. *Reports of the Immigration Commission: Immigrants in Industry (Steel and Coal).* Document no. 633, 61st Congress, 2nd Session, 1910.

4. Information on the villages of origin comes from a survey of 583 applications for United States citizenship. Naturalization papers are deposited at the Birmingham Public Library Archives and at the Federal District Courthouse in Birmingham.

5. Interview with Charlie P. LaRocca, July 28, 1980; interview with Frances Lucia Oddo, March 26, 1918; interview with Rose Maenza, March 25, 1981. The estimate of the number of Italians living in Birmingham's "Little Italy" was arrived at by counting Italian surnames in the Birmingham City Directories for 1914 and 1932. Although it is not always accurate, the use of surnames to determine ethnicity is reasonably safe here. Birmingham Italians rarely changed their names and I am aware of at least some of those who did.

6. *Immigrants in Industry (Steel),* 177. I have used the figures here for "South Italians," because the number of "North Italians" in the survey was very small and would have not appreciably changed the average, though the northerners made slightly more.

7. LaRocca, Oddo, and Maenza interviews; interview with Paul Lorino, April 2, 1981; interview with Mary Tortorici, May 12, 1981. The num-

ber of Italian groceries comes from a listing of retail grocers in the 1932 Birmingham City Directory.

8. In fact, they climbed out more often than these figures indicate. Because Birmingham's City Directories before 1910 did not cover many areas where Italians lived, I was not able to determine the first jobs of some of the early immigrants. Consequently, I counted some Italians who no doubt started as laborers but who entered the grocery business before 1910 as having started as white-collar, because that was the only information I had. This problem makes the figure for those starting as white-collar too high. Complete data on late-arriving immigrants suggests that forty-one percent started white-collar. Other figures indicate, somewhat surprisingly, that early arrivals and late arrivals performed very similarly, which may tell us that a forty-percent figure on white-collar starters is a reasonable guess.

9.   The sample of Italian immigrants for this study was taken from a group of 583 Italian men who applied for citizenship between 1890 and 1930. The naturalization papers listed place and date of birth, date and port of arrival in the United States, village of birth, occupation at the time of application, the names of wife and children, and the date and place of birth of children. The immigrant men were then tracked through the City Directories from 1900 to 1956. Sons were tracked from 1922 to 1956. Only men who could be followed for at least ten years were used in the sample.

Out of concern that the naturalization papers may have yielded a biased sample, I found 257 men with Italian surnames in the 1918 City Directory who had not applied for citizenship by 1930. After ten years, only sixty-six could be found in the Directories. Among the men who persisted, mobility was high, though somewhat lower than in the larger sample drawn from the naturalization papers. Fifty-two percent ended in the middle-class, as compared with sixty-seven in the main sample. Although the small sample means that the difference could fall within the margin of error, the men who did not apply for citizenship were probably less successful occupationally. Clearly, however, the great majority of men who stayed in the community did apply for citizenship. On that basis, the sample used herein seems reasonably, if not perfectly, valid.

I have shamelessly borrowed table structure, statistics, and observations from Josef Barton's seminal study of immigrants in Cleveland, *Peasants and Strangers: Italians, Rumanians, and Slovaks in an American City, 1890-1950* (Cambridge: Harvard University Press, 1975), 91-116. Almost as influential was Stephen Thernstrom, *The Other Bostonians; Poverty and Progress in the American Metropolis 1880-1970* (Cambridge: Harvard University Press, 1973). I used the occupational classification scheme listed in Appendix B of *The Other Bostonians* to determine which class stratum particular occupations belonged in.

10.   I have included among the second-generation sample a few Italian men who were born in Italy but who arrived in the United States before

they were ten years old. Professor Thernstrom calls these men *de facto* second-generation because their experience was much more like a second-generation person's. I also excluded from the first-generation sample the men who belonged in the first-generation cohort but who arrived before their tenth birthday.

The success among second-generation Italians in Birmingham is somewhat surprising because they overcame the virtual collapse of the Birmingham economy during the Great Depression. The Roosevelt Administration called Birmingham "the hardest hit city in the nation" by the Depression. One would expect an Italian grocer to fare better than a steelworker because he was in a service industry, but still the low rates of skidding and the high rates of climbing are impressive.

In Cleveland, Barton traced success among second-generation Rumanians to relatively high levels of education and greater assistance from families — usually young adults remaining in their fathers' homes into their mid- and late twenties. Impressionistic evidence on Birmingham's Italians suggests that education did not account for second-generation success; success in a grocery store did not depend on a college, or even a high school education, though most second-generation Italian men did complete high school. Families did help second-generation men get started in business, usually by taking them in as partners and sometimes by giving them a business of their own.

11. Barton, *Peasants,* 93-95.
12. *Immigrants in Industry, (Steel),* 172; E.J. Hobsbawm, *Social Bandits and Primitive Rebels: Studies in Archaic Forms of Social Movement in the 19th and 20th Centuries* (Manchester: Manchester University Press, 1959), 93-100.

It should be noted that immigrants from Sicilian coastal villages were notably more successful than those from the interior. Eighty-nine percent of immigrants from coastal villages ended in the middle class, as compared with fifty-nine percent of immigrants from the interior. I cannot explain this intriguing statistic, though Professor Barton's observation about fishermen may be a clue.

13. Scarpaci, *Italian Immigrants in Louisiana's Sugar Parishes,* 210-213.
14. On nativism among southern whites, see John Higham, *Strangers in the Land: Patterns of American Nativism 1860-1925* (New York: Atheneum, 1965), 164-171; *Congressional Record,* 59 Congress, 1 Session, 553.
15. LaRocca, Oddo, Maenza, Lorino, and Tortorici interviews.
16. Jewish immigrants were largely clothing merchants and Greeks usually operated restaurants and fruit stands. The very small number of Lebanese immigrants also ran grocery stores. Most immigrants from central and northern Europe were industrial workers.
17. Paul B. Worthman, "Working Class Mobility in Birmingham, Alabama, 1880-1914," in Tamara K. Hareven, ed., *Anonymous Americans: Explorations in Nineteenth-Century Social History* (Englewood Cliffs, New Jersey: Prentice-Hall, 1971), 195.

18. Thernstrom, *The Other Bostonians,* 145-175.
19. Richard Hopkins, "Occupational and Geographic Mobility in Atlanta, 1870-1890," *Journal of Southern History* XXXIV (1968), 200-213; Alwyn Barr, "Occupational and Geographic Mobility in San Antonio, 1870-1890," *Social Sciences Quarterly* LI (1970), 396-403.

Chapter **10** THE LIFE OF ROSA CAVALLERI:
AN APPLICATION OF
ABRAMSON'S MODEL OF
ROOTEDNESS/ROOTLESSNESS
Vaneeta-marie D'Andrea
University of Connecticut

ROSA: THE LIFE OF AN ITALIAN IMMIGRANT recounts the immigration experience of Rosa Cavalleri, one of a ½ million Italians to come to the United States in 1884. More than 4½ million of Rosa's[1] compatriots shared a similar experience during the period of the "great migration" — 1880-1930 (Dinnerstein, 1971: 11).[2] Few descriptions of the immigrant people of this period in U.S. history have delineated the circumstances of those less renowned; fewer still concern the lives of immigrant women.[3] Rosa's biographical account, a rare, first-hand glimpse into the daily life — the challenges, the struggles and the routines — of a working-class immigrant woman, does both.

Rosa's biography was prepared by Marie Hall Ets, a social worker at the Chicago Commons Settlement House where Rosa was employed as a cleaning woman. For more than a decade, 1918-1931, Ets and Rosa shared life almost daily. Ets made notes of her conversations with Rosa and organized them chronologically to recreate Rosa's life story.

Rosa's vivid recollections enabled Ets not only to describe Rosa's personal feelings and experiences, but to also chronicle life in the Italian-American communities where she lived. Rosa's story is probably not unique, but because it has been recorded it is an important research document.[4] The rich qualitative data contained within it remain, as far as I know, an untapped resource for sociological analysis. A plethora of questions related to issues in migration research, ethnic studies and social change analysis, to name a few, have potential for fruitful exploration through an analysis of Rosa's biography.

This paper uses Rosa's biography as a case study. It examines outcomes of the migration experience[5] (social change) on ethnicity (social rootedness). The major question considered is: What components of ethnicity, either cultural or structural, remain (or, the reverse, are lost), following migration? Abramson's model of ethnic rootedness/rootlessness is applied to the findings.

Ethnicity: Rootedness vs. Rootlessness

An analysis of the sociological outcomes[6] of migration are especially suited to an application of Abramson's model of rootedness/rootlessness.

112

This model, first of all, distinguishes between ethnic culture and ethnic structure.[7] Ethnic culture refers to individual attachments to subcultural symbols of the ethnic group such as: language, history, religion or customs etc., while ethnic structure refers to subcultural relationships such as: patterns of friendship or organizational membership etc. "Analytically then we can speak of *symbolic* ethnicity (as culture) and *relational* ethnicity (as structure)" (Abramson, 1977a: 5).

Further the model illustrates how continuity and change, or combinations of each, may occur in either cultural or structural dimensions of ethnicity, by delineating four "ideal type" responses available to individuals experiencing change in their ethnic milieu. Abramson organizes each of these into a fourfold typological model of ethnic rootedness/rootlessness (see below).

As Abramson explains:

> In the typology presented here, two of these individual responses are group-connected and group constrained, the Traditionalist and the Convert. The remaining two individual responses are isolating and without relationships, those of the Exile and Eunuch. Two of the responses are guided and constrained by symbolism, the Traditionalist and the Exile. And the other two function without ethos and symbolism, the Convert and the Eunuch (Abramson, 1976: 57).

Figure 1: MODEL OF ROOTEDNESS AND ROOTLESSNESS

	Subcultural Symbols and Culture of Ethnicity	
	Present (+)	Absent (−)
Present (+)	Socio-cultural Traditionalist (+, +) (Cell a)	Socio-cultural Convert (−, +) (Cell b)
Subcultural relationships and Structure of Ethnicity		
Absent (−)	Socio-cultural Exile (+, −) (Cell c)	Socio-cultural Eunuch[a] (−, −) (Cell d)

Source: Harold J. Abramson, "On the Sociology of Ethnicity and Social Change: A Model of Rootedness and Rootlessness," *Economic and Social Review*, 8, (1976), p. 49.

[a]Abramson has recently changed this category to Socio-cultural isolate (Personal communication).

Since a "shift in residence involves not only new places, but new faces and new norms" (Brody, 1970: 15), the combinations outlined in Figure 1 represent the logical alternatives available to an immigrant who leaves one social setting to enter another different from the former. Rosa Cavalleri's experience will be examined in order to determine her response to the sociological factors related to migration.[8]

After reviewing Rosa's life story, her move to America shortly after her arranged marriage appears, at first, to follow a pattern of rootlessness which started with her placement in an orphan hospital at birth. Rosa's childhood and adolescence were continuously punctuated by moving. She lived with three separate foster parents before she was three years of age; at six she was returned to her birthparents for a short while, after which she was officially adopted. Her adoptive family then sent her away to work first, in a convent mill and then, to a dormitory mill, each located some distance from her home village. These various up-rooting experiences might suggest that by the time Rosa emigrated to the United States she would predictably fall in one of the rootless cells (b, c or d) of the Abramson model. Yet upon closer examination of the ethnic symbols and relationships in Rosa's life, numerous links to a concrete social heritage can be identified. In order to understand how this might be possible a brief consideration of Rosa's life in Italy is necessary.

Life in Italy: The Childhood Years

Rosa's first parenting experience was provided by a wet-nurse, named Visella.[9] She took Rosa from the hospital in Milan to live in the village of Bugiarno about 18 miles away. Soon Visella became pregnant again and could no longer serve as wet-nurse for Rosa. Visella's mother-in-law, Marietta, however, offered to keep Rosa by bottle feeding her. Rosa lived with Marietta for the next few years. At this point, Marietta, in her seventies, felt that she might not live long enough to raise Rosa until she was fully grown, so she located a third woman from Bugiarno, Maddalena, to take care of Rosa.

Life for Rosa in the village of Bugiarno included an extended network of caring family relationships, Marietta, in effect, her *nonna* (grandmother), Maddalena, her mamma and Maddalena's husband Gigulur, her papa.[10] Mamma Lena's sister Teresa, and her family, lived close by too. Rosa's relational network in Bugiarno also went beyond her family. She had two special friends who were close to her in age, Caterina and Toni. Beppo, a bachelor who lived in her courtyard, Carlo, the mailman, and Don Domenic, the village priest, also spent time entertaining and comforting Rosa. In her biography, Rosa noted that each time she had to leave Bugiarno she missed Zia Teresa and her village friends as much as she missed

Mamma Lena and Papa Lur. All of these people were there each time to see her off and to welcome her back.

It is clear from Rosa's description that group connections were available and important in her early life. Equally important were the symbolic connections acquired during this time. Here, Mama Lena's role was all important. It was she who changed Rosa's name from Inez, taught Rosa to have a strong religious faith and sought formal adoption rights. Each provided Rosa with cultural ties to her social milieu.

When Rosa was about six years of age, her birthmother, Diodata sought to have Rosa returned to her. Diodata was a well-known Italian actress whose lifestyle was, even by today's standards, *avant-garde*. Diodata lived in Milan with an artist who had fathered her second child, and whom she had not married. To the people in Rosa's primary network, Diodata was defined as the "Devil's daughter." Rosa claimed that she hated Diodata from the start:

> I hated her! I hated her, just as I knew I was going to! But as I looked at her and smelled the flowers in her perfume I felt a little bit happy anyway. If I had to have another mother I was glad she was so pretty (Ets: 53).

Rosa poignantly describes leaving Bugiarno to go to live with Diodata.

> Diodata came and took my hand and pulled me away from Mamma Lena and out through the door. 'No!' I cried. 'Don't make me go!' But somehow I knew I had to. She was taking me away from everyone and everything I knew and loved and there was no one who could help me. Such a hurt filled my chest that I couldn't stand it! I burst out screaming and crying as she dragged me across the court and out the gate. (Just as Diodata and Rosa got to the waiting carriage Mamma Lena rushed over to them). She put something in my arms. 'Here, Rosa,' she said. 'Take it! Take it!' And I was wiping the tears from my eyes and trying to see. At first I couldn't believe it! It was the little Madonna from over the chicken coop. Mamma Lena knew how much I loved that little statue and she was giving it to me! 'Take it, Rosa' she said. Take it! And when you get in trouble you pray the little Madonna. The Madonna is going to help you' (Ets: 61, my parenthesis).

Rosa's attachment to the symbolic and relational ties in Bugiarno not only made it difficult for her to leave, it also made life in Milan, with Diodata, unbearable for her. Diodata insisted on calling her by her birth-name, Inez. Rosa insisted she be called Rosa. Rosa also noted the difference in her way of speaking and the *Milanesa* manner of speaking. Each of these coupled with Diodata's indifference to Rosa's religious beliefs contributed to Rosa's feeling unconnected to her new home. Rosa's biological roots did not matter to her. What was important were the ethnic roots she had acquired in the social milieu of her village.[11] By Abramson's definition she was now a Socio-cultural Traditionalist with "persisting allegiance to networks of primary group relationships as well as to enduring symbols and values of memories" (1977b: 5).

Life In Italy: The Adolescent Years

According to Rosa, Mamma Lena was a strict parent, who did not hesitate to severely punish Rosa if she did not meet Mamma Lena's expectations. Rosa explained that it was Mamma Lena's deep religious commitment that caused her to be so serious about Rosa's moral development. These concerns became acute as Rosa reached adolescence and puberty. Mamma Lena's solution was to send Rosa away where she could be watched and protected. The first place she was sent was the convent at Canaletto.

The first two years at Canaletto Rosa heard nothing from Bugiarno. Mamma Lena couldn't write and no one else had written for her. When Mamma Lena finally came for a visit her news explained the communication hiatus. Papa Lur had become ill and died while Rosa was gone. Rosa was shaken by the news.

> Papa Lur dead! Papa Lur gone forever...I couldn't believe it — that I would never see Papa Lur again! And suddenly I was full of loneliness that I busted out crying too. The best friend I had in the world has deserted me. He had gone away and left me alone (Ets: 114).

Mamma Lena wanted Rosa to come home as soon as her three year commitment was completed. Rosa thought, "It would be nice to see Caterina and Toni and Zia Teresa and Don Domenic, but without Papa Lur there to save me from Mamma Lena I didn't want to go home" (Ets: 114).

When Rosa did get back to Bugiarno Mamma Lena's loneliness became secondary to her concern for Rosa's morality. With so many suitors seeking to marry Rosa it would be better to send her away again. This time Rosa was sent, along with many other girls and women in Bugiarno, to a silk mill some distance from their village. Although the women were locked in their dormitory each night, Rosa felt freer than ever before. At this place she was with friends she knew and loved (Caterina had been sent too), and she was away from the severe punishments of Mamma Lena.

While Rosa was away this time, Mamma Lena decided to accept the suit of Santino, an older man who frequently came to her *Osteria* (inn). Once married[12] Rosa's life changed dramatically. As she described it, "I was around fifteen years old and I had been like an old woman. I couldn't even sit with the young girls at lunchtime at the mill" (Ets: 160). Worse yet, Santino was cruel beyond belief. Finally, during one particularly severe beating Mamma Lena interceded and forced Santino to move out of her house. By now, however, Rosa was pregnant with her first child.

Soon after Santino left for America. Before long word came for Rosa to join him there. Rosa's choice was constrained by social expectations.

> 'Yes, Rosa,' she (Mamma Lena) said. 'You must go. However bad that man is, he is your husband—he has the right to command you. It would be a sin against God not to obey. You must go. But not Francesco. He didn't ask for Francesco and I would be too lonesome without him' (Ets: 160).

The contradictions between Rosa's inner feelings concerning this matter and the social expectations are evident in her response. "Me, I was even wanting to sin against God and the Madonna before I would leave my baby and go off to Santino in America! But Mamma Lena said I must go (Ets: 160). She left Mamma Lena and her baby and went to America with her *paesani*.[13]

Life In Italy: A Summary

Although Rosa had experienced several potentially anomic situations during her early life in Italy, she had the resources of a network of people and the guidance of her religious beliefs to help her. Rosa was certainly not alienated or anomic (Vecoli in Ets: vii), when she left Italy for America. Although she had been born in Milan, she knew she was not *Milanesa,* she was one of the *paesani* from the village of Bugiarno; although born the daughter of Diodata, she had become the daughter of Mamma Lena and then a wife and mother. Rosa came to the U.S. a Socio-cultural Traditionalist. Now, in a totally unfamiliar social environment, the question was: would she be able to hold onto the cultural and structural links to her past?

Life In America: The Missouri Years

Rosa's trip from Bugiarno was in the company of her *paesani;* in Missouri, her destination, others, mostly young men she had known in Bugiarno, were waiting when the group arrived. Similar to other Italian immigrants from northern Italy at this time, Rosa viewed herself and her *paesani* as different from Italians who came from outside her region (Femminella & Quadagno, 1976: 62). She makes this point several times in her biography. For example, when she met the cousin of one of her friends from Bugiarno she says, "He was not *Lombardo* like the others — he and his friend were *Toscani*. I had to listen careful to understand his words" (Ets: 170). Life in Missouri would be among Italians but not all would be Rosa's *paesani*.

If Rosa's relationships could not remain solely limited to *paesani*, she could however, live among the symbols of her life in Bugiarno. Rosa described some of these in a story about unpacking her luggage. I

> found the featherbed and sheets Mamma Lena and Zia Teresa had put in. And I found the little Madonna and the crucifix Don Domenic had blessed. I kissed the feet of Jesus and said a prayer. With that crucifix over my bed I would not feel so alone — so afraid.

Soon Rosa's definition of *paesani* would extend to others from northern Italy, as well as those from her region of Lombardy. Gionin, the *Toscano,* became her first real friend in America. In times of crisis Rosa always preferred her *paesani,* old and new, to her new American friends. For example, it was Gionin to whom she looked for protection from Santino's beatings and it was Domiana, another Italian woman, who she wanted to help her at the birth of her baby.

Rosa's life in Missouri was in many ways similar to that in Bugiarno. The community was small and although everyone was not from the same region in Italy they were, for the most part, from the north. Rosa's primary network continued to be among her *paesani,* thus her customs and beliefs were easy to maintain. Although she lived in a physically different environment, little ambiguity existed in her life because of the certainty of her cultural and structural ties. During this period she remained a Sociocultural Traditionalist.

Soon, however, Rosa would face a major life decision that would change her lifestyle dramatically. Santino had decided to buy a whorehouse and have Rosa run it for him. Rosa resisted his decision more forcefully than ever before. She knew it was right to disobey Santino in this situation because the priest in Bugiarno had told her when a husband wants his wife to sin against God and the Madonna she must disobey.

Rosa sought Gionin's help. He suggested she leave Missouri and go to his cousin's in Chicago. So Rosa left Santino, her *paesani* and went alone to Chicago, a place she had never seen before.[14]

After Santino divorced Rosa, she married Gionin. Rosa was now married to a man not only from a different village than her own, but a different region too. Together they lived in a building which housed ten Norwegian families and two Italian men from Genoa. Rosa's primary network was as different as it had ever been. Gionin and Rosa did, however, share a strong faith in God and the Madonna, so her symbolic ties to her past were not severed. This pattern of living in the "presence of cultural memories and symbols and the absence of any sustaining primary group network" (Abramson, 1977b: 11) is more like that of the Socio-cultural Exile than a Socio-cultural Traditionalist.

While in Chicago Rosa and Gionin had to move several times. Each time circumstances made them move further from their ethnic ties. Finally they were living in a neighborhood made up mostly of Norwegians, Irish, Dutch and Germans. They lived in the only building in the neighborhood that would rent to Italians. When Rosa and her neighbors were forced to move from this building because it had been rented to the Chicago Commons Settlement House group, she took action. In her halting English she made it clear to the people at the Commons that she had been forced, by them, to move to living conditions which were below standard. She told them about the discrimination against Italians and that no one would rent decent housing to her. She convinced them to help her get a better place to live. Not only did they agree to do so but they also loaned Rosa the money for the first month's rent. From then on Rosa became the

> Chicago Commons most devoted friend and neighbor. She came to their evening classes and social groups, and as soon as the Commons could afford hired help she stopped cleaning floors in a saloon and washing clothes for a group of plasterers and came every day to work in the Commons (Ets: 4).

Eventually Italians would move into the neighborhood replacing the Norwegians but in Rosa's words, "they were not (really) Italians — they were Sicilians" (Ets: 232, my parenthesis). Now in times of need, Rosa had no *paesani* to help her. The Commons people became her primary network and like her *paesani* had done in the past, they helped her survive difficult times.

Life In America: A Summary

Rosa lived until her late seventies; by then she had been in America more than three-quarters of her life. Throughout this time she remained strongly attached to the cultural customs symbolic of her past life in Bugiarno. Each time she had a child she would have "that hot water with the bread and butter in, like us Italian women always drink when we have the baby just born" (Ets: 217). And with few exceptions[15] "she wore a neckerchief pinned with a safety pin, for in her girlhood in Bugiarno to expose a naked neck was a sin" (Ets: 4). In these ways life remained continuous for her.

But as the years went by she found her relationships from the past slowly slipping away. When she first lost contact with her *paesani,* after moving into a predominantly non-Italian neighborhood, she had found the Commons to replace these primary ties. The Commons had, in fact, reunited her with her past through the development of the Italian Mothers Club (IMC). But eventually Rosa felt that, "the old Commons, when everybody was like one family is gone" (Ets: 240). When we last hear of Rosa, her best friend Ollie, a Chicago-born American, who worked at the Commons with Rosa and shared a strong religious belief similar to Rosa's, has just died.

Discussion

Within the fourfold classification of Abramson's typology, Rosa remained a Socio-cultural Traditionalist at least up until the time she moved to Chicago. Each move in Chicago, however, moved her further and further away from her relational past and established the conditions within which she would become more like a Socio-cultural Exile. "Although she associated more with Americans than did most Italian immigrants, her basic beliefs seem to have remained those of the girl of Bugiarno" (Vecoli, in Ets: xi). Thus, she could never be said to have "converted." With her husband gone, her children married, the old Commons family gone and her nearest *paesani* in Joliet,[16] as far for Rosa as *Italia* itself, she had only her symbolic ties to give her a sense of rootedness to her past. At the end of her life Rosa affiliated with a past and a rooted cultural base but had fewer and fewer people with which to share it (Abramson, 1977b: 12). She could be described as a Socio-cultural Exile.

Rosa asserted these ethnic ties most clearly through her continued belief in Italian Catholicism.[17] The God and the Madonna had kept her rooted to her past.[18] Because of her faith Rosa would always be group constrained if not group connected. But Rosa knew she would never be really alone, she always had the Madonna. "The Madonna, She helped me all through my life, and now She gives me peace" (Ets: 254).

Notes

1. Throughout the biography of Rosa Cavalleri the familiar forms of "Rosa" and "Mrs. C" are used to refer to the biographee. I have chosen to simplify this by only using "Rosa" throughout this paper. In addition, it should be noted that Rosa and all other names used are not the real names of the persons and places involved.

2. The massive influx of people from southern and eastern Europe, between 1880 and 1930 has been termed the period of "new immigration." The "old immigration" occurred from 1820-1880 and included immigrants primarily from northern and western Europe (Dinnerstein and Reimers, 1977: 10). The term "new immigration" is somewhat anachronistic, however, since recent immigration from Latin America and Asia could also be called "new immigration." See especially: Juliani (1982: 369) for a discussion of this point.

3. Seller (1975) and Vecoli (1972) have noted that the experience of immigrant women has been especially neglected by scholars. The past decade has seen some growth in this literature, yet

> the humble, unsung stories of women whose lives are the warp and woof of the many-colored fabric that is the United States, lives never proclaimed in the headlines, but cherished in the memories of their children and grandchildren (Colecchia, 1978: 258),

remain relatively unresearched.

4. Caroli (1976: 248) describes Rosa's story as "a more typical immigrant experience."

5. Migration defined as, "the physical transition of an individual or a group from one society to another" (Eisenstadt, 1954: 5).

6. It should be noted that most migration research has focused on the psychological outcomes of the experience (Brody, 1970; Child, 1943; Stonequist, 1937 and Park, 1928 for example). Dickie-Clark (1966) makes a similar point.

7. This distinction is based on a definition of ethnicity which Abramson generated from the work of Bell (1974). Abramson defines ethnic groups as categories:

(1) with a past-oriented group identification emphasizing origins;

(2) with some conception of cultural and social distinctiveness;

(3) which are component units in a broader system of social relations;

(4) which are larger than kin or locality groups and transcend face-to-face interaction;

(5) which have different meanings both in different social settings and for different individuals;

(6) which are *emblematic,* having names with meaning both for members, outsiders, and for analysis (1977b: 6).

8. Abramson's model unlike earlier explanations of immigrant behavior, especially Park's (1928), does not contain sexist biases. Thus it can be applied equally well to the analysis of male or female immigrants. For a discussion of the sexist bias in the work of Park and others see: Smith, 1980: 78.

9. Orphan hospitals would hire poor women, who needed money, to take care of the babies left with them. Frequently, as was the case with Visella, these women had lost a child at birth or shortly thereafter.

10. In her biography Rosa makes an interesting comment on the role of the male parent in Italian society.

> People had always told me that I had another mother, so I could understand a little about my real mother. But nobody ever told me about another father, so I was not prepared (for an introduction to her birthfather). 'This man is not my father!' I said. 'Papa Lur in Bugiarno is my father!' (Ets: 66).

11. The various distinctions between Rosa's lifestyle in Bugiarno and the way of life in Milan illustrates her distinct ethnic identity. If she had stayed in Bugiarno all of her life these distinctions may not have become known to her. See: Abramson (1977a: 11 & 1977b: 8) for a discussion of this phenomenon.

12. Rosa's description of the marriage ceremony indicated that she never said yes. The priest, who was hard of hearing, assumed she did and married her to Santino anyway.

13. The word *paesano* in Italian has several meanings. It can be used to refer to a person from the same country, region, province, town or village. Rosa uses it in its various forms throughout her biography.

14. The power of Rosa's belief system is impressive in this instance considering as Winsey notes:

> Whether they got along or not, most of these unhappily married Italian-born immigrant women remained with their husbands, partly through fear of being ostracized by the Italian community, partly for the sake of their children, but above all, for economic reasons (1975: 204).

15. Once Rosa's daughter had a special dress made for her when she was to give a talk to a large women's club downtown. "But Rosa didn't wear that dress very much. She felt more 'comfortable' in her old clothes" (Ets: 5).

16. Rosa's friend from Bugiarno, Caterina, had moved to Joliet while Rosa was living in Chicago. But Rosa was able to visit her only once and that was arranged through the help of one of the people at the Commons.

17. As Vecoli has noted, Italian "peasants, to be sure, thought of themselves as *cristiani*...their brand of Christianity, however, had little in common with American Catholicism" (1969: 230).

18. Rosa's experience was typical as Gallo notes, "most of the immigrants look to religion as a guide or a foundation for a person's life. Some expressed it in terms of having to believe in something" (1974: 171).

Bibliography

Abramson, Harold J. "Ethnicity and Marginality in Diverse Societies: The Case of the Ottoman Empire." Unpublished paper. June, 1977a.

———. "Ethnicity, Persistence and Change: A Comparative View of Italians and Jews in America." Presented at the Second Joint Conference of the American Italian Historical Association and the American Jewish Historical Society. March, 1977b.

———. "On the Sociology of Ethnicity and Social Change: A Model of Rootedness and Rootlessness." *Economic and Social Review.* 8 (1976), 43-59.

Bell, Wendell. "Comparative Research on Ethnicity: A Conference Report." *Items.* 28 (1974), 61-64.

Brody, Eugene B. *Behavior in New Environments: Adaptation of Migrant Populations.* Beverly Hills, Ca: Sage Publications. 1970.

Caroli, Betty Boyd, et al. (eds.) *The Italian Immigrant Woman in North America.* Toronto: The Multicultural History Society of Ontario. 1978.

Caroli, Betty Boyd. "Italian Women in America: Sources for Study." *Italian Americana.* 2 (1976), 242-253.

Child, Irvin L. *Italian or American?: The Second Generation in Conflict.* New Haven: Yale University Press. 1943.

Colecchia, Francesca. "Women, Ethnicity and Mental Health: The Italian Woman, Impressions and Observations." In *The Italian Immigrant Woman in North America.* Ed. Betty Boyd Caroli, Robert F. Harney and Lydio F. Tomasi. Toronto: The Multicultural History Society of Ontario, 1978, pp. 252-258.

Dickie-Clark, H.F. "The Marginal Situation: A contribution to Marginality Theory." *Social Forces.* 44 (1966), 363-370.

Dinnerstein, Leonard and David M. Reimers. *Ethnic Americans: A History of Immigration and Assimilation.* New York: New York University Press. 1977.

Eisenstadt, S.N. *The Absorption of Immigrants: A Comparative Study Based Mainly on the Jewish Community in Palestine and the State of Israel.* London: Routledge and Kegan Paul. 1954.

Ets, Marie Hall. *Rosa: The Life of an Italian Immigrant.* Minneapolis: University of Minnesota Press. 1970.

Femminella, Francis X. and Jill S. Quadagno. "The Italian American Family." In *Ethnic Families in America: Patterns and Variations.* Ed. Charles H. Mindel and Robert W. Habenstein. New York: Elsevier, 1976, pp. 61-88.

Gallo, Patrick J. *Ethnic Alientation: The Italian-Americans.* Teaneck, N.J.: Farleigh Dickinson University Press. 1974.

Juliani, Robert N. "Ethnicity: Myth, Social Reality and Ideology." *Contemporary Sociology.* 11 (1982), 368-373.

Park, Robert E. "Human Migration and the Marginal Man." *American Journal of Sociology.* 33 (1928), 881-893.

Seller, Maxine S. "Beyond the Stereotype: A New Look at the Immigrant Woman." *Journal of Ethnic Studies.* 3 (1975), 59-70.

Smith, M. Estellie. "The Portuguese Female Immigrant: The 'Marginal Man'." *International Migration Review.* 14 (1980), 77-92.

Stonequist, Everett V. *The Marginal Man: A Study in Personality and Culture Conflict.* New York: Charles Scribner's Sons. 1937.

Vecoli, Rudolph. "European Americans: From Immigrant to Ethnics." *International Migration Review.* 6 (1972), 403-434.

_____ "Prelates and Peasants: Italian Immigrants and the Catholic Church." *Journal of Social History.* 2 (1969), 217-268.

Winsey, Valentine Rossilli. "The Italian Immigrant Women Who Arrived in the United States Before World War I." In *Studies in Italian-American Social History: Essays in Honor of Leonard Covello.* Ed. Francesco Cordasco. Totowa, N.J.: Rowman and Little Field, 1975, pp. 199-210.

PART IV

Images of Italian Americans: Collective and Individual Traits

Chapter **11**   CULTURAL TRAITS OF ITALIAN
AMERICANS WHICH TRANSCEND
GENERATIONAL DIFFERENCES
Valentine J. Belfiglio
Texas Woman's University

> Ethnic Group: A Population that is
> distinguished socially and that has its own
> distinctive cultural and social patterns.
> (Jonathan H. Turner, *Studying the Human
> System,* p. 567.)

Wedding receptions without folk music, evening meals without wine,
Sunday afternoons spent watching the Dallas Cowboys, and Texas drawls.
These behaviors are shared similarly by Italian Americans, and many other
ethnic groups living in Texas today. Paradoxically, Italian clubs currently
flourish in Texas. A few examples are: The Italian Club of Dallas, the Italy
in America Association of Houston, The Christopher Columbus Italian
Society of San Antonio, and the American Italian Association of El Paso.
These clubs host Italian cultural events, festivals, dinners, sporting events
including *bocce* tournaments, and symposiums. They also sponsor inex-
pensive Italian language classes, charter tours to Italy, and engage in
charitable and civic affairs, and mutual aid programs. Together in 1980,
they raised thousands of dollars in aid for the Italian earthquake victims.

What is the nature of the corporate will that seeks to preserve
Italianism by institutionalizing it in the form of Italian clubs? This study
will attempt to isolate and identify distinguishing cultural traits which appear to be common among Italian Americans of different generations.
Because the American society places a premium on conformity and mobility,
assimilationist pressures have been strong, and the maintenance of group
identity has been very difficult. Three broad concepts of assimilation and
acculturation have emerged in this century, and new theories are currently
being advanced. The "melting pot" theory suggests the desirability and in-
evitability of biological and cultural amalgamation,[1] whereas, some writers
advocate separation and segregation,[2] as ways of strengthening group life,
bolstering individual identity and psychological wholeness, and furthering
group interests in a competitive multicultural society. "Cultural pluralism"
is an attempt to live in both worlds at the same time in order to take advantage of primary group associations for personal, familial, and cultural

needs, while utilizing secondary group contacts in the civic, economic, and political environments.[3]

Assimilation and acculturation also have been the subject of differing theories about the predicted decline or resurgence of ethnicity. "Hansen's Law" pointed to an anticipated decline of ethnicity in the second generation and a resurgence in the third, with the group gradually thinning out in the fourth and succeeding generations. Empirical observations by Patti and Herrmann (1981) in Bloomfield, an Italian working class neighborhood within the city of Pittsburgh, Pennsylvania, "indicates Hansen's Law is at work" there. "Youthful boosterism in Bloomfield coincides with the emergence of the third generation, the grandchildren about whom Hansen wrote."[4] Another theory suggests that ethnic differences tend to disappear in the third generation in the "triple melting pot," resulting in religiously identified Catholics, Protestants, and Jews who have lost their national identifications.[5] Some writers perceive a more or less straight line of cultural and social assimilation, with ethnic consciousness diminishing in each succeeding generation. Other writers identify another aspect of the situation by pointing out the relatedness of ethnic values and social class factors.[6] Milton M. Gordon amplifies this by suggesting that people of the same social class tend to act alike and have the same social values, adding that they often confine their primary group social participation to the "ethclass," the social class segment within their own ethnic group.[7] It appears that people of the same social class tend to think and behave similarly even when they have different ethnic backgrounds. Consequently, social class groupings may also become interethnic, especially where opportunities for in-group association are more limited.

Rudolph L. Biesele (1930) and Terry G. Jordan (1966) have conducted studies of German rural settlements in Texas during the nineteenth century, and T. Lindsay Baker (1979) has researched the first Polish residents in the state. Biesele wrote a monumental book, titled *The History of the German Settlements in Texas, 1831-1861,* in which he documented the contributions of German settlers to the political, economic, and social life of Texas.[8] The book is an excellent general source on the early German rural communities in the state. Jordan reveals the importance of cultural heritage in the agricultural systems of immigrant groups. The partial assimilation of the German farmers in Texas was facilitated by emigrant guidebooks, and by direct contact with the southern Anglo-American population of Texas. Assimilation was also facilitated through an apprenticeship period in which many newly arrived immigrants worked for several years on the farms of other Germans who had come previously and already been partially assimilated agriculturally, and by the numerous agricultural societies founded by Germans in Texas.

However, Jordan also points out that the Germans were an alien group to Texas, whose agricultural heritage was greatly different from that of the native southerners in the state, and, as a result, those important farming traits which survived tended to differentiate them from the Americans. Examples include the greater intensity, productivity, and locational stability of the German farmers, as well as their high rate of land ownership. Jordan concludes that "... the German-American farmers of Texas still retain a measure of distinctiveness today."[9] Baker gives a detailed account of the founding and history of the oldest Polish communities in the United States. Established in south-central Texas in the 1850's by immigrants from the region of Upper Silesia, to this day, those settlements continue to retain elements of their regional folk culture, much of which has since disappeared in Europe.[10]

John P. Roche (1982), investigated ethnic attitudes among Italian Americans from two suburbs of Providence, Rhode Island. Examining attitudinal ethnicity and ethnic behavior by suburb, occupational status, and generation, Roche came to some interesting conclusions. According to his study, the dominant pattern within both communities is declining ethnic attachments with each succeeding generation.[11] The findings support those who stress the homogenizing influences present in American society. The forces of education, suburbanization, upward mobility, and succeeding generation tend to make for a decline in ethnicity. The results of the studies conducted by Roche uphold assimilationist theory and fail to support those who propose a recent rise in ethnicity or a return to the ethnic group in the third generation. "Hansen's Law" does not seem to apply to Italian Americans living in the suburbs of Providence.

However, in both suburbs sixty percent or more of the respondents in each generation and status group reported that at least half of their friends are of Italian background. In the ethnic suburb among blue-collar workers there was a steady decline for each succeeding generation, while among white-collar workers there was a slight increase reported in the third generation.[12] Roche's study demonstrates that approximately one out of four of the people surveyed shop at an Italian store frequently.[13] If it is assumed that the person purchasing the groceries is obtaining them for his or her family, then it can be further assumed that Italian food is often served in the homes of the respondents. The findings of Roche imply that ethnicity in both its attitudinal and behavioral aspects is considerably lower among those groups which represent likely future trends. However, Rhode Island's large Italian American population may serve to inhibit the kind of ethnic consciousness that comes into being when a group is a small minority, as is the case of Italian Texans.

Despite the important works of Biesele, Jordan, Baker, Roche, and others, until now there have been no serious studies of the early Italian settlements in Texas. Between May 8, 1980 and April 15, 1982, the author conducted research on Italian ethnicity in Texas. The initial funding for this program was provided by a grant from the Texas Committee for the Humanities.[14] The results of this research indicate that today's Italian Texan bears little resemblance to his forebears. Many of the cultural characteristics that once distinguished him have disappeared. Except for members of the older generation, the Italian language has fallen into disuse. In order to survive and prosper, Italian Texans gradually adapted to the dominant culture surrounding them. Eventually, they assimilated many of the values of the southern Anglo-American group. Intermarriage took place, and the Italians by degrees adopted local customs, attitudes, and skills. Today, preference for an Italian spouse and friends has become the exception, rather than the rule. Assimilation was inevitable. With so few of their countrymen in the state, the Italians were required to form increasing numbers of friendships and associations with people outside of their own ethnic group.

Hence, the Italian experience in Texas largely supports the theory of assimilation. That is, their experience offers an example of the transformation of immigrant culture: a manifold and ongoing process. While Italians discarded some aspects of their Old World culture in the adjustment to the new society, they retained other aspects. But very little of their heritage was left untouched. The experience of migration and resettlement encouraged the newcomers to regenerate their culture through the development of novel forms, which, in some cases, had little similarity to traditional forms. With regard to theories about the predicted decline or resurgence of ethnicity, research on the Italians in Texas is compatible with "Hansen's Law." That is, first and second generation Italian Texans were largely committed to assimilation, but third generation Americans living in the state demonstrate considerable interest in their ethnic identity. These people appear to feel very secure about their American citizenship, and this allows them the luxury of exploring their Italian roots. Children of marriages in which only one parent is of Italian lineage often inculcate an ethnic identity, whenever they retain the Italian surname, or live with a relative or guardian who was born in Italy. Statistics obtained from interviewing hundreds of third generation Italian Texans in Bryan, San Antonio, Montague, Dallas, Houston, Victoria, Dickinson, and Mingus, as a result of the grant from the Texas Committee for the Humanities, demonstrate that many of these people define themselves, and are defined by others, as possessing certain distinguishing cultural attributes, some of which are shared by other ethnic groups. Although there are exceptions, and individual attitudes are often ambivalent and self-contradictory, these attributes include:

(1) Membership in the Roman Catholic Church.
(2) Pride in the achievements of Italy in the fields of music and art.
(3) Knowledge of Italian terms and phrases.

(4) Knowledge of customs pertaining to the preparation, cooking, and eating of Italian cuisine.
(5) Familiarity with Italian games, folk music, dances, and other forms of entertainment.

These attributes can be operationalized to yield quantitative measurement about the nature of Italian ethnic identification.[15]

The Montague Experiment

Italians from the Alpine provinces of Northern Italy began settling in Montague County in 1882. The Italian colony reached a peak of 66 foreign-born in 1920, and the total population of Italian immigrants and their families was estimated at 300 in the first quarter of the twentieth century. During May 21-22, 1981, the author conducted a survey of Italian American families, and non-Italian American families, living in Montague County. He asked 25 fourth generation Italian American residents, and 25 non-Italian American residents of a comparable age group, the following questions:

(1) Are you a member of the Roman Catholic Church?
(2) How do you feel about the achievements of Italy in the fields of music and art?
(3) Are you very familiar with several Italian terms and phrases?
(4) Are you quite familiar with Italian customs pertaining to the preparation, cooking, and eating of Italian cuisine?
(5) Are you quite familiar with Italian games, dances, folk music, or other forms of recreation? (eg. *bocce, morra, briscola, la tarantella,* etc.)?

In order to minimize bias and maximize the amount of accurate information obtained during the interviews, the author attempted to avoid asking leading questions, and he conscientiously gathered, carefully processed, and critically examined all information.[16] An attempt was made to match the respondents in the two samples according to sex, age, and social class, but none of these factors proved to be statistically significant. Two additional questions were asked of the interviewees, which first generation Italians living in Texas had consistently answered in the affirmative, during the author's statewide interviews of 1980-1982:

(6) In your selection of a spouse, did you, or would you, give preference to Italian Americans?
(7) Do you give preference to Italians and Italian Americans in your selection of friends?

The non-Italian Americans were selected at random, except that they could not be related in any way by affinity or consanguinity to any Italian or Italian American. The results of the survey have been tested for rank correlation in Table I. The null hypothesis states that there are no significant cultural traits which distinguish fourth generation Italian Americans from non-Italian Americans living in Montague County. The alternate hypothesis states that there are significant cultural traits which distinguish the two groups. A significance level of 0.05 means that it has been decided to reject the null hypothesis only if it is found that the relationships are so high that they would be equalled or exceeded by chance only 5% of the time or less. The value of ϱ to reject the null hypothesis is 0.7 On the basis of the computations, the null hypothesis is rejected. That is, there are significant cultural traits which distinguish fourth generation Italian Americans from non-Italians living in Montague County.

Table II is designed to determine whether or not there are significant cultural traits which distinguish first and fourth generation Italian Americans of Montague County. Because all first generation family members are now deceased, the author was required to rely on certificates of birth, marriage, baptism, other County and Church records, and upon oral history interviews with descendants, in an attempt to ascertain their attitudes on the seven issues. In order to determine the accuracy of the oral history interviews, and to resolve those few cases, where there are discrepancies between the ancestors' responses to the given questions, wherever possible, the answers were compared to information obtained from County and Church records. Information was obtained about thirteen male and twelve female immigrants. On the basis of the computations, the null nypothesis for Table II is accepted. That is, there are no significant cultural traits which distinguish first and fourth generation Italian Americans living in Montague County, based upon the seven selected categories. However, it is obvious from reviewing Table II that there is a great difference between the two generations regarding their preferences of spouses and friends, as well as their knowledge of the Italian language and familiarity with Italian games. Therefore, it was necessary to apply more specific tests in order to determine what cultural characteristics, if any, transcend generational differences. Table I indicates that a majority of fourth generation Italian Americans, and a minority of non-Italian Americans:

(1) Were members of the Roman Catholic Church.
(2) Expressed pride in the achievements of Italy in the fields of music and art.
(3) Possessed knowledge of customs pertaining to the preparation, cooking, and eating of Italian cuisine.

Tables III, IV, and V, utilize the chi-square test to determine whether or not Italian lineage is significantly related to these characteristics for fourth generation Italian Americans living in Montague County. The null hypotheses state that they are not related, and the alternate hypotheses state that they are related. The significance level for the three tables is 0.05, and the degree of freedom is 1. The value of X^2 to reject the null hypotheses is 3.841. On the basis of the computations, the null hypotheses for Tables III, IV, and V, are rejected. That is, Italian lineage is related to membership in the Roman Catholic Church, knowledge of Italian foods, and pride in the achievements of Italy.

Music Preference: The Dallas Experiment

Between January 4 - April 15, 1982, the author tested and interviewed 25 fourth generation Italian Americans, and 25 non-Italian Americans of a comparable age group, in an effort to ascertain their music preferences. The Italian Americans were members of the Italian Club of Dallas, and the non-Italian Americans were students at the Institute of Health Science, of the Texas Woman's University. The latter could not be related in any way by affinity or consanguinity to any Italian or Italian American. All of the subjects were residents of Dallas County, and between the ages of 18 and 24. Of the Italian Americans, nineteen were male, and six were female. Of the non-Italian Americans, eleven were male, and fourteen were female. The premise upon which this research was based was that music preference and ethnic identity are significantly related. The participants were tested individually, in the living room of the home of the author in Garland, Texas. They were made to feel comfortable and seated on a couch directly across from a XJL Sound Stereo system with two external speakers. Music stimuli consisted of eight tapes including styles of classical, rock, jazz, Italian folk music, marches, oriental, country-western, and German folk music. Prior to testing, the subjects were required to listen to one piece from each of the eight styles of music. Then testing began. The subjects were asked to choose from among the various selections, and to play one or more of the tapes during a 30-minute period. They were told that they could listen to any one tape for as long as they liked, or to change tapes frequently, or infrequently, if that was what they wanted to do. The author recorded the amount of time participants spent listening to each style of music.

The results of the experiment have been tested for rank correlation in Table VI. The null hypothesis states that Italian lineage and music preference are not significantly related, and the alternate hypothesis states that they are related. The significance level is 0.05, and the value of ϱ to reject the null hypothesis is 0.7. On the basis of the computations, the null hypothesis is rejected. That is, music preference and Italian lineage are significantly related for the experimental groups. The Table VI indicates that the greatest difference between Italian Americans and non-Italian Americans was the amount of time they spent listening to Italian folk music. All participants were asked the question, "What style of folk music do you prefer to all other styles of folk music?" Table VII shows that 80% of the Italian Americans, but only 12% of the non-Italian Americans preferred Italian folk music to all other kinds of folk music. Table VIII utilizes the chi-square test to determine whether or not Italian lineage is significantly related to a preference for Italian folk music in Dallas County. The significance level for the table is 0.05, and the degree of freedom is 1. The value of X^2 to reject the null nypothesis is 3.841. On the basis of the computations, the null hypothesis is rejected. That is, Italian lineage is significantly related to a preference for Italian folk music for the experimental groups. An attempt was made to match the respondents in the two samples according to sex, and social class, but neither of these factors proved to be statistically significant.

Conclusion

The Montague and Dallas experiments imply that there are significant cultural traits, transcending generational differences, which distinguish Italian Americans from non-Italian Americans. The most important of these traits include:

(1) *The possession of an Italian surname or maiden name.*
(2) *Membership in the Roman Catholic Church.*
(3) *Pride in the achievements of Italy in the fields of music and art.*
(4) *Knowledge of customs pertaining to the preparation, cooking, and eating of Italian cuisine.*
(5) *A preference for Italian folk music over all other kinds of folk music.*

But taped interviews with scores of Italian Texans indicate that an "Italian consciousness" does not depend upon any of these factors. Rather, they merely facilitate the formation or maintenance of an ethnic identity. What is essential, is a group perception of having accomplished important things in the past, and the desire to accomplish them in the future. Ethnic identity depends upon common values and sympathies. Many Italian Americans appear to share an unconscious constellation of feelings, thoughts, perceptions, and memories, based upon similar experiences in childhood, which give rise to common ideas and images. Among some members of this ethnic group there is frequently an immediate, subliminal understanding, based upon shared values and attitudes, which is conveyed through body gestures and facial expressions. Ethnic identification exists when people share a common outlook and agree that they are a distinct group who ought to associate with one another and form organizations with social, cultural, and political goals. Hopefully, the hypotheses and methodology developed in this study, can be applied and adapted to other regions of the state and country.

The findings of Jordan and Baker regarding German and Polish settlements in Texas, also apply to the Italian community of Montague County. Like Baker's Poles, Italians have retained elements of their regional folk culture. Italian farmers are similar to Jordan's Germans in their intensity, productivity, and locational stability, and they have maintained a high rate of land ownership. Italians are still coming to Texas. The immigrants who have arrived since World War II are mainly trained professionals, or skilled workers who are easily acculturated into the fabric of American life. No matter when they came, most Italian Texans are proud of their ancestry. They are also proud of their contributions toward making Texas a better place in which to live.

Notes

1. Israel Zangwill, *The Melting Pot.* (New York: Macmillan, 1909).
2. Stokely Carmichael, and Charles H. Hamilton, *Black Power: The Politics of Liberation in America.* (New York: Random House, 1967).
3. Horace M. Kallen, *Culture and Democracy in the United States.* (New York: Boni and Liveright, 1924).
4. Marcus L. Hansen, "The Third Generation in America," *Commentary.* Vol. 14, no. 5, November, 1952; William Simons, Samuel Patti, and George Herrmann, "Bloomfield: An Italian Working Class Neighborhood," *Italian Americana,* Vol. 7, no. 1, Fall/Winter 1981, pp. 112-113.
5. Will Herberg, *Protestant-Catholic-Jew.* (Garden City, N.Y.: Anchor Books, 1960).
6. Herbert J. Gans, *The Urban Villagers.* (New York: The Free Press, 1962).
7. Milton M. Gordon, *Assimilation in American Life.* (New York: Oxford University Press, 1964).
8. Rudolph L. Biesele, *The History of the German Settlements in Texas: 1831-1861.* (Austin: Press of Von Boeckmann-Jones, 1930).
9. Terry G. Jordan, *German Seed in Texas Soil: Immigrant Farmers in Nineteenth-Century Texas.* (Austin: University of Texas Press, 1966), p. 202.
10. T. Lindsey Baker, *The First Polish Americans: Silesian Settlements in Texas.* (College Station: Texas A&M Press, 1979).
11. John P. Roche, "Suburban Ethnicity: Ethnic Attitudes and Behavior Among Italian Americans in Two Suburban Communities," *Social Science Quarterly.* Vol. 63, no. 1, March, 1982, p. 152.

12. *Ibid.,* p. 151.
13. *Ibid.,* p. 150.
14. Grant No. M80-710-PG — During interviews, four different types of measurements suggested by Cook and Selltiz (1975) were used as a basis for determining attitudes about Italian ethnicity. See Stuart Cook and Claire Selltiz, "A Multiple-indicator Approach to Measurement," in *Attitude Measurement.* Ed. Gene Summers, Rand McNally & Company, 1975, pp. 25-26.
15. In social research some of the most useful statistical tests are those which may be applied to distributions based on rankings, as compared with those based on specific quantitative values. Spearman's ϱ is a correlation coefficient related to the more complicated product-moment coefficient of correlation, but it is far easier to compute. Like the Q statistic and other coefficients it ranges from -1.00 (perfect negative correlation) to $+1.00$ (perfect positive correlation), with the 0.00 value indicating no association at all. Precise probabilities may be attached to its values for specified numbers of ranked pairs. The computational pattern essentially consists of attaching a rank number to each item in each of the two paired distributions, squaring the difference between each of the paired ranks, and applying the formula to the sum of these squared differences.
16. Whatever its errors, oral history memoir remains the closest thing to pure, unadulterated human memory. How someone recalls the past can provide revealing insights even if the story is of doubtful veracity. Practitioners view their work as supplementing and enriching the written record. In cases where a taped memoir is the only source available, as with many interviews of ordinary persons, oral historians acknowledge that the record is necessarily incomplete. Proficient interviewers often can steer a narrator closer to the truth by approaching the same topic from several lines of inquiry. All primary historical sources are subject to factual error, so in at least an absolute sense oral history is no less reliable than newspapers, personal correspondence, and presidential messages. The conscientious researcher adopts a skeptical view toward all data, including oral history.

TABLE I

Are There Significant Cultural Traits Which Distinguish Fourth Generation Italian Americans From Non-Italian Americans Living in Montague County?

Cultural Traits	Italian Americans Indicating an Affirmative Response N = 25.	Non-Italian Americans Indicating an Affirmative Response N = 25.
Preference for an Italian Spouse	0.0%	0.0%
Member of the Catholic Church	84.0	28.0
Pride in the Achievements of Italy	60.0	8.0
Knowledge of Italian Terms and Phrases	12.0	0.0
Preference for Italian Friends	0.0	0.0
Knowledge of Italian Foods	80.0	8.0
Knowledge of Italian Games	8.0	0.0

Source: Survey conducted by the author in Montague County on May 21, 1981. The Italian American interviewees were great-grandchildren of five Italian families from Piedmont, and Lombardy, who settled in Montague County in the 1880s. They ranged in age from 16 to 25. Sixteen were males, and nine were females. The non-Italian American interviewees were from six Anglo-American families, who settled in Montague County from Missouri in the 1870s. They ranged in age from 18 to 30. Fifteen were males, and ten were females.

H_0: There are no significant cultural traits which distinguish fourth generation Italian Americans from non-Italian Americans living in Montague County.

Alternate hypothesis: There are significant cultural traits which distinguish the two troups. $\varrho = 0.701$

Significance level: 0.5
Statistic: Spearman's ϱ Value of ϱ required to reject H_0: 0.7

TABLE II

Are There Significant Cultural Traits Which Distinguish First Generation Italian Americans From Fourth Generation Italian Americans Living in Montague County?

Cultural Traits	First Generation Italian Americans Who Possessed These Traits N = 25	Fourth Generation Italian Americans Indicating an Affirmative Response N = 25
Preference for an Italian Spouse	100.0%	0.0%
Member of the Catholic Church	100.0	84.0
Pride in the Achievements of Italy	100.0	60.0
Knowledge of Italian Terms and Phrases	100.0	12.0
Preference for Italian Friends	100.0	0.0
Knowledge of Italian Foods	100.0	80.0
Knowledge of Italian Games	100.0	8.0

Source: All of the first generation Italian Americans were deceased. Information about them was obtained from Certificates of Birth, Certificates of Marriage, Certificates of Baptism, other Church and County records, and oral history interviews of the oldest surviving offspring. Eleven families were involved in this study.

H_0: There are no significant cultural traits which distinguish fourth generation Italian Americans from non-Italian Americans living in Montague County.

Alternate hypothesis: There are significant cultural traits which distinguish the two troups. $\varrho = 0.55$

Significance level: 0.5
Statistic: Spearman's ϱ Value of ϱ required to reject H_0: 0.7

TABLE III

Catholicism as a Cultural Trait of Fourth Generation Italian Americans Living in Montague County: 1981.

Cell	Observed	Expected	Difference	D^2	D^2/E
Italian American Catholics	21	14	7	49	3.50
Other Catholics	7	14	−7	49	3.50
Italian American Non-Catholics	4	11	−7	49	4.45
Other Non-Catholics	18	11	7	49	4.45

Degrees of freedom: 1 $X^2 = 15.9$

H_0: Italian lineage and membership in the Roman Catholic Church are not related in Montague County.

Alternative: Italian lineage and membership in the Roman Catholic Church are related in Montague County.

Significance level: 0.5
Statistic: X^2

Value of X^2 required to reject H_0: 3.841

TABLE IV

Pride in the Achievements of Italy as a Cultural Trait of Fourth Generation Italian Americans Living in Montague County: 1981.

Cell	Observed	Expected	Difference	D^2	D^2/E
Italian Americans Exhibiting Pride in the Achievements of Italy	15	13.5	1.5	2.25	.167
Italian Americans Not Exhibiting Pride in the Achievements of Italy	10	11.5	−1.5	2.25	.196
Other Residents of Montague County Exhibiting Pride in the Achievements of Italy	2	13.5	−13.5	132.25	9.79
Other Residents of Montague County Not Exhibiting Pride in the Achievements of Italy	23	11.5	11.5	132.25	11.50
				$X^2 =$	$\underline{21.65}$

H_0: Italian lineage and pride in the achievements of Italy are not related in Montague County.

Alternate: Italian lineage and pride in the achievements of Italy are related in Montague County.

Significance level: 0.5

Statistic: X^2

Value of X^2 to reject H_0: 3.841

TABLE V

Knowledge of Italian Foods as a Cultural Trait of Fourth Generation Italian Americans Living in Montague County: 1981.

Cell	Observed	Expected	Difference	D^2	D^2/E
Italian Americans with Knowledge of Italian Foods	20	11	9	81	7.36
Italian Americans without Knowledge of Italian Foods	5	14	−9	81	5.79
Other Residents of Montague County with Knowledge of Italian Foods	2	11	−9	81	7.36
Other Residents of Montague County without Knowledge of Italian Foods	23	14	9	81	5.79
				$X^2 =$	26.30

H_0: Italian lineage and knowledge of Italian food are not related in Montague County.

Alternate: Italian lineage and knowledge of Italian foods are related in Montague County.

Significance level: 0.5

Statistic: X^2

Value of X^2 to reject H_0: 3.841

Table VI

Music Preference as a Cultural Trait of Fourth Generation Italian Americans Living in Dallas County: 1982

Music Style	Percentage of Total Listening Time: Italian Americans N = 25	Percentage of Total Listening Time: Others N = 25
Classical	13.0%	12.0%
Rock	39.0	44.0
Jazz	1.0	6.0
Italian Folk Music	19.0	2.0
Marches	5.0	7.0
Oriental	1.0	1.0
Country-western	22.0	26.0
German Folk Music	0.0	2.0

Source: Experiments Conducted by the Author in Dallas County between January 4-April 15, 1982.

H_0: Music Preference and Italian lineage are not significantly related.

Alternate hypothesis: Music Preference and Italian lineage are significantly related. $\varrho = 0.75$

Significance level: 0.5
Statistic: Spearman's ϱ Value of ϱ required to reject H_0: 0.7

TABLE VII

Preference for Italian Folk Music as a Cultural Trait of Fourth Generation Italian Americans Living in Dallas County: 1982

Music Preference	Italian Americans	Others
Preference for Italian Folk Music	20	3
No Preference for Italian Folk Music	3	18
Don't Know	2	4
Total (N)	25	25

Source: Author's questionnaire.

Table VIII

Preference for Italian Folk Music as a Cultural Trait of Fourth Generation Italian Americans Living in Dallas County: 1982

Cell	Observed	Expected	Difference	D^2	D^2/E
Italian Americans Preferring Italian Folk Music	20	12.02	7.98	63.68	5.30
Others Preferring Italian Folk Music	3	10.98	7.98	63.68	5.80
Italian Americans Not Preferring Italian Folk Music	3	10.98	7.98	63.68	5.80
Others Not Preferring Italian Folk Music	18	10.02	7.98	63.68	6.36

$$X^2 = \underline{23.26}$$

Degrees of freedom: 1

H_0: Italian lineage and preference for Italian folk music are not related in Dallas County.

Alternate: Italian lineage and preference for Italian folk music are related in Dallas County.

Significance level: 0.5

Statistic: X^2

Value of ϱ required to reject H_0: 3.841

Chapter **12**   THE ITALIANS OF MONTREAL:
A CRITICAL REVIEW OF
THE LITERATURE
Anthony C. Masi
McGill University

Introduction

In addressing the issue of Italian Canadian studies, Harney (1977:115) characterized the field as "frozen waste." Since his remarks referred in particular to the social history of the Italian experience in Canada, and since some six years have passed since he first made these observations, it is appropriate to broaden the scope of his initial inquiry and to assess current developments in the recent literature on Italian immigration to Canada and the modes of adaptation that have characterized these communities. Such a general survey of the field, however, is beyond the scope of this paper which will be restricted to contemporary research on the Italians of Montreal.

While the community in Quebec is not as large as that in Toronto and the rest of Southern Ontario, it nonetheless deserves careful consideration. Montreal was the initial point of contact with Canada for the first great wave of Italian immigrants in the pre-war period. Consequently, there has been a considerable amount of historical material available for some time on the character of the immigration and the experiences of this, Canada's original Italian community. In addition, according to Harney (1979a:220), fully two-thirds of Italian construction workers employed in building the yards in Montreal for the Grand Trunk and Canadian Pacific Railway companies entered via the United States.[1] Another factor that makes Montreal worthy of consideration in the study of Italian emigration is that many used it as a step or "second chance" to obtain entry to the United States (Harney, 1977:117; cf. H. Palmer, 1972). Further, the Italian community in Montreal has developed in the most unique corner of North America, in a province where eighty per cent of the population speak French, rather than English, as their mother tongue. Therefore, in the context of this different milieu in which the Italians of Montreal have evolved their institutions, as compared to other Italian enclaves in North America, this community offers an opportunity to test several crucial hypotheses which distinguish various schools of thought on immigration, ethnicity, assimilation, acculturation, adaptation, and multiculturalism.[2]

However, it must be emphasized that the present paper is simply a critical review of the state of the present research, both historical and socio-

143

logical, on the Italians of Montreal. The organization of this review, however, will suggest several important avenues of research that can be undertaken and which stand a chance of melting some of Harney's "frozen waste." First, this paper will review the state of the social history of the Italian community of Montreal. While reference will be made to the works cited by Harney, emphasis will be on materials that have appeared since his critique was first published. In the second section, the sociological literature on "Little Italy, Montreal" will be examined critically. Finally, the third part of this paper will provide an agenda for future research oriented toward quantitative and qualitative studies to fill the gaps in knowledge of the social structure and historical development of Montreal's Italian community.

Historical Research on the Montreal Italian Community

On the basis of Harney's (1977) critique, and following his efforts in the study of Italian Toronto (1974a; 1976; 1978a; 1978b), as well as his influential piece on "padronismo" in Montreal at the turn of the century (Harney,1979b), Ramirez (1980; 1981; 1982a; 1982b) has produced a series of articles, and together with Del Balso (1980) a short monograph, which attempt to reconstruct the social history, or as Ramirez (1982c) calls it in his own review of the state of Italian-Quebec studies, "la nuova storia sociale," of the Italian community of Montreal.

The principal hypothesis of the Ramirez argument is that by the second decade of the current century, there occurred a transition from temporary sojourning to permanent settlement on the part of Italian immigrants to Montreal. Accompanying this shift in migrant intentions and behaviour, new institutional arrangements for mutual aid, and new networks of information on working and living conditions replaced the old labour mediators and led to chain migrations from specific locations on the Italian peninsula to Montreal.[3] With the shift from sojourning to settling, the composition of immigrants to Montreal changed as well, with an ever increasing number of women entering along with the men (cf. Harney, 1978b). Finally, residential patterns responded to this new socio-cultural composition of the Italian community of Montreal and a complete institutional structure emerged as the center of Little Italy moved away from the old railway yards toward the northeastern end of the city.

The claim is that the sojourner left Italy with the idea of returning at the end of a work period, while a settler is a true emigrant who left thinking of remaining permanently in the new country. In fact, an early writer on Canadian immigration (Scott, 1914:413) noted that Italians did not come with the intention of making permanent homes in Canada and that "by working at the lowest possible expense and by working diligently, hope to accumulate sufficient wealth to enable them to live comfortably in 'Sunny Italy.'" In addition, as will be seen below, one analyst of the contemporary community has argued that today for the Italian Montrealer, "the drive to buy a house, to own property, is one of the fundamental reasons why the immigrant left his country (Boissevain, 1970:17)." It is this transition that Ramirez tries to understand in the period at the end of the first great wave of Italian migration to Montreal.

Ramirez provides a very suggestive scenario which is documented carefully with the available quantitative and qualitative information, including (apparently not without controversy in historiographic circles) "oral histories" with surviving first-wave Italian immigrants to Montreal. He has dug into the parish archives on marriages and baptisms, immigration statistics, and most recently the personnel files of the Canadian Pacific Railroad (personal communication). However, there are still important gaps in this socio-historical reconstruction of the Italian community of Montreal.

First, the changes in the character of the waves of early Italian immigration to Montreal from sojourning to settlement need to be considered in terms of the particular place that Italian workers played in the labour market of the day. As Harney (1979b), Ramirez (1981; Ramirez and Del Balso, 1980), and Foerester (1919), all basing themselves on the "Royal Commission Appointed to Inquire into the Immigration of Italian Labourers to Montreal and the Alleged Fraudulent Practices of Employment Agencies" (Canada, 1905a; cf. also Canada, 1905b) have pointed out, the *padrone* system overextended itself in a "war" between two important labour bosses. This crisis, however, was followed by larger cohorts of new Italian arrivals. In 1905 there were 5,930 Italian immigrants to Canada, followed by 10,032 in 1906, 10,436 in 1907, dropping to 5,988 in 1908, but rising to a peak of 30,699 in 1913 (Centro Studi Emigrazione, 1978:passim). The First World War and restrictive Canadian immigration laws then slowed the growth in the 1920s. Fascist emigration restrictions (Treves, 1976; Cannistraro and Rosoli, 1979) and the Great Depression, and then the Second World War, kept immigration to Canada at much lower levels thereafter until the mid-1950s when "ten times as many Italians (came) to Canada between 1951 and 1961 as had arrived in the great age of immigration in the period from 1885 to 1914 (Harney, 1977:117)."

The point here is that the transition from sojourning to settlement needs to be given a more exact "timing." Was it simply a gradual response to favourable working and living conditions in Montreal? Was it a sudden change based on the spontaneous formation of new institutions to respond to the crisis caused by the breakdown of *padronismo* and the loss of railway construction subcontracting jobs? What changes accompanied it in terms of the structure of occupations held by Italians, and their overall position in the labour market? Were there changes in the conditions of life in the places of origin at this time? How does this compare to the experiences of other Italian communities in North America or elsewhere? Did previous so-journers become settlers, or were there always two distinct groups of migrants?

Second, the demographic evolution of Montreal's "Little Italy" needs to be more carefully analyzed. Specifically, with the arrival of women and children the community must have become concerned with the provision of social services, most importantly education. What services did the community develop on its own and which were claimed from the host society? Did an enclave economy evolve or was the Italian community interdependent with Montreal society in general? Did any internal conflicts characterize the development of the community during the period of transition? How quickly was it growing by natural increase? What tensions were there between immigrants and the native-born Canadians of Italian origin? Did the transition from labour mediation to chain migrations based on informal networks witness a change in the internal composition of the community? Were there disputes between various "paesani" associations?[4]

Third, Italian Montrealers were clearly not the only immigrant group in the city. In addition, Quebec was undergoing a massive rural to urban migration of its own, while previously this society itself had been a net-emigration area for some time before the Italians and others started arriving. What was the relation of the Italians to the overall class structure of the city during the first two decades of this century? With which other groups were they in competition for jobs? for housing? for other services?[5]

Notwithstanding these limitations in the current research, it is worth emphasizing that the work of Ramirez represents a major leap forward with regard to the previous efforts at writing Italian Quebec history. In a real sense, it has just opened the door to the possibilities. His attempts to reconstruct the social history of the Italian experiences in Montreal takes us beyond the simple noting of Italian names in various contexts in Quebec's past (Canada, 1951; Hardwick, 1976), well beyond the very myopic parish history that Vangelisti (1956) wrote in dealing with the community, and in a different direction than the journalistic "histories and analyses" written by Spada (1969) and Mastrangelo (1979).

Sociological Research on Italian Montrealers

As noted above, between the two world wars Italian immigration to Montreal was severely limited. Two studies, both master's theses were produced at McGill University prior to the defining of Italians as "enemy aliens." Bayley (1939) compared the institutional arrangements of Italian and Ukranian immigrants. Gibbard (1935), examined the economic mechanisms and documented the emergence of what has since been labelled the ethnic labour market phenomenon among immigrant groups in the city of Montreal. However, during the time when the community was growing most rapidly, i.e., between 1955-1965, there were no in-depth analyses such as Jansen's (1969; 1978) on the organization of "Toronto Italia," save, as noted above, Vangelisti's historical account and the first edition of Mingarelli's (1980) little "who's who and what they do."

The first major study of the Italian community of Montreal by a professional social scientist was Boissevain's (1970) anthropological and sociological research on "adjustment in a plural society." The piece was produced for a Royal Commission on Biculturalism and Bilingualism, and attempts to place in perspective the role played by language in the internal and external dynamics of the Italian community of Montreal. The attempt, however, is seriously flawed, and the author himself apologizes in the introduction for the partial nature of the fieldwork and the presentation of the results. In fact, Boissevain (1970:xii) notes that "contact with the Italians of Montreal was relatively superficial by the standards of anthropological field research," and further, that "the sample of Canadian-born persons of Italian descent is too small to have much [sic] statistical significance."

A decade after this first attempt, a major research funded by the federal Minister of State for Multiculturalism was undertaken. Only the preliminary report, in manuscript form, is available to the public (Painchaud and Poulin, 1981). This massive work attempts to deal with the intersection of two issues: the reasons for the massive emigration from Italy in general and to Canada-Quebec in particular, and the formation of the Italian-Quebec community. It employs several important statistical sources on Italian emigration and Canadian immigration, contains the results of a major sociological survey, and bases part of its analysis on in-depth privileged witness interviews and discussions with "leaders" of the Italian community. While the attempt seems well designed, problems in the carrying out of the fieldwork (see Painchaud and Poulin, 1981: Notes methodologiques), apparently led to a very different report than was anticipated when the project was begun.

The first section on Italian emigration is little more than a summary of the major work in Italian, *Un Secolo Di Emigrazione Italiana* (Centro Studi Emigrazione, 1978), which is oft-quoted and whose tables are reproduced, rather than being reanalyzed. The substantive analysis is not new and it does not resolve the issue of the reasons for Italian emigration and will not be further discussed.[6] In the second part of this manuscript, the authors attempt to deal with the formation of the Italian community of Montreal. This is a potentially important contribution. Potentially, because in its present form it does not integrate arguments very well and the presentation of data is sometimes overwhelming rather than informative. At this point, it is perhaps best to review the Boissevain (1970) and Painchaud and Poulin (1981) researches comparatively.

Boissevain's (1970) study consisted of 197 "usable" completed interviews of which 132 (67%) were with family heads at addresses originally drawn from a random sample of 219 addresses obtained from the Italian national parishes and missions. From four randomly chosen census tracks outside of the community's core, another 38 (19%) interviews were conducted with individuals having Italian names. The remaining 27 (12%) family heads were apparently "searched for" by interviewers who could not find Italians at the addresses. Computing a goodness of fit chi-square for the occupational distribution of this sample compared to values from the 1961 Canadian census (both sets of figures provided by Boissevain, 1970:15), yields a probability value of only 0.005. In other words, only 5 times in 1000 tries would you expect to get a sample with this occupational distribution if it truly were randomly drawn from the population whose characteristics are given from the census. Even though Boissevain does not use any measures of statistical inference in his study, the percentages themselves may be very misleading unless the reader is aware of the nonrepresentativeness of this group.[7]

Boissevain documents all of the traditional features of Italian immigrant community life from contact with relatives to political orientation and illustrates these findings with his sample data. Two of his insights, notwithstanding the limitations of the survey and other aspects of the fieldwork, however, are indeed important contributions to our understanding of the Italian community of Montreal. First, Boissevain (1970:27-36) provides several lines of cleavage or "internal segmentation and conflict" among various groups. Principal among these divisions are "generation gaps" between first wave immigrants, native-born Montrealers of Italian descent, and more recent arrivals. The data limitations noted above, however, still leave this an open question—one worth in depth-analysis. Second, the place of the Italians in the linguistic conflict between French and English is given much attention by Boissevain (1970:37-68). Of particular interest is his finding that old-wave immigrants who were upwardly mobile were francophone, while post-war professionals were increasingly choosing English as the language of instruction. This linguistic issue is still an important defining characteristic of the Italian community of Montreal (cf., Cappon, 1974; Masi, 1981).

The sample from Painchaud and Poulin (1981) is much larger (n = 400), and chosen with more care toward being representative on the basis of the ecological distribution of Montreal's Italians in terms of the "ethnic concentration" of the neighborhoods in which they reside.[8] They pursue the above-mentioned issues of generational conflict and linguistic assimilation, updating the arguments to account for the turmoil of Quebec nationalist policies and institution of a "Conseil de la langue française" in Quebec in the 1970s.[9] In addition, they note other sources of conflict in the internal dynamics of Montreal's Italian community. Regional differences in the places of origin in Italy are shown to play some role in generational as well as contemporary conflicts (Painchaud and Poulin, 1981:222,353-377). Finally, this research attempts to analyse the "enclave" aspects of the Italian "ghetto" (Painchaud and Poulin, 1981:463-504) in terms of isolation from the concerns of Quebecois nationalism.

The major limitation of the Painchaud and Poulin (1981) study is the almost total lack of a multivariate analysis even though they state that the interview schedule contained some 813 items.[10] In fact, much of the data simply document, using the sample, information that was available from other sources. In the simple percentage tables, however, two characteristics of the community do emerge that had not been previously noted. First, for some 20 per cent of the sample their arrival in Canada was from a country other than Italy (Painchaud and Poulin, 1981:221), therefore indicating a step-migration process may be at work.[11] Second, the relatively unique composition of the Italian community of Montreal is illustrated in terms of the regional dominance by Molisani-Abruzzesi overall, and Agrigentini among those from Sicilia (Painchaud and Poulin, 1981:222). This argues in favour of comparing Italian Montreal to other Little Italies on this dimension to assess its importance in giving a specific character to the community. However, since the documentation of internal conflicts by these researchers depended on even less contact with the community than was the case for Boissevain (see above), the significance of these two pieces of information has yet to be determined.

The emphasis placed on the issue of language in both the Boissevain (1970) and Painchaud and Poulin (1981) studies clearly demarks it as the defining characteristic of Little Italy, Montreal. The essential trilingualism of the community, however, has not been subject to rigorous analysis by either of these two previous research efforts. While both spend time analysing language retention rates (apparently high by United States standards), language used at home and at work, and various other indicators, they do not see the issue of conflict between English and French as actually creating an environment in which Italian has been able to survive (cf. Masi, 1981). The Italian community is in many ways, as Boissevain (1970:85) points out, strategically located in Montreal's social ecology — even its physical location is on the border between the French "East End" and the English "downtown." However, since both studies focused attention on choice in terms of the language of adoption, insufficient attention has been given to the dynamics of seeing Italian as a viable language for family and community use.

Some Suggestions for Future Research

In concluding this brief critical review of the current state of research on the Italians of Montreal it is appropriate to offer some potential research questions that would help fill in the gaps in the social historical development of the community and in the current state of our knowledge concerning the contemporary social and economic structure of "Little Italy, Montreal."

It would seem absolutely essential that some basic demographic analyses of the evolution of the Italian community of Montreal precede or accompany any other research efforts. Some manuscript census materials are now available and greater attention should be paid to the possibility of linking information for the same person from different sources, for example employment records from the Canadian Pacific Railway with parish records from one of the Italian national missions. The role of women in the transition from sojourning to settling must be considered in this process, particularly as it relates to childbearing, natural increase, and non-market resources among immigrant Italians in the city.

Also along demographic lines the impact of changes in the Canadian immigration laws (and more recently some changes in Quebec regulations governing residence in the province itself) should be analysed in a search for changes in the character of arrivals from Italy in the different periods. In this context the relationship between origin and destination needs to be considered in detail (and not just in broad generalities as was done by Painchaud and Poulin, 1981). In fact, this may be one of the last chances to study the dynamics of origin and destination in the study of Italian emigration and the adaptation and/or return of migrants.[12] Given the chain migration patterns and the regional and even village level dominance of some migration patterns to Montreal it may even be possible to examine the choice of destination among several alternatives. Fieldwork both in Montreal and Italy, obviously, would be required. In this context, the role of paesani associations could also be given serious attention.[13]

Finally, the labour market position of Italians in Montreal needs to be scrutinized. This needs to be done both for the historical period of the transition from sojourning to settlement as well as for the post-war period. Split labour markets or ethnic segmentation in the labour market have been examined for other groups in Montreal (Laura Pao-Mercier, 1982), but not for Montreal's largest ethnic minority, i.e., the Italians. This could be corrected by a major survey research effort directed toward those in the labour force. In addition, some additional ethnographic work on Italians, along the lines of Gans's (1982) classic study of Boston's West End could yield valuable insights into the class versus group aspects of the position of Italians in Montreal.

In short, there is much left to learn about the Italians of Montreal.

Notes

1. Harney (1977:123) actually argues that "in the early years of un-monitored exploitation and crude capitalist flux, two-thirds of the Italians in Canada came through American ports of entry. They were overwhelmingly young males, and they had little thought of staying after earning a season's wages." However, no sources are cited to substantiate the numbers presented, nor the "intentions" of these early arrivals.

2. While the literature in the United States has tended to place an emphasis on assimilation, Canadian research has been more inclined to deal with multiculturalism. This in part may be due to the fact that Canada is an officially "bilingual" country, albeit not without conflict (cf. Lieberson, 1970). In this context, as will be argued below, Italian has flourished in Montreal as a so-called "non-official language" (cf. O'Bryan, et al., 1976).

3. It has been oft-quoted that the "stamp is the most powerful agent of migration." In the context of Montreal, therefore, it should be possible to develop a research framework for sorting out origin and destination conditions for some of the first wave arrivals. Given, as will be seen below, that many Italians arrive in Montreal today after having resided previously outside of Italy, the second-wave offers the opportunity to study step-migration processes as well as the factor of choice among destinations. These are important questions in the general migration literature and deserve careful empirical work.

4. Schmitter's (1980) work on the role of associations in immigrant integration in West Germany and Switzerland could serve as a model for such a research, particularly since the Canadian system of seasonal work permits at the turn of the century seems to resemble the current "guestworker" patterns of those European countries.

5. It is Ramirez's position (personal communication), however, that much of the groundwork for such analyses of the Italian community of Montreal will depend on the evolution of the general historical writing on Quebec. Apparently, the social history of this province has not kept pace with developments elsewhere in North America, and Ramirez himself is looking into the quebecois emigration to New England mill towns during the end of the last century (cf. Ramirez, 1980).

6. Much of the presentation of data in the first part of the Painchaud and Poulin (1981) study is simply regurgitation of tables prepared by the Italian scholars who contributed to *Un Secolo Di Emigrazione* (Centro Studi Emigrazione, 1978). Some misinterpretations are also contained in their reporting of these results. For example, the ratio of the number of returnees to Italy from Canada to the number arriving in Canada for a single year is not, as erroneously presented, a percentage. The population at risk in the numerator is drawn from all the immigrants who have arrived in Canada up to that year (and who did not die before

then), while the denominator refers only to one year's worth of immigrants. It may be a valuable "index" number or ratio, but it can be
very misleading to speak of it as a percentage.

7. One of the principal sources of error contributing to this large chi-
square value, which Boissevain himself could have computed, is the
low percentage of craftsmen and the high percentage of labourers in his
sample. In any case so few multivariate tables are reported it is difficult
to assess the significance of these distortions. It may be easier to
understand how the difference between the census and his sample came
about. By using the parish registries he was ignoring an important component of the community in the late 1960s, i.e., Italians that were born
in Canada and not registered with the missions. Since these individuals
were more likely to have skilled rather than labourer occupations, by
missing them his sample became heavily weighted with Italian-born individuals who do not have the same skill levels as the native-born individuals of Italian origins.

8. The Painchaud and Poulin (1981) sampling technique is discussed in
their "Notes methodologiques." In searching for a balance in the
geographic dispersion of Italian Montrealers by the density of "ethnic
concentration" in their neighborhoods, they may have introduced an
"ecological fallacy" into logic. In any case, since the fieldwork was
done in 1979-1980, when the 1981 census becomes available, it will be
possible to assess the overall representativeness of their sample on
characteristics other than density of Italians in the areas sampled.

9. While it is difficult to assess the biases of researchers unless they are
overwhelmingly candid in their remarks, it seems that Painchaud and
Poulin are most interested in the ways Quebec nationalists can gain an
alliance with the big Italian minority in Quebec. The fact that the
Italians have increasingly aligned with the English, linguistically and
politically, is a problem to which they seek a "corrective" rather than an
aspect of the community to be studied and understood.

10. The astounding number of questions to which the sample of 400 was
subjected probably led to a large number of incomplete interview
schedules. In any case, the report does not reproduce the questionnaire
that was used, nor does it provide information on the marginals for
anything more than a dozen or so of the background and attitude questions. For more information on the apparent difficulties in fieldwork
organization and the write-up we will have to await word from the
original study group, the authors themselves, or the funding agency,
the Minister of State for Multiculturalism.

11. The Québec Ministère de l'Immigration 1973 provided a three way
crosstabulation of country of birth by country of citizenship by country
of last residence for those arriving there from abroad in 1973. The findings for the Italians coming to Québec are almost identical to those
reported by Painchaud and Poulin (1981:221). See Table 3 of that special
report by the Québec government for details (cf. Québec 1977, 1979).

12. On the basis of data presented by Painchaud and Poulin (1981:Chapitre VII, pp. 185-236), it seems that there was a significant return migration even during the "second wave" of Italian immigrants in the 1950s and 1960s. This finding necessitates a reevaluation of the transition from sojourning to settlement to account for a continued portion of the Italian migrant community being transitory. In other words, the relative importance of this component of the population of "Little Italy, Montreal" needs to be explored in more detail.

13. The extent to which *paesani* ties were important to the establishment of the "settlers" can also be seen in the patterns of endogamous marriage by village, province, and region for the Italian parishes. Sylvie Taschereau (personal communication) is presently working on a master's thesis at the Université de Québec à Montréal using these sources and addressing, among other things, precisely this issue.

Bibliography

Charles M. Bayley
1939   "Social Structure of the Italian and Ukrainian Community in Montreal, 1935-1937," M.A. Thesis, Department of Sociology, McGill University.

Jeremy Boissevain
1970   *The Italians of Montreal: Social Adjustment in a Plural Society* (Ottawa: Royal Commission on Bilingualism and Biculturalism, Information Canada)

CANADA
1905a   *The Royal Commission Appointed to Inquire into the Immigration of Italian Labourers to Montreal and the Alleged Fraudulent Practices of Employment Agencies: Report of the Commissioner and Evidence* (Ottawa: The King's Printer)
1905b   *The Royal Commission in re the Alleged Employment of Aliens in Connection with the Surveys of the Proposed Grand Trunk Pacific Railway* (Ottawa: The King's Printer)
1951   *The Italians in Canada* (Ottawa: Research and Publications Division, Department of Citizenship and Immigration)

P.V. Cannistraro and G. Rosoli
1979   "Fascist Emigration Policy in the 1920s: An Interpretive Framework," *International Migration Review,* 13(4)

P. Cappon
1974   *Conflict entre les Neo-Canadiens et les Francophones de Montréal* (Québec: Presses de l'Université Laval)

E.F. Foerester
1919   *The Italian Emigration of our Times* (Cambridge, Mass.: Harvard University Press)

H. Gans
1982   *The Urban Villagers* (New York: The Free Press, updated and expanded edition).

H.A. Gibbard
    1935   "European Immigrants in Montreal: Their Means and Modes of Living," M.A. Thesis, Department of Sociology, McGill University
Francis C. Hardwick
    1976   *From an Antique Land: Italians in Canada*, (Ottawa: Tantalus Research Ltd., Canadian Culture Series, no. 6)
Robert F. Harney
    1974   "The Padrone and the Immigrant," *Canadian Review of American Studies,* 5(2, Fall)
    1975   "Ambiente and Social Class in North American Little Italies," *Canadian Review of Studies in Nationalism,* 2(2)
    1976   "Chiaroscuro: Italians in Toronto, 1985-1915," *Italian Americana,* 1(2, Spring)
    1977   "Frozen Wastes: The State of Italian Canadian Studies," in S.M. Tomasi (ed.), *Perspectives in Italian Emigration and Ethnicity* (Staten Island: Center for Migration Studies)
    1978a   "Boarding and Belonging: Thoughts on Sojourning Institutions," *Urban History Review,* 2
    1978b   "Men Without Women: Italian Migrants in Canada, 1880-1930," in B. Caroli, R.F. Harney, and I. Tomasi (eds.), *The Italian Immigrant Women in North America* (Toronto: Multicultural Historical Society of Ontario)
    1979a   "The Italian Community in Toronto," in Jean Leonard Elliott (ed.), *Two Nations, Many Cultures: Ethnic Groups in Canada* (Scarborough, Ont.: Prentice-Hall)
    1979b   "Montreal's King of Italian Labour: A Case Study of Padronism," *Labour/Le Travailieur,* 4
Clifford J. Jansen
    1969   "Leadership in the Toronto Italian Ethnic Group," *International Migration Review,* 4(1), Fall
    1978   "Community Organizations of Italians in Toronto," in Leo Driedger (ed.), *The Canadian Ethnic Mosaic* (Toronto: McClellend and Stewart)
Stanley Lieberson
    1970   *Language and Ethnic Relations in Canada* (Toronto: John Wiley & Sons, Inc.)
Anthony C. Masi
    1981   "Little Italy Now: Montreal," a background paper submitted under contract to *Attenzione.*
Rocco Mastrangelo
    1979   *The Italian Canadians* (Toronto: Van Nostrand and Reinhold)
Giosafat Mingarelli
    1980   *Gli Italiani di Montreal: Note e Profili* (Montreal: Centro Italiano Attivita Commerciali, Artistiche, 3rd edizione)

K.G. O'Bryan, J.G. Reitz, and O.M. Kuplowska
1976 *Non-Official Languages: A Study in Canadian Multiculturalism* (Ottawa: Minister of Supply and Services)
Claude Painchaud and Richard Poulin
1982 "Le phenomene migratoire italien et la formation de la communaute italo-québecoise," unpublished manuscript, Université du Québec à Montréal
Howard Palmer
1972 *Land of the Second Chance: A History of Ethnic Groups in Southern Alberta* (Lethbridge: The Lethbridge Herald)
Lauro Pao-Mercier
1982 "Ethnicity and Labour Market Segmentation: The Case of Chinese in Montreal," *Working Papers in Migration and Ethnicity,* no. 82-1
QUEBEC
Bruno Ramirez
1973 *L'Immigration au Québec,* Bulletin spécial No. 1, Annexe au Bulletin Statistique annuel (Québec: Gouvernement du Québec, Ministère de l'Immigration, Direction de la Recherche)
1977 *L'Immigration au Québec,* Bulletin spécial No. 5, Travailleurs immigrants, 1968-1975 (Montréal: Gouvernement du Québec, Ministère de l'Immigration, Direction de la Recherche)
1979 *L'Immigration au Québec,* Bulletin Statistique annuel, Vol. 6, 1978 (Montréal: Gouvernement du Québec, Ministères des Communautés culturelles et de l'Immigration, Direction de la Recherche)
1980 "L'Immigration, la Récomposition de Classe, et la Crise du Marché du Travail au Canada," *Cahiers du Socialisme,* automne, 6
1981 "Montreal's Italians and the Socio-Economy of Settlement, 1900-1930: Some Historical Hypotheses," *Urban History Review*, June, 10, 1
1982a "L'Immigration Italienne: Rapports Familiaux chez les Italiens du Québec," *Critére*, printemps, numero 33
1982b "La Recherche sur les Italiens du Québec," *Questions de Culture,* 2
1982c "La ricerca sugli italiani del Quebec," *Quaderni Culturali,* anno I, n. 3-4 n.s.
Bruno Ramirez and Michael Del Balso
1980 *The Italians of Montreal: From Sojourning to Settlement,* 1900-1921 (Montreal: Les Éditions du Courant, Inc.)
Barbara E. Schmitter
1980 "Immigrants and Associations: Their Role in the Socio-Political Process of Immigrant Worker Integration in West Germany and Switzerland," *International Migration Review*, 14(2), Summer
W.D. Scott
1914 "The Immigration by Races," in A. Short and A.C. Doughty

(eds.), *Canada and its Provinces: A History of the Canadian People and their Institutions,* Vol. 7, Political Evolution, 2 (Toronto, Glascow), reprinted in B. Hodgins and R. Page (eds.), *Canadian History Since Confederation: Essays and Interpretations* (Georgetown, Ontario: Irwin-Dorsey Limited, 1979, Second Edition)

Antonio Spada
    1969   *The Italians in Canada* (Montreal: Riviera Printers and Publishers)

A. Treves
    1976   *Le Migrazioni Interne nell' Italia Fascista* (Torino: Einaudi)

Giugliemo Vangelisti
    1956   *Gli Italiani in Canada* (Montreal: N.S. de la Defense)

Chapter **13** BEYOND THE "GODFATHER"
IMAGE: THE ROLE OF
ITALIAN AMERICANS IN THE
DEVELOPMENT OF AMERICA
Anthony Peter Alessandrini
Fairleigh Dickinson University

Prominently displayed on the dust jacket of Andrew Rolle's *The Italian Americans: Troubled Roots* appears a short and direct statement by the prominent Italian-American educator, Peter Sammartino. That statement reads as follows:

> "No other ethnic group has had as wide an influence on the birth
> and early development of the United States as the Italians. It is
> as simple as that."

While the cautious historian will argue that it may *not* be "as simple as that," Sammartino's statement ought to be remembered by every Italian-American who seeks his true identity in American society and comes to realize that he must look beyond the "Godfather" image to find himself.

In this paper I propose to show that the generations of Italian-Americans can resolve their contradictory feelings about their *Italo-americanità* only by learning about the *whole* Italian-American experience. It is the common experience of *all* the generations of Italian-Americans that is their heritage. Its origins predate the period of mass migration by several centuries and are intertwined with the roots of the new nation. That experience developed with the growing nation. It influenced the nation's growth and grew with it. But, the development of that experience has been increasingly obscured by the rise of the "Godfather" image, as much recent scholarship has tended to emphasize the more recent past and to neglect the long past of that experience.

Every major bibliography on the Italian-American experience includes the works of that great pioneer in the field, Giovanni Schiavo. I have come to know those works well, particularly his *Four Centuries of Italian-American History.* While I may not agree with Schiavo that his book "...is the most important work on the Italians in the United States ever written..."[1] because it is my fervent hope that "the most important work" hasn't been written yet, I think many can join me in agreeing with LaGumina and Cavaioli that "...if not classic," it is "basic."[2] Also, if Schiavo is correct — as he appears to be — in saying that "...writing about the

Italians in America without a reference to my *Four Centuries* is like writing about the Catholic Church without mentioning the Pope..."³ then this mention makes it possible to establish my credentials early. It also makes it possible to avoid his wrath, from wherever it may be directed, for that wrath can be withering as demonstrated in the "Bibliographical Appendices" that appear at the end of his 1976 edition of *The Italians in America Before the Revolution.*⁴ These Appendices are both instructive and entertaining — as long as the vitriole isn't directed at the reader.

But, it is in order to refer to a personal experience of his that he relates in the Introduction to this last-mentioned work that I have turned to Schiavo. These are Schiavo's words:

"Actually, for years after I became naturalized...I hesitated to refer to our founding fathers as "our", because I felt that the Italians had done nothing to create the American republic. It was only later, when I began to dig into that unexplored mine that still is the story of the Italians in America before the Civil War, that I acquired confidence in myself as an American, not only by conviction and devotion, but also because I had learned that I belonged, and, as an American of Italian origin or birth, I had as much right as anybody else, historically or otherwise."⁵

"I had learned that I belonged," writes Schiavo. In an article he wrote about two years before his book *Blood of My Blood* was published, Richard Gambino wrote of the dilemma that a later generation of Italian-Americans face in trying to achieve that same sense of belonging:

"When the third-generation person leaves school and his parents' home, he finds himself in a peculiar situation. A member of one of the largest minority groups in the country, he feels isolated, with no affiliation with or affinity for other Italian-Americans. This young person often wants and needs to go beyond the minimum security his parents sought in the world; ... this descendant of immigrants despised by the old WASP establishment embodies one of the latter's cherished myths. He sees himself as purely American, a blank slate upon which his individual experiences in American culture will inscribe what is to be his personality and his destiny. ... it is a myth that is untenable psychologically and sociologically. ... self-confidence ... is undermined by his yearning for ego integrity."⁶

Obviously, Schiavo acquired something to give him his sense of "belonging" that the young Italian-Americans of the third and fourth generation have sought and not found according to Gambino. Can it be that this something is the "Italo-americanità" that we are seeking to discover here, an awareness of their Italian ethnicity that "comes with the blood"[7] as Gambino puts it, but which at the same time threatens to isolate and submerge them to the lower socio-economic levels of our society unless that ethnicity can somehow be melded with their also being "American"? And yet, how can one be American in the fullest sense if one can only trace his American "origins" to a horde of "Giovanni-come-latelies" who were hated, abused and reviled by that very American tribe to which one now wants to belong? This, if Gambino will pardon me, appears to me to be the real dilemma of the Italian-American today that creates for him "a lonely, quiet crisis."[8] Certainly, for the resolution of this dilemma, the Italian-American must be provided with a very long historical view. Even four hundred years won't do it if the Italian-American is to escape the shadow of the "Godfather image".

At this point I must hasten to explain that by the "Godfather image" — perhaps a more scientific term might be the "Godfather syndrome" — I do *not* mean merely the stereotyping of Italian-Americans as criminals and gangsters. I may be overly optimistic but I think the time is past when, as actually happened not too long ago on a popular quiz show, a participant, asked to identify three persons whose surnames were those of three recent Popes, could get an easy laugh by replying, "Three guys who, if you pay them protection, will not blow up your candy store."[9] Contestants might guess that the three surnames were those of baseball players, the "real" names of popular singers — perhaps even three Nobel Prize winners. But they would not immediately conclude that they were three gangsters — certainly not aloud at least.

By the "Godfather image" I *do* mean the entire environment, the larger *ambience* conveyed most particularly by the movie adaptations of Mario Puzo's bestselling novel and the television inclusions of nearly every foot of film shot in the production of the movies *Godfather I* and *Godfather II* with all its flashbacks and futures related to the Corleone family. I include not only the Corleones and those immediately or even remotely related to them and affected by them — the major actors and the bit players — but also the cast of millions. I include the views of Ellis Island, the Jacob-Riis-like shots of the streets of Little Italy in livid color — and, yes, the pastoral scenes of Sicily.

I include in the Godfather image the Italian-American as *lazzarone* (bum), *delinquente* (criminal), *carogna* (louse), *Cafone* (clown), and *disgraziato* (slob), as well as *un amico degli amici* (Mafioso). I include not only *gli uomini di rispetto* (powerful criminal leaders) but also many so-called *prominenti,* the "celebrities", the "success-stories" like many of those embraced in the title of an article describing Italian-American groups organized to combat the Godfather image written by Nicholas Pileggi. The article, which he wrote for *Esquire Magazine* in 1968 is rather irreverently titled, "How We Italians Discovered America and Kept It Clean and Pure While Giving It Lots of Singers, Judges, and Other Swell People."[10]

The Godfather image as I use the term is made largely in the likeness of what Iorizzo and Mondello have termed the "five stereotypes of the Italian-American male (racketeer, lover, artist, showman, and family man)."[11] It is the mustached organ grinder and his monkey, Chico Marx in his clown's hat, Jimmy Durante destroying a piano along with the English language, only to be outdone in the latter occupation by Don Ameche as Professor Guzzolla. It is the monosyllabic baseball player marrying the blonde American sex goddess. And, as Iorizzo and Mondello point out

> "It seems that the public considered Italian organ grinders and their monkeys, and Italian immigrants in general rather comical, always good for a laugh."[12]

Good for a laugh, that is, as long as it was recognized that these Italian-Americans could also be dangerous and subversive as well as comical. So that the symbols of the Godfather image included stilettoes, anarchists bombs, black hands, severed horse's heads and large dead fish! Gambino has distilled the Godfather image into a set of key words:

> "the Mafia; pizza and other food; hard hats; blue collar; emotional, jealous people; dusky, sexy girls; overweight mammas; frightening, rough, tough men; pop singers;"[13]

It is ironic that Italian-Americans of all the generations—sometimes knowingly, more often unwittingly—have contributed to the development of that image. And, the greatest irony of all is that it may well be the scholarship and research of those interested in advancing Italian-American studies toward the development of *Italo-americanità* who will contribute to the perpetuation of the Godfather image into the future. How can this be? you will ask. Even a superficial survey of the literature on the Italian-American experience will, I feel make my meaning perfectly clear.

At first blush this literature appears to be positively immense and diverse. One looks at the work of that untiring bibliographer Francisco Cordasco and his colleagues and one's first reaction is amazement that so much has been written about the Italian-American. Doesn't the most recent edition of his bibliography contain 163 pages of references?[14] In fact, the 1974 edition lists five full pages of "bibliographies and archives!"[15] One cannot help but be impressed.

However, when one examines the entries on those pages more closely and assesses the total value of the accumulated literature, amazement must turn into disappointment. Two things immediately become apparent: First, how little the total bulk amounts to when it is carefully analyzed—it is a paucity of great wealth—or should we say a great wealth of paucity? and secondly, that almost all of the literature is devoted to the Godfather image as I have described it here, or, if that is too strong, perhaps you will settle for the Godfather era—the period of mass immigration and the generations after; that is, what the title of this Conference calls, "The First Hundred Years."

Non è vero? You will admit that Andrew Rolle is not, like me, a newcomer to the vineyard. In his "Essay on Sources" appended to his most recent work published in 1980 he writes:

> "Those who have written about Italian-Americans know how remiss this group has been about acknowledging its history. For decades these particular immigrants hardly seemed to want to fill the gaps in their knowledge of themselves."[16]

I shall be returning to this lack and to Rolle's estimate of its significance in a little while, but as to the literature on the Italian-Americans he continues:

> "Yet, the time has passed when one could say that there are no adequate histories of the Italians in America. Building upon the earlier work of Schiavo and Prezzolini, the books of Iorizzo and Mondello, De Conde, Rolle, Gambino and Amfitheatrof have filled this gap."[17]

Let us, then, examine briefly three of those works he mentions, leaving aside for the moment the work of Schiavo and of Rolle himself. (Let me state in a brief parenthesis here that I consider Rolle's *The Immigrant Upraised*[18] a classic example of good writing about the Italian-American experience.)

It is to the credit of Iorizzo and Mondello that they provide a kind of disclaimer in the very first paragraph of their Preface to *The Italian Americans*. They write:

> "The reader who is looking for a Who's Who of famous Italian-Americans or a definitive treatment of Italian immigration need go no further. The former has already been done and the latter will have to wait until scholars produce the monographs upon which such a study depends."[19]

Not indicating how well they thought the "former" had been done, they add that their work is a "textbook on the Italian-American experience."[20] But it becomes immediately clear that for them this experience is limited to the period after the "great migration" since of the 267 pages of text, all of them except for 38 pages, from Chapter 4 on, are devoted to the Godfather era. Chapter 1 is a six-page chapter on Italian history entitled "Prelude to Emigration." Chapter 2 is entitled "Italian Adventurers and Pioneers" and includes the following paragraph:

> "The story of this Italian migration to colonial and pre-Civil-War America is little known to most Americans. Even some of those who have studied the movement have tried to dismiss it on grounds of numerical insignificance. However, the value of the Italian contribution to America, as it must be with all immigrant groups, lies in its enduring characteristics which helped to make up the fiber of the American nation. In assessing the contribution scholars have hardly begun to scratch the surface."[21]

The authors do some scratching for the remaining 13 pages of this chapter and in the 14 pages devoted to Chapter 3, "Early Italian Colonies in America." Chapter 4 is entitled "The Great Migration." There follows a good book on the Godfather era.

Alexander De Conde's book *Half Bitter, Half Sweet* while subtitled *An Excursion Into Italian-American History*[22] is admittedly more a book about relations between Italy and the United States. In this work of 386 pages, all but 59 of those pages are devoted to the Godfather era. Even that is not the entire picture. Of those 59 pages only the first 17 (Chapter 1) are devoted to "Early Encounters", that is, Colombo, the Waldensians, Mazzei, Vigo, Botta, Beltrami, etc. Chapter 2, titled "Wanderers in Arcadia" is an interesting Chapter on early American travelers in Italy. Chapter 3 is titled "Risorgimento" and fills in some Italian history while Chapter 4 brings us to "Unification and Emigration." In sum, De Conde's book gives us 17 pages of the Italian American experience other than the Godfather image – out of a total of nearly 400 pages.

Richard Gambino's examination of *The Dilemma of the Italian-American* as his *Blood of My Blood* is subtitled, is easy to deal with. This important work, useful as it may be in other respects (I shall be referring to it again very soon) because of the very nature of the work, gives us exactly zero pages on the Italian-American experience before the Godfather era. (I purposely looked, and neither Colombo nor Mazzei are listed in Gambino's index, but Dante and Machiavelli *are* included!)

Let us look at two other sources not mentioned in the quote from Rolle's essay. (He does mention them later in the essay.) That obvious labor-of-love laboriously compiled by Lawrence Frank Pisani and published in 1957 is entitled *The Italian in America*.[23] Pisani devotes 29 pages of his 251 pages of text to the Italian-American experience preceding the period of mass migration before he begins to tell the story of Italian-American success achieved in spite of the Godfather image.

Finally, to rest my case, allow me to describe the contents of *A Documentary History of the Italian-Americans,* edited by two non-Italian-Americans (although Francis A. J. Ianni, as Consulting Editor, did "provide advice on topics and sources.")[24] There are six "parts" of uneven length to the book. Part One is entitled "The Italian-American Presence in the New World, 1492-1850." This appears promising but a closer examination reveals that Part I covers Columbus (sic), John Cabot (sic), Vespucci, Verrazzano, Enrico di Tonti, Kino, Mazzei, Italian opera and Da Ponte, and Lawrence Talliaferro, the indian agent — all in 33 pages out of a total of 432 pages in the book. Interestingly, the title of Part Two is actually misleading as it begins to document the Godfather image. It is titled "Immigration and the Patterns of Settlement, *1850*-1929" but in fact the very first "document" in that part is dated 1881.

Part Four of this apparently important work is sub-titled "Organized Crime and The Italian-American, 1890-1973. (Please note the dates, 1890-1973 — the book was published in 1974.) This section devotes some 90 pages to that specific aspect of the Godfather image. Another 42 pages that constitute the entire contents of Part V are dedicated to "Violence and Polemics" directed against Italian-Americans with heavy emphasis on violence, lynchings and beatings as well as diverse aspects of Italophobia. It includes that monument to bigotry and masterpiece of stereotyping produced by the respected scholar on Shakespeare, J. Appleton Morgan which was published in 1890 in *Popular Science Monthly* entitled "What Shall We Do With the Dago?"[25]

This work is an illustrated text and an enumeration of the two sets of good quality illustrations is enlightening in itself. The first set includes Colombo, of course, Vespucci, Kino, a photograph of immigrants on the crowded deck of one of the "cattle boats", a rather tidy scene at Ellis Island, a view of what appears to be a section of a mural depicting four pick-and-shovel workers on a railroad "track-gang" (one of the four with an obvious "Italian-type" mustache), a photograph of Sacco and Vanzetti handcuffed together, a lovely pen-and-ink drawing of "Little Italy in Manhattan in New York City" during a *festa,* a photograph of Anthony J. Celebrezze with President Kennedy (*not* in the Oval Office), John Volpe with President Johnson (*perhaps* in the Oval Office), an action shot of Senator John Pastore, and a photograph of Enrico Caruso dressed for *La Forza del Destino.*

The second set of illustrations opens with a photograph of Enrico Fermi, followed by a full-page photograph of Frank Rizzo, mayor of Philadelphia, followed by two other mayors of major cities, Joseph Alioto and Fiorello La Guardia, who are forced to share a page between them, as well as a view of two workers operating some sort of wine-making machinery apparently in California. Amadeo P. Giannini, the banker-magnate, and Joseph Valachi, the Mafia stool-pigeon, confront each other from opposite pages. There follow action photographs of Nick Buoniconti (a football star with the Miami Dolphins), Rocky Marciano the prizefighter, and Joe Pepitone (a baseball player with the New York Yankees). Joe Di Maggio is shown with his father who is identified as a "retired fisherman." The section closes with a highly idealized painting of Mother Frances Cabrini and a photograph of Francis J. Mugavero, "the first Italian-American bishop", hugging two little children, one of them black. How much better can my point be made? Pileggi's funny title doesn't seem funny any more!

Now, the usual justification for this strange phenomenon of the God-father image, an image which makes it appear that the "roots" of the Italian-American go back a mere hundred years and totally ignores centuries of *gloria e grandezza,* is to be found succinctly stated in the very first sentence of the last work discussed above:

> "Because Italians were numerically so conspicuous in the 'new immigration' after 1880, it is sometimes forgotten that Italian-American history is as old as American history itself."[26]

Actually, Italian-American history is much, much *older* than American history, but *non importa,* the message is clear. Philip M. Rose makes the same point in fewer words. "Only 30 Italians came to the United States in 1820,"[27] he writes. Is that important? Only *one* came in 1492!

Of course, that is the height of hyperbole because we all know that many of Colombo's crews were also Italians. But it helps us to demolish that other explanation for the undue and unfortunate emphasis on the Italian-American experience during the last hundred years — that, before 1860, there *was* no Italy except for the "geographical expression" of Talleyrand's sneer. Given this logic of history I must feel great compassion for the Polish-American attempting to find his roots and sense of belonging in America among the cohorts of his countrymen since there was no Poland until 1920 according to the same logic. That logic is false, of course, because there may have been no Poland but there certainly were Poles.

In this regard, Rose found it useful to quote an Italian who wrote to his English friend,

> "You English are always writing books about Italy and the Italians — but it never seems to strike you that there are many Italies and many Italians; and you forget that the plebiscites which gave us political unity and liberty did not at the same time miraculously create a new race."[28]

However this may be (certainly what Rose's Italian said about many Italies and many Italians would apply to the history of quite a few other nations) there is only *one* Italian-American and he must come to realize that he is the descendant of all the Italies and of all the Italians if he is to find his place in American society. To do otherwise is to play the "Mayflower descendant" game. It should matter little to the Italian-Americans of the so-called "fourth" and "fifth" generations *when* their closest ancestors arrived here and whether they were *Genovesi, Abbruzzesi, Calabresi, Siciliani,* or *Romani.* The *provincialismo* and *campanilismo* that this view represents has no applicability for the Italian-American of today. Only when that view is put behind him and forgotten will he begin to resolve his dilemma.

Let me begin to conclude this excerpt from a paper with a not-too-profound observation. That the Italian-American experience is replete with ironies has been remarked repeatedly in the literature, and each irony appears to loom larger than the one before it. But, it certainly would be the crowning incongruity if the destiny of the Italian-American through four or five generations is simply to complete a cycle that begins with the lonely sadness of separation, deprivation, and despair of the period of mass migration only to return to that sad, deprived state of not belonging that is as lonely and separate and desperate as the cruel beginning.

I am reminded of a short passage in Oscar Handlin's *The Uprooted.* Rolle calls this work a "rather maudlin book"[29] and he clearly means that the book oversentimentalizes the immigrant experience. However, it should be remembered that the word "maudlin" also invokes the meaning of "a tearful repentance." Certainly, America has much to repent of in its treatment of the immigrant during the period of the "new immigration". I would like to think that Rolle would agree with me that Handlin's expression of some of that repentance may be depressing and "tearful" at times, but that Handlin also expresses it graciously and with a minimum of condescension.

For the immigrant to America during this unfortunate era, Handlin asserts, "Sadness was the tone of life..."[30] He adds:

> "Loneliness, separation from the community of the village, and despair at the insignificance of their own human abilities, these were the elements that, in America, colored the peasants' view of their world. From the depths of a dark pessimism, they looked up at a frustrating universe ruled by haphazard, capricious forces. Without the capacity to control or influence these forces men could rarely gratify their hopes or wills."[31]

How similar this description is to the description which we quoted earlier from Gambino of the third-generation Italian-American who chooses to reject his ethnicity with its heavy baggage of the Godfather image and attempts to become "purely American". Is this then the fate of the Italian-American who does not wish to assert his *Italo-americanità* if that assertion means joining the ranks of the militant white ethnics in "defending their turf" and thereby assuming the role that the nativist bigot played in the shameful confrontation with his father or grandfather or great-grandfather? The dilemma again: to play the part of the persecutor, or to accept the sad loneliness of the new immigration all over again!

I will not pretend to be an expert on ethnicity. I do not know too much about it, frankly. I have done some reading and will do more, though some of these recent studies like that of James A. Crispino[32] have left me with many unanswered questions and some grave doubts. I *do* know some formal definitions of ethnicity—that it "... refers to the cultural ethos of a group, its values, expectations, behavior, and the cultural characteristics that distinguish it,"[33] and that "... ethnicity is one of a number of ways in which Americans may identify themselves and which they may use as part of their self-definition."[34] I also know some functions of ethnicity, described and so neatly summarized by Andrew M. Greeley:

> "... the functions of ethnic groups in American society are multiple. They keep cultural traditions alive, provide us with preferred associates, help organize the social structure, offer opportunities for mobility and success and enable men to identify themselves in the face of the threatening chaos of a large and impersonal society."[35]

It is the last of these functions—that ethnicity enables individuals to identify themselves within a large and increasingly impersonal society—which is of most concern to the Italian-American of today. Ethnicity defined in these terms is not a matter of whether one consumes home-made *pasta* in his household or puts *battuto*[36] in the tomato sauce, or wears a "Kiss Me, I'm Italian" button! Marcus L. Hansen, I think, has said it best:

> "... whenever any immigrant group reaches the third-generation stage in its development a spontaneous and almost irrestible impulse arises which forces the thoughts of many people of different professions, different positions in life, and different points of view to interest themselves in that one factor which they have in common: heritage—the heritage of blood."[37]

"Heritage of blood", of course, is a romantic way of referring to the product of a common history. The phenomenon that Hansen describes is true for all 'ethnics", apparently, but it is particularly true of Italian-Americans. "It comes with the blood," said Gambino. And, what it is that "comes with the blood" is the history of the Italians in America.

Michael J. Parenti exhorted those present at the fourth Annual Conference of this Association in 1971 in the following terms:

"So my people, the Italian-Americans, we still have to learn our history. Italian-Americans are in fact historical illiterates in terms of their own group, not only in Italy but, in fact, with concern to Italians in this country."[38]

I should like to add to Parenti's advice, "Let us learn *all* our history. Let us not retain our fixation with the relatively small portion of that history—the mere hundred years since the new immigration—that lends itself so easily to the calumnies of the Godfather image. Let us broaden our horizons to include all the history that came before "The Troubled Roots" and find our real roots beyond the Godfather image.

Notes

1. *Italians in America Before The Revolution,* New York and Dallas, 1976, p. 148.
2. Salvatore J. La Gumina and Frank J. Cavaioli, *The Ethic Dimension in American Society,* Boston, 1974, p. 187.
3. *Op. cit.,* p. 146.
4. *Ibid.,* pp. 139-182.
5. *Ibid.,* p. 4.
6. "Italian Americans Today," in Wayne Moquin and Charles Van Doren, (eds.), *A Documentary History of the Italian-Americans,* New York and Washington, 1974, p. 432.
7. Richard Gambino, *Blood of My Blood,* Garden City, 1974, p. 341.
8. *Ibid.,* p. 332.
9. Nicholas and Mary Spilotro, (eds.), *Study Guide On Italian-Americans,* New York, 1979, p. 208.
10. In Wayne Moquin and Charles Van Doren, (Eds.), *op. cit.,* pp. 235-242.
11. Luciano J. Iorizzo and Salvatore Mondello, *The Italian-Americans,* (Revised Edition), Boston, 1980, p. 273.
12. *Ibid.,* p. 266.
13. *Blood of My Blood,* p. 320.
14. Francisco Cordasco, *Italian-Americans: A Guide to Information Sources,* Detroit, 1978.
15. Francisco Cordasco, *The Italian American Experience,* New York, 1974.
16. *The Italian Americans: Troubled Roots,* New York, 1980, p. 196.
17. *Idem.*
18. Andrew F. Rolle, *The Immigrant Upraised: Italian Adventurers and Colonists In An Expanding America,* Norman, Oklahoma, 1968.

19. *Op. cit.,* p. 11.
20. *Idem.*
21. *Ibid.,* p. 25.
22. New York, 1971.
23. Lawrence F. Pisani, *The Italian in America: A Social Study and History,* New York, 1957.
24. Moquin and Van Doren, *op. cit.,* p. xii.
25. *Ibid.,* pp. 259-262. The article is followed by a response to the editor from a reader published in a later issue of the magazine that attempted to defend the Italian immigrant which ends with the words, "What shall we do with the Dago? Give him a chance."
26. *Ibid.,* p. 1.
27. *The Italians In America,* New York, 1975, (Arno Press reprint of the 1922 edition), p. 25. The figures that Rose used have been, of course, the subject of much controversy and debate.
28. *Ibid.,* p. 14.
29. *Op. cit.,* p. 23.
30. Oscar Handlin, *The Uprooted,* (Second Edition Enlarged), Boston and Toronto, 1973, p. 97.
31. *Idem.*
32. *The Assimilation of Ethnic Groups: The Italian Case,* New York, 1980.
33. Charles F. Marden and Gladys Meyer, *Minorities in American Society,* New York, 1968, quoted in Neil C. Sandberg, *Ethnic Identity and Assimilation: The Polish-American Community,* New York, 1974, p. 1.
34. *Why Can't They Be Like Us?: America's White Ethnic Groups,* New York, 1975, p. 45.
35. *Ibid.,* pp. 51-52.
36. Minced meat, usually fatty, or salt-pork, used to flavor tomato gravy.
37. "The Third Generation In America," *Commentary* 14, No. 5, (November, 1952), pp. 496-497, quoted in Neil C. Sandberg, *op. cit.,* p. 33.
38. *Power and Class: The Italian-American Experience Today,* (Proceedings of the Fourth Annual Conference, The American Italian Historical Association), Staten Island, New York, 1973, p. 31.

Chapter **14** SOCIAL PSYCHIATRY IN THE
ITALIAN AMERICAN COMMUNITY
Francis X. Femminella
State University of New York at Albany
Henry A. Camperlengo
Albany Medical College

Studies dealing with Italian and Italian American families have abounded since the early classic study by Paul Campisi in 1948.[1] Without in anyway gainsaying this contribution, his orientation to a straight line theory of ethnic assimilation in a melting pot society would be less than accepted today given the new pluralist rather than either melting pot or traditional cultural pluralist ideologies. The former change in theoretical positioning evolved out of the neo-Hegelian and even Maxist social science. The latter derives from what has been called the "Black revolution" — the demand on the part of Afro-Americans for their rights, as Americans, to the fullness of participation in America and in its heritage.

Studies of the underlying cultural dimensions of the etiology of psychiatric illness have also been extensive during the same time span over the last 3 or 4 decades. Simultaneously the practice of psychiatry in community settings outside of large state hospitals has become commonplace and with it there has been a heightening of awareness of the influence of social and cultural change on psychiatric functioning.

More recently there has been the specific clinical recognition that not only do certain kinds of disorders have their etiology in the socio-cultural context; but the socio-cultural situation may itself be utilized in the very treatment of the disorder or distress. Specifically, with the work of Price Cobbs,[2] Judith Weinstein Klein,[3] Joseph Giordano,[4] and the authors of this paper, a form of group therapy for persons of similar ethnic background has been developed and referred to as "Ethnotherapy." This form of treatment seems particularly suited to adult individuals suffering with what is technically referred to as Identity Disorder, the essential feature of which is severe distress regarding inability to reconcile aspects of the self into a relatively coherent and acceptable sense of self. "There is uncertainty about a variety of issues relating to identity, including long term goals, career choice, friendship patterns, sexual orientation and behavior, religious identification, moral values, and group loyalties." (DSM III-313.82)[5] It is this

169

last symptom, namely difficulty and inner conflict regarding one's loyalties and identifications with one's loyalties and identification with one's ancestral socio-cultural heritage, i.e., one's ethnic group, that is particularly distressful and painful to Italian Americans for whom family life is so central; ethnicity is passed on through families by the processes of socialization. Nevertheless, in the modern, urban, industrial society of our times the evolution of values that conflict with the traditional village, agrarian value system we inherited, is inevitable. These conflicts, as Del Russo and Tropea[6] have pointed out, go back and forth through individuals, families and larger social groupings.

The theoretical explanation of the persistence and change of these values has been presented elsewhere. Briefly we refer to the fact that Italian and Italian American is not the same. Through the process of socialization, the inner identification of Italian Americans with the historical heritage is found in their individual ego-identities which persist because of what we have theoretically posited as the presence of "ethnic ideological themes." "Ideological themes" as used here refer operationally to "the generalized leit-motifs and underlying principle features (of which an individual may or may not have awareness) of one's ideals, aspirations and interests, and the specific pattern of variation (i.e., rank ordering) of value orientations of individuals. When we refer to these topics and value orientations which are held in common by members of an ethnic group, we refer to them as *"ethnic ideological themes."* Ethnic ideological themes are "located" deep in the foundation of that dimension of individuals, where social and ideological structures constitute a unitary process, i.e., the personality structure itself. These themes are not easily eradicated—at least not without seriously weakening either or both the individual and the society."[7] They operate in a variety of ways not yet fully understood. In fact, their presence is theoretically posited and they are in reality undefined terms. Now and then they are discerned in values or in cultural traits, in styles of thought and expression and even in actions. When they are explicit patterns of behavior they are susceptible to historical derivation and selection. It is this that explains how they can evolve. Viewing the appropriateness of any given conduct to a specific time and place, the individual with or without the concurrence of his "significant others" can modify his life.

So, for example, if an individual is confronted by a conflict between an inherited behavior or value system and a behavior which is perceived as necessary for today's society, he may experience pain and suffering. The emotionally mature individual finds ways to reconcile and resolve the conflict. The individual who attempts a wholesale rejection of his heritage risks what might be called a positive or negative disorder. A positive disorder is of the nature described above. A negative disorder appears on the surface as a total and even "successful" acculturation but is in fact a view of self as inherently without worth or value. The individual suffering with a negative identity disorder organizes his life around a process of ideological centrism (opposite of the process of ideological polarization) that directs him to uncritical acceptance of the dominant culture and the acting out of its expected behaviors. Throughout the world, all immigrants and their progeny have had to reconcile and resolve value and behavior conflicts. In the United States, what makes our culture unique is our ability to evolve new forms as each new immigrant group has impacted and integrated with us.

For Italians in America, a crucial value conflict has been their traditional and changing perspectives on mental health and the use of professions for the treatment of mental disorders. Fandetti,[8] Rotuno and McGoldrick,[9] Giordano,[10] and Rabkin and Struening,[11] all make reference to the traditional Italian bias *against* seeking professional treatment for emotional disturbances, and *in favor of* the use of some respected family members or a priest. This view of mental disorders as a family problem to be solved by the individual himself or at least resolved within the family, operates to a large degree against Italian Americans whose traditional structures by themselves, are insufficient for meeting the crises caused by this society. As Italian Americans perceive this, they reconcile and accommodate and begin to use the help available to them, thereby diminishing a little the traditional orientations. At the same time, however, they recognize and, so also, should the professionals, that the strengths that exist in cohesive families is by no means all negative. As the Italian Americans are changing so the practitioners in all the helping professions should learn to utilize the existing social and cultural systems of their patients, clients, students, etc. in their practice.[12] Few family therapists that I know would deny the inestimable value to the mental health of all our citizens that more family cohesiveness, with all that that implies, would engender.

II

Having addressed, however peripherally, the issue of cultural continuity and change, this paper will now address another paradox: the differential diagnoses and responses to illness of and among Italian Americans. From this we will see that the process of utilizing diverse sociocultural systems is not an easy one to integrate into practice.

It was very early in the history of Italians in America that they were found by Dr. John Kirby (first New York State Mental Health Department Commissioner) to behave differently from patients of other ethnic groups having the same diseases. His studies of the cultural factors in GPI (general paresis of the insane) focused on immigrants. A large number of descriptive studies over the years, and our own clinical practice, have confirmed this observation. Rotuno and McGoldrick have reviewed this literature carefully.[9]

To illustrate this behavior variability we may cite the finding that Italians appear to be more somatically oriented, focusing on physical symptoms and expressing their discomfort by use of body language.[13] Their low tolerance to pain combined with their uninhibitedness about complaining earned for them the animadversion of "whiner" in nursing circles in American hospitals. The admired patient in an American hospital is the one who, more than merely suffering quietly, actually denies his pain. The picture conjured by this is of a John Wayne having just been shot, thrown and dragged by his horse, run over by a wagon and hurled over a cliff, protests to the beautiful heroine who is nursing him, "It's just a scratch, sweetheart." In the United States complaints about physical pain are acceptable only from babies. For Italians, concern with physical adjustments and complaints about physical symptoms are fully acceptable. Not only physical pain but psychic suffering may be and is expressed physically. The cultural base for this derives from the attitude that men are risk takers. They are supposed to take chances. But when they are frightened their social or psychological feelings are hidden and they are encouraged to talk about physical symptoms or convert their emotional feelings into physical complaints.

In attempting to make a meaningful diagnosis based on an assessment of a patient's behavior, feelings, transferences, etc. in culturally strange situations of this kind, it is not difficult to see how mistakes can be made. In the case of Italian Americans, where behavioral or psychological problems may be related specifically to social heritage, misdiagnosis is even more possible.

The now classical studies of Opler and Singer[14] of twenty five years ago were followed by a related study by Fantl and Schiro[15] shortly afterward, comparing Irish and Italian schizophrenic patients on a variety of variables. Here we shall report on the findings of a preliminary exploration that was originally meant to be preparatory to a larger investigation replicating in part those earlier works. Our early tentative findings have led us to redirect the forms of that study.

The population of the present study consisted of all adult patients in our case files seen during the last 10 years; of Italian origin or descent, who resided in the capital district of New York State, which includes urban, suburban and rural areas. Patients with Organic Mental Disorders were excluded from the Opler and Fantl studies and from our survey also. The sample consisted of 41 upper working and middle class persons. Each case chart was analyzed for the following information:

A. Sex
B. Generational status, i.e., 1st generation—born in Italy; 2nd generation—born in U.S. of Italian born parents; 3rd and beyond

generation—born in U.S. of U.S. born (Italian descendant) parents or grandparents.

C. Major diagnosis.

The results of the survey are shown in the accompanying tables:

Table 1
Distribution by Diagnosis and Sex

Diagnosis	Sex	
	Male	Female
Hypochondriasis	5	1
Depressive Disorders	11	11
Paranoid Disorders	10	3
Total	26	15

Table 2
Distribution by Diagnosis and Generation

Diagnosis	Generation		
	First	Second	Beyond
Hypochondriasis	5	1	0
Depressive Disorders	2	16	4
Paranoid Disorders	0	5	8
Total	7	22	12

Table 3
Distribution by Sex and Generation

Sex	Generation			
	First	Second	Beyond	Total
Male	5	10	11	26
Female	2	12	1	15
Total	7	22	12	41

Table 4
Distribution by Sex, Diagnosis and Generation

Sex	Diagnosis	First	Second	Beyond	Total
Male	Hypochondriasis	5	0	0	5
	Depressive Disorders	0	7	4	11
	Paranoid Disorders	0	3	7	10
Sub-total male		5	10	11	26
Female	Hypochondriasis	0	1	0	1
	Depressive Disorders	2	9	0	1
	Paranoid Disorders	0	2	1	3
Sub-total female		2	12	1	15
TOTAL		7	22	12	41

(Header spanning "First, Second, Beyond, Total": Generation)

About 63% of the sample was male, 20% of whom were 1st generation, the rest evenly divided between 2nd and beyond generations. The females constituted only about 33% of the sample of whom 80% were 2nd generation.

Three major diagnostic categories were found: Hypochondriasis, Depressive Disorders and Paranoid Disorders. Put in non-technical language these categories answer the question: "What makes people feel psychologically bad?" In hypochondriasis the patient is judging that his body is bad; in depressive disorders he judges that he is a bad person; and in paranoid disorders, he is asserting that someone outside of himself is making him feel bad. A total of about 15% of the patients suffered from hypochondriasis. Thirteen percent suffered from paranoid disorders; and more than half — fifty-four percent suffered from depressive disorders.

Our findings on hypochondriasis resembled Opler's findings and were in contrast to Fantls. They are consistent with what was said about the somatic focus of Italian males. Our findings on depressive disorders were consistent with two facts of literature: a) the literature on 2nd generation marginality; and b) the developing literature on women.

Finally, our findings on paranoid disorders serve as a reflection of the inexorable process of ethnic change in the United States.

Notes

1. Campisi, Paul J., "Ethnic Family Patterns: The Italian Family in the United States." *American Journal of Sociology,* May, 1948, pp. 443-49.

2. Cobbs, Price, "Ethnotherapy in Groups" in L. Solomon and B. Berzib (eds.), *New Perspectives on Encounter Groups,* San Francisco: Jossey-Bass, 1972.

3. Klein, Judith Weinstein, *Jewish Identity and Self-Esteem: Healing Wounds Through Enthotherapy,* New York: Institute on Pluralism and Group Identity, 1980.

4. Giordano, Joseph, "Basic Group Identity: The Hidden Dimension in Therapy", paper presented at the American Group Psychotherapy Association Conference, Atlanta, 1972.

5. American Psychiatric Association, *Diagnostic and Statistical Manual of Mental Disorders, Third Edition,* Washington, D.C. APA, 1980.

6. del Russo, Carl and Tropea, Joseph L., "Identity and Contradictions: *La Via Vecchia e i Giovanetti",* paper presented at the American Italian Historical Association Conference, Chicago, Ill., 1980.

7. Femminella, Francis X., "The Ethnic Ideological Themes of Italian Americans", paper presented at the American Italian Historical Association, Chicago, Ill., 1980. See also Femminella, F.X. "Rural Urban Contrasts in Identity Elements of Rural Italian Americans", paper read at the American Italian Historical Association, St. Paul, Minn., 1981.

8. Fandetti, D., "Sources of Assistance in a White Working Class Ethnic Neighborhood", unpublished Ph.D. dissertation, Columbia University, School of Social Work, N.Y.C., 1974.

9. Rotuno, Marie and McGoldrick, Monica, "Italian American Families" in M. McGoldrick, J. Giordano and Pearce, *Ethnicity and Family Therapy,* New York: Guilford Press, 1982

10. Giordano, Joseph, "Families: Staying Alive" *Attenzione,* Sept. 1980, p 80. _____ "Families: Health and Culture" *Attenzione,* July/August, 1981, p. 68.

11. Rabkin, Judith G. and Struening, Elmer L., "Ethnicity, Social Class and Mental Illness", Working paper Number 17, New York, Institute on Pluralism and Group Identity, 1976.

12. Gordon, Andrew J., "Ethnicity Old and New: Implications for Mental Health Care", in A.J. Gordon (ed.) "Ethnicity and the Delivery of Mental Health Services," Working paper Number 23, New York, Institute on Pluralism and Group Identity, 1979.

13. Ragucci, A.T., "Italian Americans" in A. Hargood (ed.), *Ethnicity and Medical Care,* Cambridge, Mass., Harvard University Press, 1981.

14. Opler, Marvin K. and Singer, Jerome, "Ethnic Differences in Behavior and Psychopathology", *International Journal of Social Psychiatry,* Vol. II, No. 1, Summer 1956.

15. Fantl, Berta and Schiro, Joseph, "Cultural Variables in the Behavior Patterns and Symptom Formation of 15 Irish and 15 Italian Female Schizophrenics," *International Journal of Social Psychiatry,* Vol. IV, No. 4, Spring 1959.

Chapter **15** THE EVOLUTION OF
PIETRO DI DONATO'S
PERCEPTIONS OF
ITALIAN-AMERICANS
Michael D. Esposito
Exxon Corporation, New Jersey

With the theme of this Conference being "Italian-Americans Through
the Generations: The First Hundred Years," this is an opportune time to
consider the evolution of Pietro di Donato's perceptions of Italian-
Americans, since he has devoted the better part of seventy-one years to
documenting their progress. Why di Donato? Because, as a pioneer among
Italo-American writers, his early works stirred the American public to
recognize the condition of the Italian immigrants, and he did so with such
energy, such passion, and such pain that it is unlikely his achievement will
ever be duplicated. By capturing the sights, sounds, and smells of his
Italian-American community, di Donato crystallized the spirit of his life
and, by extension, the lives of many Italian-Americans during the early
years of the twentieth century. If only for that achievement, his voice
deserves to be heard and his thoughts preserved.

As a child, when he went to Ellis Island with his father to meet
relatives, di Donato found people packed into steerage no differently than
were livestock. They were fleeing from such economic and political injustices as starvation, conscription, and crushing taxes. He remembered
that these "mustachioed men with their rag bundles were from the lowest
class in Italy and had the perspective of the medieval vassal." They brought
no notions of democracy, but rather, fig and vine cuttings, Catholicism,
their village patron saint, and an unconquerable pride and passion for their
families.[1]

Di Donato's recollections of his youth before World War I represent
the immigrant world he found himself in and later provided the substance
of much of his fiction. Because he grew up in an Italian ghetto in West
Hoboken, New Jersey, di Donato's ethnic identity was indelibly etched in
his mind and consequently, his most powerful works deal with the plight of
the Italians in America.

The unique shaping of di Donato's life, and later, his fiction, may be
attributed largely to the Italian immigrants' transferred ideas of community,
labor, education, and family primacy. Not surprisingly, these customs were
expressed by his parents as they acclimated themselves to the New World.

Di Donato was remarkably adept at distancing himself from his people and documenting "a process of interaction between two established cultures, each participating in the growth of the American race or nation."[2] In effect, he has witnessed the evolution of the primitive, Italian immigrant into what he calls a "grasping materialistically-minded melting pot creature."[3] In this paper, I will trace the evolution of di Donato's perceptions of this "creature" from the author's childhood to the present.

But first, to better appreciate the genesis of di Donato's perspective, one needs to understand the Italo-American milieu from which he sprang. The ancient culture of his people, for instance, included a deep reverence for masonry, and he captured this veneration in *Three Circles of Light:*

> Masonry was the great, revered art of my people. To have been accepted and honored by them you had to be both Vastese and a master mason; otherwise, even if you were the King of England or the President of the United States you would have been contemptuously spurned.[4]

In fact, because tailors and barbers did not wield the pick and the trowel they were considered "anemic aristocrats" by di Donato's people.[5]

This attitude, lauding the virtues of bricklaying and, by implication, other forms of skilled, manual labor, reinforced the Italian immigrants' low opinion of a formal education. As di Donato put it, "my people disdained books; they spurned, they curled their lips at anybody who studied. Theirs was a completely ... muscles and sweat physical life. As a result, the practice of reading was foreign to young Italo-Americans."[6] Because of this aversion towards reading, the older immigrants often discouraged their young from furthering their educations. This seriously restricted their movement out of the blue-collar ranks.

All in all, di Donato's childhood was no different from that of most second-generation Italian-Americans, that is, until his father, Geremio, died in 1923. When Geremio was killed in a construction accident four days before Pietro's twelfth birthday, his son's life and view of the world were irrevocably shaken. Pietro firmly believed the contractor was responsible for the building's collapse for insisting on using cheap materials to reduce expenses. Even though officials of New York's Building Department claimed the accident was caused by the criminal negligence of the workers themselves,[7] Pietro was convinced then as he is now that the accident resulted from the greedy profiteering of the project's contractor. Henceforth, di Donato came to realize that his father, the Italian immigrants, and the laboring masses suffered irreparable injustices at the hands of the rich. Geremio's death illuminated the workers' condition for young di Donato and propelled him to the conviction years later that he was "class-conscious and in sympathy with the dream of some kind of revolution and the uplifting of the working man."[8]

When asked in an interview in 1939 about his father's death, di Donato said "my belief in goodness and beauty was upset.... I didn't believe that adults were gods anymore. Even the *paesani* — kinfolk — didn't help us. For three years we had no relief, no help from anyone, except one dollar a week in bread tickets from the local poormaster."[9] The eldest male in his family, di Donato quit school in the eighth grade to support his mother and seven brothers and sisters, and faithful to the tradition of his ancestors, who came from a generation of builders, he became a bricklayer.

Di Donato's maturing affinity for the masses led him to join the Communist Party on the night Sacco and Vanzetti were executed, August 23, 1927. He had been part of a demonstration in Union Square protesting their innocence. Beside himself at the time and overwhelmed with emotion and anger, di Donato remembered the crowd keeping vigil in the Square the night Sacco and Vanzetti were electrocuted. In one of his short stories, di Donato relived that night:

> There must have been a hundred thousand people in the park across the way. The Union Square crowds were looking at the floor above the co-op where the office of the Communist newspaper, *The Daily Worker,* ran huge bulletins about Sacco and Vanzetti. The people received the news that first Sacco, and then Vanzetti had been put to death in the electric chair. A hush fell over the people. Then there were murmurings. The murmurings grew and wrathful cries broke out against Capitalism. Cops on foot, horseback, on motorcycles and in motorcycle sidecars went berserk attacking the people.[10]

This trauma further intensified his disenchantment with American politics and heightened his compassion for the oppressed Italian immigrants. He saw them as a people who, under desperate conditions fled their homeland and who, upon settling in America were exploited and persecuted.

About two years after the Sacco and Vanzetti incident, the Great Depression hit and, though employed, di Donato's despondency grew as he watched his people evicted from their homes. He noted his observations in *Christ in Concrete:*

> NINETEEN TWENTY-NINE!
> The building boom lay back — and disappeared. Builders stopped giving out plans to contractors, building owners lost their holdings, building-loan corporations liquidated, the active world of Job shrunk and overnight men were wandering the streets trowel on hip and lunch beneath arm in futile search for work.[11]

Di Donato's godfather was one of these unemployed *paesani*. By kicking back ten dollars of his own paycheck to help cover his godfather's, di Donato was able to secure employment for the aging bricklayer.

Shortly after his godfather started work, di Donato watched him plummet twenty stories to his death as he was working on a construction project in New York City. Sickened by the catastrophe, di Donato left the site dazed, believing that like his father and his paternal grandfather (who was killed in Italy while building an aqueduct), and now his godfather, he, too, was destined to perish in a construction accident. This event, coupled with his father's violent death and the executions of Sacco and Vanzetti, exacerbated di Donato's disillusionment with what he believed to be a bankrupt society. He also lost faith in Catholicism, since he could no longer believe in a God who allowed such injustices to continue unabated. Consequently, at nineteen di Donato discarded all the myths, superstitions, and religious beliefs that had bred in his people an attitude of passive resignation to the inequities they suffered. In the process, he acquired a consciousness of himself and of his relationship to the world based on a reverence for life here and now, and this realization ultimately drove him to record his feelings on paper.

Di Donato's empathy for the masses characterized his first attempts at writing. In 1932, he wrote several letters to Franklin D. Roosevelt urging him to be the social messiah and to save the working class from the grip of the Depression. In one letter he told FDR that as President he had been chosen by Christ "to lead the poor and hungry, the old and ill, and the oppressed unemployed out of the Valley of Economic Despair and into the Light of the Promised Land...." As di Donato put it, he "pleaded only for what was decently and reasonably possible."[12] FDR ignored these impassioned appeals, and di Donato's identification with the working class intensified because he knew the President "was not familiar with the ways of the masses, that it could never be so, and that the only way he could save the masses would be by sending them to die in war."[13]

Meanwhile, di Donato's first literary efforts were interrupted by yet another tragedy: his mother died of cancer in 1932. Emotionally shattered, di Donato said her death brought to mind the deaths of his father and godfather, and he realized he was "part of the masses and was class-conscious, conscious of the inequalities and injustices of the Depression." He then bought a ticket for the Soviet Union because, he recalled, "I wanted a new world and, wishful thinking, I idealistically dreamt of helping to build the proletarian society because I identified myself with the proletariat."[14] Despite his class-consciousness, di Donato was forced to abandon his dream and remain in the States to fulfill his familial responsibilities.

In 1937, when he was twenty-five, di Donato was on relief. As he explained:

> God, relief was a godsend to me. I was supporting my seven
> brothers and sisters in Northport [Long Island].... There was a
> building strike, and for the first time in my life I was free and
> didn't have to work. The government was paying our rent. We
> dug clams and filched corn and vegetables from the farmers.[15]

Once freed from the constrictions of the scaffold, he strayed into the
Northport Public Library and began reading serious literature for the first
time. It is significant in di Donato's development as a class-conscious writer
that he began to correlate the injustices suffered by his people with the corresponding injustices endured by the workers described by Tolstoy,
Turgenev, and Dostoevsky. Di Donato's admission that he "felt kin not only
to those who expressed themselves but also to those who had no voice"[16]
demonstrates clearly his camaraderie with those Russian writers who shared
his sentiments for the working class. Soon thereafter, di Donato wrote his
first short story, entitled "Christ in Concrete." He sent the story to *Esquire,*
and amidst much fanfare, saw it published in March 1937. Letting his
original story stand as the first chapter in what became *Christ in Concrete*
the novel, di Donato published his book in 1939.

A brief mention of *Christ in Concrete* is necessary in order to appreciate di Donato's perceptions of Italian-Americans when he wrote the
novel. In recreating his own story, di Donato dramatized the condition of
the exploited Italian immigrant worker and his family as they embraced the
American ethos. As one critic explained, *Christ in Concrete* is a tale of the
poor, the confused, the wretched, written not from outside, but from
within—not by one seeking out of hatred to whip up revolutionary fervor,
but motivated rather by an overwhelming love for his clan, his culture, and
his calling."[17] With almost reckless intensity and deliberate purpose, di
Donato related the problems of the immigrant family to the brutal
pressures of the construction workers' world. In essence, he recorded the
entrance of the Italian immigrant into the foreign world of industrial
capitalism. Di Donato claimed that by faithfully reconstructing "things as
they are" in *Christ in Concrete,* he hoped "the thinking or sensitive reader
would become emotionalized against the constrictions and the oppressive
nature of the environment to which the immigrant and the poor were subjected."[18] By accurately reporting the facts and carefully reproducing settings and events, di Donato expected his audience to pause and re-evaluate
the present economic disparities in this country.

In telling his story, di Donato credited no capitalist institution with
helping his people in what he argued was class warfare. When he wrote
Christ in Concrete, di Donato said "I was bitter in my heart against the
money system, the capitalists' world," and so compressed his "social passions into the local family and job scene."[19] One need only examine the

title *Christ in Concrete* to grasp di Donato's feelings. He chose the title, which represents the destiny of Italian-American construction workers and their families, because he saw in the immigrants' work ethic and humble acceptance of America's inequities reflections of Jesus Christ.

Heralded as one of the best works of 1939, *Christ in Concrete* was highly praised by readers and critics, but soon after its release di Donato's literary career and enthusiasm and passion for the working class declined. He said he had begun "to see humanity in a different light, ... the supine masses and the predatory masters."[20] Unable to document his thoughts, di Donato reluctantly returned to bricklaying, broken and humiliated. He thought the *paesani* had preferred he remain a celebrity and a successful writer: "My coming back and joining them seemed a betrayal of their expectations of me." Consequently, di Donato drank and lived sensuously during what he called his "dark ages."[21]

By 1970, di Donato's attitude towards the working class, Italian-Americans in particular, had undergone a striking metamorphosis. His regard for the Italians living in America turned to disgust and shame because he felt they had turned their backs on the dignity of the immigrant:

> The Italian has become homogenized. He does not compare with the original immigrant. My father took me to the Metropolitan Opera when I was five, and he had concrete on his shoes. The Italians then were full of legends; they were self-regulating and self-entertaining.
>
> But now the species has degenerated. The Italian-American has become a vociferous, rotund breed, endomorphs in the anarchy of freedom over freedom. A good people gone wrong.[22]

Di Donato was especially critical of working-class Italo-Americans for not overcoming the limitations associated with a lack of education and motivation: "There are few things they enthuse over, except football and baseball. This is the age of the ugly people and the Italians are adapting to it."[23] In short, di Donato has accused the Italians in this country of becoming Americanized; instead of preserving the best traditions and customs of their culture, they have abandoned their ethnic identity for the anonymity of American mores.

Di Donato's bitterness towards Italian-Americans — fueled largely by their indifference towards his work — is paradoxical in view of his own seemingly valueless life following the success of *Christ in Concrete*. He was a young writer, overwhelmed with the pressing concerns of his past, who wrote a powerful first novel, and for years succumbed to the worst blandishments of the capitalist enterprise he despised. In fact, as evidenced from an examination of his fiction, the burden of his past is so great that he can never completely free himself from the Italo-American milieu of his childhood. In reality, it seems di Donato has lived what may be called the "Hollywood Paradigm": acquiescing to the perils of money and fame, di Donato was robbed of his higher ideals and artistic impulses.

Today, though he admits he is experiencing "all sorts of moods and impressions, feelings, cynicisms, and pessimisms," di Donato advises pessimists "to be optimistic in spite of many things that discourage us" because "the world changes and better things happen, good things happen."[24] Yet, while advocating optimism it is clear his once prolific faith in America's working class has withered rather than flourished. For example, in 1977 he said, "the average American is to me a dummy, something I cannot feel for. He is such a Babylonian confusion of lies and mediocrities that I can't care what happens to him."[25] He now sees the working class and Italian-Americans quite differently than when he wrote *Christ in Concrete* over forty years ago:

> The primitive types I wrote about in my youth no longer exist, the *paesani,* the immigrants. They had come literally from the feudal world, the dark ages, and things were unadulterated by the blandishments of our consumer society.... Imagine what the impact is on the average mediocre mind of twenty or thirty hours a week of imbecilic television, of soap operas, of situation comedies. Even though I sympathize for the working man, he is still the willing recipient of the bombardment of these banalities.[26]

As the recipient of these banalities, the average American, in di Donato's opinion, must be regarded as a robot, as a potential Nazi or Fascist ready to march with another Hitler or Mussolini or with American reactionaries into another Vietnam.

Despite his contemptuous assessment of Americans and Italo-Americans, di Donato is surprisingly optimistic about the future. As far back as 1971 he predicted the advent of "the rosy-fingered rays of redemption and salvation beyond the smogged horizon."[27] He noticed more Italian-Americans attending college and studying the Italian language and culture, while scholars began seriously examining the question of ethnicity. The American Italian Historical Association and your presence here today attest to the advances made by Italian-Americans as they attempt to understand their heritage and to learn how they helped shape this country.

Indeed, di Donato's perceptions of Italian-Americans have gone full circle. Earlier, I mentioned how he witnessed the immigrants' arrival on Ellis Island, people representing Italy's lowest social stratum. As primitives, oppressed for generations and conditioned to be suspicious of strangers and government officials, these immigrants derived their strength from their families, and it is to an extended familial relationship that di Donato envisions humanity in general returning:

> I want to witness the great drama of the creation of the socialist man because inevitably we're all going to have to be brothers. There's no way out. It will come, not because it's a lyric ideal, but because man is going to have to be forced to be the brother of every other man. Our technical age, our problems, our pollution. We're going to have to be forced to collectivize our lives [in order to survive]....[28]

The time will soon come, promises di Donato, when man will break away from the confines of the existing world and create a new political and economic order energized by love and by brotherhood. This new world will evolve, in part, in response to the people's demand to equally distribute the wealth of the world among all men of all nations. Di Donato's compelling and hopelessly idealistic tone is, to some extent, what makes *Christ in Concrete* such a moving novel and what, to this day, makes his voice truly a distinctive one among Italian-American writers.

Notes

1. Pietro di Donato, "A Rinascimento on L.I.," *The New York Times,* 14 November 71, Section 1A, p. 16; Helen Geracimos Chapin, "If You Seek Justice, Put a Gift on the Scale: Concepts of Justice in White Ethnic American Literature," *U.S. Department of Health, Education, and Welfare.* National Institute of Education, 1977, pp. 2-3.
2. Rose Green, *The Italian-American Novel* (Rutherford, N.J.: Fairleigh Dickinson University Press, 1974), p. 23.
3. Personal interview with Pietro di Donato, March 21, 1977.
4. Pietro di Donato, *Three Circles of Light* (New York: Julian Messner, Inc., 1960), p. 40.
5. *The New York Sun,* August 1939, p. 8.
6. Personal interview with Pietro di Donato, March 21, 1977.
7. *The New York Times,* March 31, 1923, p. 2.
8. Personal interview with Pietro di Donato, March 21, 1977.
9. *The New York Sun,* August 1939, p. 8.
10. Pietro di Donato, "Sugar, Spice and Everything Nice," in *Naked, As An Author* (New York: Pinnacle Books, 1971), p. 219.
11. Pietro di Donato, *Christ in Concrete* (New York: Bobbs-Merrill Company, 1939), p. 273.
12. Pietro di Donato, "From Laborer To Literary Lion," *Newsday,* November 15, 1981, pp. 18-19.

13. Personal interview with Pietro di Donato, March 21, 1977.
14. Personal interview with Pietro di Donato, March 26, 1977.
15. Joseph Barbato, "Once Upon a Time He Created A Classic," *The National Observer,* March 20, 1976, p. 21.
16. "A Terrific Fuss Over A Story," *Esquire,* March 1937, p. 32.
17. Warren French, *The Social Novel at the End of an Era* (Carbondale and Edwardsville: Southern Illinois University Press, 1966), p. 182.
18. Personal interview with Pietro di Donato, December 4, 1977.
19. Personal interview with Pietro di Donato, March 21, 1977.
20. Continuation of interview.
21. Personal interview with Pietro di Donato, December 4, 1977.
22. Richard Severo, "New York's Italians: A Question of Identity Within and Without," *The New York Times,* November 9, 1970, p. 43.
23. Severo, *ibid.*
24. Personal interview with Pietro di Donato, March 26, 1977.
25. Personal interview with Pietro di Donato, March 21, 1977.
26. Personal interview with Pietro di Donato, September 2, 1979.
27. di Donato, "A Rinascimento on L.I.," p. 16.
28. Personal interview with Pietro di Donato, March 26, 1977.

Chapter 16

"THE SEMIOLOGY OF SEMEN": QUESTIONING THE FATHER

Robert Viscusi
Brooklyn College, CUNY

I hope that Jerre Mangione will find some space in his forthcoming history of Italian-Americans to trace the development of their sense of ritual. Once very traditional in their observances, Italian-Americans have created some startling innovations in recent years. The Italian-American Club in Clearwater, Florida, for example, an organization comprised largely of senior American citizens who spoke Italian when they were children, appeared on Columbus Day marching down the main street of that retirement colony in a mock funeral. Everyone wore black. The women draped themselves with veils and rosaries. They followed an empty pine box painted black, and they howled and fainted and rent their garments, calling upon the saints and pretending to bare their chests. Everyone agreed that this was among the most diverting celebrations the club had ever staged.[1] Again, not long since, I attended a fund-raising dance at St. Margaret Mary Church in Astoria, Queens. The dance took the form of a "football wedding." The organizers, husky middle-aged people with grown children, took the parts of bride, groom, bridesmaids, ushers, flower girl, ring bearer, priest, parents, and so on. The band played "Let Me Call You Sweetheart" and a long *tarantella*. The bride had a large silk bag for envelopes. Every detail recalled the weddings of thirty and forty years ago, and each was hailed with general hilarity and delight.[2] These funeral and wedding ceremonies had in common a striking, and rather surprising, quality of burlesque. This quality would seem to call for some explanation. What leads Italian-Americans to travesty with such exuberance sacred rituals which their parents, and even they themselves not many years back, practiced with a remarkable degree of intensity and solemnity?

Most evident in the travesties is the exaggeration. Becoming Americans, Italian immigrants and their children learned to look upon their own rituals as excessive, laden with affect that other people's rituals avoided. No one raised, as I was, mostly among Italian immigrants can forget the shock of his first visit to a non-Italian funeral: the absence of tears, the muted conversation, the undisturbed hairdos, and the pink dresses all seemed to us shockingly inadequate to the occasion. These people, we said to one another, do not know how to grieve properly. But soon enough we began wondering whether it might not be ourselves who were doing it wrong.

Likewise with weddings. How dull the "American" weddings seemed, with their expensive bland dinners and their absence of children, their spastic foxtrots and insipid toasts; compared with our marathon bouts of drinking and dancing and eating and laughing, how pointless, how inappropriate they were! How useless were their presents: their butter knives and tea services and Revere bowls were as so much wind next to a great white *peau de soie* satchel fat with cash. But, then, soon enough we were all having formal dinners with no children and began buying sterling-silver pickle forks and mint trays. We loved our ancient customs so much, it now seems, that we cannot bear our repudiation of them in silence as we move towards American manners; we must drive out our memory of how we once did things as if we were driving out devils, making elaborate public fun of them. We rid ourselves of our past by ridiculing it.

We are, perhaps, in the adolescence of our history in Italian America, where even our old folk still struggle through travesty and sarcasm to free themselves of their parents. We possess no more talented or determined ancient teenager than Pietro di Donato. Those who have had the good fortune to hear him at one of our ritual convocations of Italian-American scholars will recognize that on such occasions he is almost unfailingly the spirit of burlesque. His performance in Chicago three years ago is still spoken of under raised eyebrows. Last May, invited to address the theme "The Italians of Brooklyn" at a conference at Brooklyn College, di Donato elected to read a story about attempting to lose his virginity in Prospect Park the same year he was about to be confirmed in a church in Bensonhurst. This charming tale, when it was first printed in the pages of *Oui*, must have seemed positively innocent in its evocation of a teenager's fantasy of what awaited him under a woman's clothes.[3] But as an offering at a celebration and "serious" discussion of the sort we were conducting at Brooklyn, di Donato's story sounded thoroughly scandalous. A young boy's appraisal of his sexual object often echoes the language of sexist oppression, and some women quite understandably stood up and walked out as di Donato was reading. His use of the demotic dialect of seduction in his narrative was flawless: such terms as *gash, cunt, ass, fuck, blow, suck, prick,* and *cock* floated along in his sentences with the irreproachable plausibility of used condoms in a sewer pipe. And di Donato read these terms with gusto. As a septuagenarian he retains the vivid sexual fury of the fourteen-year-old who has just decided there had better not be God. This fury, and the powerful longings that fuel it, come across very plainly in di Donato's reading of such a story, and they never fail to shock those in the audience who have come to hear the man who wrote *Christ in Concrete* forty-five years ago, the man who, as they suppose, must by now be a wise elder, a Solomon, a Pope John. When instead they encounter this randy old village atheist, they raise their hands in horror and in general grow terribly dignified, outraged, and foolish. This, of course, is very funny and is, moreover, exactly what di Donato wants. Indeed, an unsympathetic reader might say that di Donato, throughout his career, has played the professional adolescent.

But a fuller comprehension might lead us to decide that di Donato has rather acted the part that fate allotted him, that of the bewildered and abandoned son. It is a resonant role, and di Donato has played it with all of the generous energy at his command. He has done so in, I think, three ways: his first move was to create a language that kept in the immigrant son's English as much as possible of the lost father's Italian; this was a poetic victory, but it did not go far to ease the son's pain at his loss. Thus, at the same time, there was a second move, the raising of an insistent question, the question of Jesus to *his* Father: "My God, my God, why hast thou forsaken me?" This question, as we shall see, contains in it a good deal of anger as well as the obvious frustration and pain we hear on its surface. Finally, di Donato has acted as if he had received an answer to this question, not from the heavens but from his own body, which speaks to him in the secret language of genes by which our fathers transmit themselves to us. Di Donato's effort to read his father's answer in his own body and behavior I call a semiology, an attempt to understand the sign-language, of semen. But this is to leap ahead. I will take these three moves in order.

1. The Language of Recovery

Christ in Concrete is written in a dialect never spoken by anyone except the American son of the lost Italian father. Take, for example, the following passage, describing the arrival home of the corpse of the slaughtered parent:

> On the entrance door-jamb was pinned a visiting sign of thin ribbons and white carnations. Hands clutched breasts, and mute respect cried, "Attend! By the love of God, attend! The man of the house has come home!"[4]

This is the language of impossible desire, the son bringing with him into his lucid, literary, and even elegant English as much as he can carry of the complex codes of symbol and gesture which belong to the poor, illiterate *paisani* of the preceding generation, so that the ribbons, the carnations, and the hands clutching breasts are transformed into a ritual dance which demonstrates that these immigrants are subtle and civilized even if they have not been much to school. The careful poetic English of the prose just misses being ridiculous. What saves it is the intensity of emotion. Thus, when di Donato renders "Attenti!" as "Attend!" we do not laugh, as we might in some other circumstance; instead, the cognate mistranslation gives to the English an orotund poetic knell of circumstance which the verb signally lacks in Italian.[5] The effect resembles what Shakespeare obtained by sprinkling his Warwickshire proverbs with sesquipedalian coinages out of Latin, French and Italian, but there is a notable difference: the Italian rises always to the surface of di Donato's English in this book because of the overwhelming motive it everywhere indicates — the desire to recover the lost Italian father and godfather whose deaths are the great forces in this novel's action. I have called this desire impossible because that is precisely how di Donato presents it: *impossible,* he says, because death is final, the father is dead, the godfather is dead, and so, he decides, God too is dead. But however hopeless it is, the desire persists. And the persistence of impossible desire is the theme of di Donato's career, just as it is the driving force with the language of *Christ in Concrete.*

2. The Persistence of Desire

The son's desire for the father is not only impossible; it is, as it persists, also criminal. When Jesus calls out to his father across the blackness, "My God, my God, why hast thou forsaken me?" we feel we hear him in his most human moment, when he most resembles that most human of his great forebears, King David, whose 22nd Psalm he is in fact quoting at this crisis.[6] The full measure of this divine humanity is that Christ's question, when we consider it, tells us that he feels the emotion which can be the unforgiveable sin: despair. Orthodoxy might say that Christ's despair is shown as a sign of his fleshly weakness, which is the absolute weakness of all mankind, and therefore, by complement, the full measure of his divinity, which can suffer even this, the coldest torture of Hell. But when di Donato asks the same question, and in *Christ in Concrete* he does little else, it is more the human weakness than the divine reply which we are given to explore. Let us consider the scene of the loss of the father, the burial of Geremio in the concrete, surely one of the few passages in modern American fiction that people will still want to read five hundred years from now:

> The rescue men cleaved grimly with pick and ax.
>   Geremio came to with a start...far from their efforts. His brain told him instantly what had happened and where he was. He shouted wildly. "Save me! I'm being buried alive!" He paused exhausted. His genitals convulsed. The cold steel rod upon which they were impaled froze his spine.

Notice that he has begun this passage by castrating the father, and remember, as we go along, that all of this is purely imaginary, since there were no witnesses to this scene when it actually took place.

He shouted louder and louder. "Save me! I am hurt badly! I can be saved I can — save me before it's too late!" But the cries went no farther than his own ears. The icy wet concrete reached his chin. His heart appalled. "In a few seconds I will be entombed. If I can only breathe, they will reach me. Surely, they will!" His face was quickly covered, its flesh yielding to the solid sharp-cut stones. "Air! Air!" screamed his lungs as he was completely sealed. Savagely he bit into the wooden form pressed upon his mouth. An eighth of an inch of its surface splintered off. Oh, if he could only hold out long enough to bite even the smallest hole through the air! He must! There can be no other way! He is responsible for his family! He cannot leave them like this! He didn't want to die! This could not be the answer to life! He had bitten halfway through when his teeth snapped off to the gums in the uneven conflict. The pressure of the concrete was such, and its effectiveness so thorough, that the wooden splinters, stumps of teeth, and blood never left the closing mouth.[8]

The fever pitch of this writing puts one in mind of di Donato's dictum that "the scene is a spike that you drive through the reader's head."[9] Our pain, however, should not prevent us from making a few pointed inquiries. What, for example, is the real theme of this passage? It begins with the father's castration, and it ends with the breaking off of his teeth, and in the next few paragraphs it will turn to his suffocation. All these themes — castration, burial alive, splintering of teeth, loss of breath, and suffocation — come straight out of Edgar Allan Poe,[10] but here they are transformed by the very clear message we receive that the author is writing, under thin fictional allegory, about his own imaginings of the death of his own father.

And it is hard to avoid the recognition that, as he writes, the author makes himself guilty of that death: driving the spike through not so much the reader's head as the imaginary father's. There is in the vividness of the writing an emotion almost of glory, certainly of fury, as the writer's pen grows in monstrous power precisely as he details the removal of the father's power to express himself. We have here the very primal scene of writing, the Son stealing the power of words from the Father. It is a *terrible* scene, in the old Italian sense that it displays and makes us feel the absolute terror of terror. To read it is to see, actually to see, di Donato in the moment of becoming a great writer by assuming, through the fury of the writing, the guilt for his father's murder. Next to this scene, even *Macbeth* reads like polite literature.

Why did di Donato write this scene? The risks involved were enormous. And, while the rewards were great, the price, as we shall see, was greater.

The risks were enormous, because to write this was to commit the most vivid possible sacrilege, and to perpetrate in writing the primal crime. Why did he do it? Di Donato's whole subsequent career has attempted to provide the answer, which, I suggest, is and has always been that he felt an intolerable and irrepressible anger at his father for dying and abandoning him, as he did, just as the boy was crossing the threshold of puberty. "My God, my God, why hast thou forsaken me?" Jesus, we might say, allows himself to be crucified as a measure of his willingness to suffer what all Sons in their fury have wished upon all Fathers in their distance. Jesus' meekness, eternal and boundless, is the exact measure of the wrath his love must deny. It is this stunning truth in the heart of Christianity that di Donato in his career has tried to make clear.

His later work demonstrates the point endlessly. The novel *This Woman*,[11] published in 1943, as well as the manuscript which he is still writing, entitled *The Venus Odyssey*,[12] detail the story of an obsessive marriage. Paul, the hero of *Christ in Concrete*, has grown up and become a successful author, rich and famous, squanders his money and marries a beautiful widow: this marriage, from the first, is shadowed by his inability to stop thinking of the woman's dead husband, whose ghost he encounters in the most private moments and places, and whose body he finally exhumes and pommels into a foul amorphous jelly, just as, we might say, he had done with his father's body in the pages of *Christ in Concrete*. Di Donato is under no illusions about the source of this obsession: *The Venus Odyssey*, in particular, is filled with detailed comparisons between Paul's dead father and Helen's dead husband. In both novels, di Donato paints Paul as a man paying the price of Oedipus, experiencing a profound love which is a form of eternal punishment. Di Donato is always aware that the only way out of this dilemma is the way that Jesus took: to sacrifice himself on the altar of the violated father. He tries, sometimes, to follow that path. The two hagiographies he wrote, *Immigrant Saint*[13] and *The Pentitent*[14] suggest by their titles the preoccupations that moved him to undertake them. It must have been a heavy labor to write them, as indeed it is to read them. They are uninspired and willful work. Di Donato's imitation of Christ has had to look elsewhere: it has needed, in the event, to follow a very unorthodox path.

In *Three Circles of Light*,[15] he abandoned the simple Christianity he had been attempting, and tried instead to justify his fury, outlining the treacheries and double identities and fornications of his father, almost making it seem that his death was a just punishment for the life he had led. If it had been, then the son's murder of him in the pages of *Christ in Concrete* would have been excusable as well. But *The Venus Odyssey*, a more recent work, suggests that neither the prayers of *The Pentitent* nor the excuses of *Three Circles of Light* have been very effective. Di Donato could not play the saint, nor could he play the defense lawyer at the throne of judg-ment. There was only one thing for him to do: he became, and he is today, a fool for Christ.

This is a precise term: it means that he has elected to work out his salvation, — or, if you will, the meaning of his career — by confessing his sins publicly and in the antic mode, endlessly. In *The Venus Odyssey,* he makes abundantly clear that this has made him an absurdly literal reader of the semiology of semen: the semiology of semen is the genetic language by which our fathers transmit themselves to us, making us resemble them in surprisingly elaborate and unpredictable and inescapable ways. We all do this, but few of us carry it so far as di Donato in *The Venus Odyssey,* where he writes, for example, "[Paul] wrote about [his father's mistress], and in the fiction laid her the way his father did."[16] Di Donato's penance has been that he has immured himself in his imaginary father's imaginary identity as if it were a concrete coffin: like his father, he feels obliged to play the great lover; like his father, he feels condemned to be an eternal scandal.

Christ in Concrete, in this light, seems an ambiguous title. Di Donato meant it, at first, to suggest the heroism of the martyred plebeian im-migrant bricklayer. But by the end of that novel, Paul seemed as stuck in the cement as Geremio. Di Donato's subsequent career has only intensified the immersion. This, as much as the great language of his great novel, is di Donato's noble achievement, that in his career he has impaled himself endlessly upon the contradictory emotions, the love and hate, the nearness and absence, the faith and despair, that moved not only him who as a child lost his father in a cloud of love and fury but also the rest of us, who have seen our immigrant progenitors disappear into a growing foreignness, a growing incomprehensibility, an incommensureable distance. When di Donato questions the father, "Why hast thou forsaken me?" he echoes not only King David and King Jesus, but also every boy who, coming home from college, sits down again to the wine and the hard bread and looks up to the head of the table to see the red face and the strange manners of a man from a world where the boy may visit but can never live again. Di Donato asks his question for us all. And when he makes us move restlessly about in our seats at the scholarly convocation as he dreams aloud of the divine vagina and the innumerable hells of desire and need, he simply confesses for us all, like the priest he has always been — confesses that he, like us, finds written in his fingers the semiology of semen, the secret language of the genes we have stolen before we could inherit them, the stolen goods, which like the ghost of the murdered God, possesses us forever.

Guilt and confession, these are the unmistakeable themes of di Donato's burlesque. So are they of ours. In this we differ not at all from all sons and daughters. What is characteristic of us, I suspect, is the way we do it, the florid liturgical inventiveness by virtue of which we atone to our parents with a mock funeral in the streets of a retirement village or a mock wedding in a catholic-school gymnasium, or the mock suffering of Paul who ascends his wife's bed as it were a scaffold, or the mock scandalousness of di Donato himself, who tells his terrible stories, stories of guilt and horror worthy of Poe or the Ancient Mariner, but tells them with a boyish relish for the gory details that puts us in mind, not of the haunted hero he feels he is sentenced to play upon the stage, but rather of the Abruzzese peasant child his father must have been, scaring his sister with tales of the slaughtered pig and the mating bull. He is his Father, but he is his Father as a boy.

The Son, it appears, becomes the Father, and yet he is always the Son. He never grows up. God, it appears, is dead, and yet one never can think of anything else. And di Donato, it is certain, is that fool who is inscrutably wise, who questions his father, endlessly, obnoxiously, embarrassingly, but who stays, as some do not, to decipher the answers he receives, to read the riddles in the seed. His books, then, for us, have the canonical status of scriptures in the history of Italian America. For what he has been — a Catholic, a hero, a fool, a lost child, and a traveling man — we begin to see, as we examine the hands of our own fathers' sons, is what our fathers and our deeds have written in the marks we make ourselves.

Epilogue, 1985

Often we wonder what it might be like, after reading some absolutely wonderful book, to sit comfortably alongside the person whose name appears on its title page and have a long conversation about exactly how and why the book possesses the virtues it does. Most of the time this pleasure is not a possible one. Dead people do not converse. Sometimes it is possible but not feasible. Live people are not always willing or available. Sometimes it is feasible but turns out to be disappointing. Willing people are not always capable. But once in a while this pleasure is possible, feasible, available, and spectacularly satisfying. Such an occasion, for me, was the one in October 1982 when I delivered this paper. After I had begun thinking about it, I called Pietro di Donato on the phone and asked him if he would be willing to listen and reply to Michael Esposito and myself on the subject of his life and works. He knows both of us, has extended innumerable kindnesses to us both, and, fully in character, agreed with enthusiasm to the proposal.

Facing so rare an opportunity I was troubled what to write. The time allotted was brief: how to say in ten typed pages what needed saying? I took comfort from the thought that Mr. Esposito, who had written a master's thesis on di Donato, would be sure to say all which was most necessary to an understanding of this noble writer. I decided, not without fear and trembling, to restrict myself to what I knew best. I had read di Donato's books, written about them, taught students ways of reading them. I had heard him speak several times at conferences of students of Italian-American history and culture. I had invited him more than once to speak to students and faculty at Brooklyn College and New York University. We had broken bread in one another's houses. We had shared many long hours of memorable conversation. He had allowed me to read unpublished manuscripts of fiction and drama. We were friends and allies. Thinking of all of this, I was most struck with a similarity between Pietro di Donato and some other great writers who were also great rebels: Lord Byron, Oscar Wilde, Allen Ginsberg. I can put this similarity into two clauses: he wrote his books as a form of living; he lived his life as a form of writing.

There were other similarities. All of these writers were what is called "uneven." Not for them the simonize of the model essayist. Not for them the chamois rag of the Yale professor. They wrote, they published, and they lived, largely without revision. They were, one might say, without shame. One might say it, but it would be imprecise. They were not *without* shame, they were *against* shame. All of them allowed more public glimpses into their sexual habits and desires than the model essayist generally will do. Byron had a child by his half-sister and promptly wrote a poem, *The Bride of Abydos,* about incest. Oscar Wilde sat in Reading Gaol writing letters about homosexual love as if he were St. Paul writing about the resurrection. Allen Ginsberg published a poem which announced that it was typed with one hand while the other was stroking the penis of his male lover. Di Donato wrote novels about sexual rivalry with a dead man. *Against,* not without, shame, I say, because these were all of them embattled men. Byron lived in exile. Wilde went to jail. Ginsberg likewise has done his time. Di Donato spent most of his middle years in absolute obscurity, a great writer forced to return to laying brick. One does not write about Byron's poetry without his life, nor Wilde's dialogues, nor Ginsberg's *Howl.* In such writers, life itself is a form of literary activity.

But what form?

It varies very considerably. Byron's life, with all its turns and leaps, best reveals itself in his letters. Oscar Wilde on the witness stand and in the newspaper interview belongs as fully to literary history as does the author of *The Importance of Being Earnest.* Allen Ginsberg has played the antic bard, chanting his mantras to the sound of a concertina in parks and public squares and church basements all over the world. Di Donato, it seemed to me, had made a specialty of turning up at all the serious rituals by which Italian-American professionals seek to raise up some public reflection of the dignity of their collective enterprise — turning up, that is, and turning everything over. I have seen many an offended propriety strut out of a room where di Donato was holding spectacularly forth. I have also seen many classrooms of Italian-American undergraduate students sit magnificently engaged for hours and hours in discourse with this remarkable man who answers their questions with the fury of Nietzsche alone with a pencil and the self-possession of a Roman senator played by Ralph Richardson. These performances, with all they contain of a passionately whirling rage of ceaseless reconsideration, seemed (and seem) to me as much a part of the historical and literary record as the extraordinary speeches of Oscar Wilde in the dock or Allen Ginsberg's monumental attempt to cause the Pentagon to rise from the ground by chanting at it. Accordingly, I wrote this paper with the aim of finding the thread which joined together for me, and for Italian-Americans in general, the varied enterprises of our most accomplished and memorable writer of fiction.

Di Donato, when he heard the paper read, rose, according to his custom, first *to*, and then *beyond*, the occasion. Taking my thesis as his theme, he wove a wonderful fabric of meditative and even rhapsodic reminiscence of his father — of what he had meant, of what he continued to mean, to the son who had sung his elegy for sixty years. This was — I hope I will be forgiven for saying — a high point, an extraordinary and definitive moment — in my own life. I had meant the essay as a compliment to a brilliantly paradoxical career. Naturally, the compliment itself was full of paradox. Di Donato not only recognized this, he exuberantly trumped it. "Viscusi," he said, "Viscous Viscusi has nailed me." But not nailed him very tightly, for he went energetically (and still goes energetically) on.

A few days later, I received a long, offended letter from a professor of psychology who accused me of "character assassination" and "a classical case of projection" and a good deal else. Nothing you may be sure, could have more fully convinced me that I had succeeded in entering the spirit of di Donato's own masquerade than this professor's succession of violent huffs and sniffs. I will not quote from the letter, and I will likewise refrain from citing the retort which I wrote with considerable pleasure to my correspondent. But one thing must be made clear: *we are all of us absolutely visible.* No reverent lowering of the eyes or raising of an index finger to the pursing lip can ever remedy this painful situation. Di Donato not only understands this simple truth, well known to every intelligent twelve-year-old in creation, but he glories in it. He has made for himself a special vocation of reminding the rest of us of it.

We Italian-Americans of professional rank are in danger, I think, of Respectability. Perhaps it is no great harm that we have taken to bringing useless chafing-dishes instead of flexible cash as wedding presents. But it will have been very great harm indeed if we turn and look back at ourselves after long, active, chatty careers and can only see there the manufactured simpers of the well-established, upwardly mobile, endlessly aspirant dullards we are likely to become if we insist always upon putting our dignity before our conscience or our desire to be accepted before our desire to tell the truth.

Notes

1. Letter from Mr. & Mrs. Joseph Viscusi, February 1979.
2. I attended this event.
3. Pietro di Donato, "The First Time," *Oui,* 5, 9 (September, 1976), 42-44.
4. Pietro di Donato, *Christ in Concrete* (New York: Bobbs-Merrill 1939), p. 32.
5. I have discussed this effect in more detail in *"De Vulgari Eloquentia:* An approach to the Language of Italian American Fiction," *Yale Italian Studies,* I, 3 (Winter 1981), 21-38.
6. For a discussion of this in its relation to psychoanalytic and literary theory, see Robert Viscusi, "The Other Speaking: Allegory and Lacan" in *The Writer's Mind: Writing as a Mode of Thinking,* ed. Janice Hayes *et al.* (Urbana, Illinois: National Council of Teachers of English, 1984), pp. 231-238.
7. *Christ in Concrete,* p. 20.
8. *Christ in Concrete,* pp. 20-21.
9. Pietro di Donato, private conversation, September 1981.
10. Very fully surveyed in Marie Bonaparte, *The Life and Works of Edgar Allan Poe,* trans. John Rodker (London: Imago, 1949).
11. Pietro di Donato, *This Woman,* (New York: Ballantine Books, 1958).
12. Mr. di Donato had kindly allowed me to study this manuscript.
13. Pietro di Donato, *Immigrant Saint* (New York: McGraw-Hill, 1962).
14. *The Penitent* (New York: Englewood Cliffs, New Jersey: Hawthorne Press, 1960).
15. *Three Circles of Light* (New York: Julian Messner, 1960).
16. *The Venus Odyssey,* unpublished manuscript, p. 109.

PART V

Education as a Frontier

Chapter **17** ITALIAN-AMERICAN
EDUCATIONAL ATTAINMENT: AN
ANALYSIS BASED ON CURRENT
POPULATION SURVEY DATA
William S. Egelman
Iona College

I

This paper seeks to explore changes in the levels of educational attainment of Italian-Americans.[1] The first part of the paper will present a brief historical overview on the subject, and traces some of the changes that have occurred. In the second part of the paper data drawn from the latest report on ethnicity published by the Bureau of the Census will be analyzed.

II

There is a long history of antipathy towards formal education by Italian immigrants. This antipathy is based upon a complex interweaving of social, historical, cultural and economic experiences.[2]

This anti-education position had a number of root causes. As Rosen notes, school was seen as an upper class institution, and those with too much learning were not to be trusted.[3] Rolle in a more recent work supports this idea by stating the following: "There was precious little learning in the Little Italys of America. Parents saw a 'bad' child as one who left home to get an education. The 'good' child stayed home to help."[4]

Perhaps the most important reason for the anti-education position lies in the fact that the Italians who emigrated from Italy were primarily from the rural south. Their tradition was a peasant tradition. In such a peasant society, children's labor was highly valued. The idea that children, in their early teens should attend school was an anathema to the adult members of the community. Children by the age of thirteen or fourteen were expected to make a meaningful contribution to the family income.[5]

The economic value of children is also emphasized in Covello's classic work on the Italian-American school child. "The most overt conflict between the American school and the Italian parental home," Covello writes, "seems to derive from the economic values of Italian family life.... Thus the old world tradition which demands of the child a share in the economic upkeep of the family, regardless of the child's age and capacity, was invoked in America."[6]

197

For the children of these immigrants, the problem becomes one of trying to live in two worlds. The two worlds being on the one hand, the world of southern Italian rural peasantry, and on the other hand, the world of modern urban America. An added dimension to this problem is that these worlds are both critical and suspicious of each other. Gambino discusses this reciprocal distrust when he writes:

> To the immigrant generation of Italians, the task was clear: Hold to the psychological sovereignty of the old ways and thereby seal out the threats of the new 'conqueror,' the American society that surrounded them. This ingrained disposition was strongly reinforced by the hatred and insult with which the Italian immigrant was assaulted by American bigots who regarded him as racially inferior — a 'dago,' a 'wop' a 'guinea.' [7]

Thus, this mutual distrust is brought about by reciprocal ignorance. Hatred and insult emerge out of a lack of understanding. The school child, in turn, is caught in the midst of this dilemma. As a result of this, Covello asserts that the child may easily develop a sense of inferiority or inadequacy. Child notes, while the family is emphasizing values of the "old world," the school represents a completely different world. The school is populated with individuals who identify themselves as being American. American behavior patterns are encouraged. Following these patterns of behavior is "rewarded by approval on the part of the teachers and by specific acts of friendship on the part of the classmates, and are thus reinforced."[8]

From the point of view of the family, the ideas and experiences the children received in the educational system were a direct attack on their traditional way of life. Vander Zanden has stressed the importance of the public school in the breaking down of traditional forms of family interaction. For a large part of each day, the children of Italian immigrants attended public school classes. Here, they were immersed with the mainstream of American life. Old world traits were looked upon as being "foreign" or "alien." A certain number of these children developed contempt for their parents. They viewed their parents as being "stupid" or "greenhorns." Parents might try to instill old world customs and beliefs on their children, while the children might attempt to teach their parents the ways of the new land.[9]

Lopreato in summing up why Italian parents were not overly zealous about having their children engage in the formal educational process suggests the following factors: school and teachers were seen as being hostile to traditional family values; parents saw no intrinsic value in having their children attend school; the Italian children were directed towards vocational programs and vocational skills could be better mastered in actual apprenticeships rather than in classrooms; and, as already noted, many families needed the additional earning power of their children in order to survive.[10]

These early Italian immigrants lived in a new and oftentimes hostile environment. The "urban jungles of Little Italy" did little to enhance their appreciation of formal education.[11] Also, the ideal of individual achievement, so highly valued in the system was an anathema to them. "Individual achievement (in school)" as Parrillo notes, "was not heavily encouraged. What mattered most were family honor, group stability, and social cohesion and cooperation."[12] This is not to say that achievement itself was not important. Achievement is a value-laden term. Achievement in one area may be highly valued by one culture but not by another culture. For example, Vecoli points out that Italian American culture contained several "core values" which were central to its social and cultural life.[13] These core values included the primacy of personal relationships; the importance of reciprocal obligations; a strong sense of authority; and, a strong allegiance to domesticity, or the overriding importance of home and family. Within the Italian-American community success in any or all of these areas would have been defined as an achievement.

III

Although tradition-oriented societies tend to be highly resistant to change, they cannot totally withstand the forces of change that exist in any society. The strong anti-education position just described could not, in fact, last forever. Within the group as new generations came on the scene the "old ways" began to meet with challenges from the young. In addition, as time progressed there were changes outside the group in the general cultural environment. Any particular traditional attitude or perception may undergo change because of both internal and external pressures. To be more specific, Cohen reports that by the 1930's there was a dramatic upsurge in Italian-American school attendance. She attributes this upswing to three factors: a decrease in the birthrate; government efforts to put a halt to child labor; and, the growing availability of more white collar jobs for high school graduates.[14]

Gans also points out how changes in the external environment can affect change within a particular group. In specifically discussing the Italian-American experience he writes:

> New occupational and educational attainments are likely to have repercussions on the structure of the family. For one thing, they will create more social and cultural differences between people. This, in turn, will affect the family circle, for relatives

who have responded to the widening opportunities may begin to find that they have less in common and are no longer compatible in their interests.[15]

Gans notes that this process does not occur instantaneously. It can take place gradually over time. It is not that Italian-Americans instantly developed a favorable attitude towards education. Instead, education began to be viewed in a more pragmatic manner. It was seen that through education one could obtain better employment. There was a realization that education could be a means for achieving social mobility.

This brief analysis of changing attitudes should not be interpreted as meaning that all Italian-Americans followed this pattern of change. As with all subgroups in society, there is great internal diversity and variation. Many members of the group still maintained the traditional viewpoint. However, these changes did begin to affect growing numbers of Italian-Americans.

IV

In a recent article Robert Marc has written: "The American population has undergone an educational revolution during the middle part of the twentieth century."[16] In 1940 the median years of schooling for the population was 8.6 years. By 1978 this had increased to a median of 12.4 years.

Italian-Americans were part of this "educational revolution." Greeley believes that if one examines educational mobility Italian-Americans along with Polish and Irish Catholics are among the most mobile groups.[17] Greeley utilized a nationwide representative sample for his analysis. His data (see Table 1) indicate a clear pattern of educational advancement, and in the early 1970's educational achievement was higher for Italian-Americans than for the total sample studied.

Richard Alba has recently analyzed N.O.R.C. data for the years 1973 through 1978. In discussing the Italian-American subsample he notes that:

> They frequently have been portrayed as bearers of cultural values that inhibit educational achievement.... amoral familism, fatalism, and a constricting loyalty to the family above all else...[18]

Alba, however, goes on to argue against this point of view. His data indicate a clear and dramatic upswing in educational achievement. Specifically, prior to World War II 6 percent of all Italian-Americans attended college. In the post World War II period 49 percent have attended college. When compared to other white ethnic Catholics, Italians are second in educational achievement only to Irish-Americans.

In another recent study reported by Stryker there is some evidence that being Italian-American may have a positive effect on education. Stryker reports that "...Italian parents appear to value educational achievement, since Italian Catholic identity has a positive impact on perceived parental encouragement to attend college."[19] While there are some methodological problems and inconsistencies with the research, it is still interesting to note the general trend reported by Stryker.

As a further indication of change in educational attainment, Table 2 presents data taken from a 1972 Current Population Reports. The data indicate substantial increases in the number of Italian-Americans who are graduating from high school, attending college and graduating from college.[20]

V

The Bureau of Census recently released a special supplement to its monthly Current Population Reports, *Ancestry and Language in the United States: November 1979*. This is the first such report on ethnicity since the bureau's 1973 report.

The ancestry question was open-ended: "What is _____'s ancestry?" Thus ethnic origin is based upon self-identification. As the report states: "Responses to the ancestry question reflect ethnic group(s) with which persons identified but did not necessarily indicate the degree of attachment or association the person had with the particular ethnic group(s)."[21]

One of the unique aspects of this report is that multiple ancestry is also included in the data ("English and other group(s); Italian and other group(s)").

The largest ethnic group in the United States is German (see Table 3). Over fifty million Americans are of German origin. Italian Americans are the eighth largest ethnic group (11,751,000). Fifty-two percent of this group are of single ancestry; forty-eight percent are descended from Italian and other group(s).

The purpose of this paper is to examine changes in level of educational attainment. This cannot be directly derived from the data presented in the report. However, inferences about intergenerational change in education may be made by utilizing the single and multiple ancestry variable.

Nativity is a variable included for analysis in the report. There are three categories of nativity: foreign-born (first generation), native of foreign or mixed parentage (second generation), and native of native parentage (third generation or later). Table 4 presents data which show how single and multiple ancestry groups are divided along generational lines. 13.1 percent of single ancestry group are foreign-born and 44.1 percent are second generation. The remaining 42.7 percent are third generation. Almost

90 percent of the multiple ancestry group are third generation, with less than 1 percent first generation, and 10 percent second generation. In addition, the median age for single ancestry group is 42.3 years. The median age for multiple ancestry is 17.7 years. To some extent then by comparing educational data for single and multiple ancestry groups may touch upon the generational factor.

Given this very real limitation, we will now undertake an analysis of generational change in educational attainment. Table 5 compares educational attainment for the total population and for Italian-Americans.

Several observations may be made from the data presented in this table. While educational gains for males as measured by "percent high school graduates," have been made for the entire population — 9.6 percent increase between single ancestry and multiple ancestry groups — the increase for Italian-American is somewhat astounding — 23.4 percent. For females, the figures are no less dramatic — for the entire population an increase of 9.6 percent; for Italian-Americans 22.8 percent.

By examining this same variable (percent high school graduates) in another way, we can also begin to see very real changes occurring for Italian-Americans. In comparing all ethnic groups listed (see Figure 1) for single ancestry Italian males ranked second lowest, and females third lowest. However, the rank order is dramatically altered when one looks at multiple ancestry. Those males listed as descended from Italian and other group(s) are highest in educational achievement; females are second highest.

In order to verify this trend, the variable "percent college, one year or more" was also examined by rank ordering males and females by kind of ancestry (see Figure 2). For the single ancestry category, both Italian males and females were second lowest. For the multiple ancestry category, Italian males were third highest, and females fifth highest. While the female rank was not as high as the male's, the percentage increase is very substantial — 16.5 percent for single ancestry, and 34.3 percent for multiple ancestry.

VI

There are a number of limitations to this study. Four major limitations are listed below.

1. The most dramatic limitation of this study is the assumption made regarding generation and kind of ancestry. Using grouped data in this manner is very problematic. However, our intent here is to at least give hint to changes that are occurring in the area under study. The method used is totally inadequate but time does not allow the procuring of the actual computer tapes so that more precise analyses could be undertaken.

2. Non-sampling variability is another limitation. Current population surveys can attribute these type of errors to many sources including differences in interpretation of questions, coding errors, non-response, and undercoverage.

3. As with any sample survey, there is sampling variability. Standard errors are provided by the Bureau of the Census (see Appendix B of the report).

4. The data in this report is also based upon population controls utilized in the 1970 census. These controls have since been changed and anyone wishing to compare these data with that of the 1980 census should be aware of this fact.

VII

Educational systems are responsible for producing patriotic citizens. In any society, this is one of the major functions of education.

In American society this function took on even greater significance because of the large numbers of immigrants entering the society. Education was seen as being the institution responsible for Americanizing these immigrants and their children.

Whether members of an immigrant group take advantage of the society's educational system or not depends upon the group's internal structure and values. For the early Italian immigrants, evidence indicates that they did not take full advantage of the educational process. More recent evidence indicates that their descendents are taking full advantage of the educational process.

What effect will this dramatic change have on the Italian-American community? The answer is unclear. There is an assumption in the literature which may be stated as follows: the higher the level of educational attainment, the greater the degree of assimilation. Stated in another way, the greater the level of educational achievement, the more tenuous the connection with one's ethnic traditions.

Following from this one may suggest that Italian-American identity is on the wane, and may very well eventually disappear. However, it appears to be presumptuous to draw such a conclusion at this point in time.

A number of factors, other than education, may affect the continuity of ethnic identification. For example, family structure, geographical mobility patterns, religious beliefs, and economic status may all impact on ethnicity. It is even possible to hypothesize that higher educational attainment may strengthen ethnic ties. More careful analysis and further research is needed to gain a better understanding of the issues raised here.

This paper has examined the dramatic changes occurring in Italian-American educational achievement. What is now needed is research that further studies the impact these changes will have on the Italian-American community.

Table 1

Percent Attending College, Italian-Americans
And Total Population, by Cohort

	Time Period					
Group	World War I	1920's	Depression	World War II	Cold War	Vietnam
Italian-Americans	7	9	14	21	29	45
Total Population	17	18	23	29	32	43

Source: Greeley, *The American Catholic,* p. 44.

Table 2

Years of School Completed By Age (Italian-Americans):

March, 1972

Age Category	Total No. (000's)	Total %	Elementary			High School		College		Median
			0-4 yrs	5-7	8	1-3	4	1-3	4+	
25-34	3,353	100.0	0.9	2.4	3.3	13.0	51.1	12.8	16.5	12.6
35 and over	4,117	100.0	8.7	10.5	17.0	19.7	31.9	6.1	6.0	11.1

Source: "Characteristics of the Population by Ethnic Origin: March 1972 and 1971" *Current Population Reports* P-20, No. 249, April 1973.

Table 3

Reported Single and Multiple Ancestries, by Ancestry Group:

November, 1979

Ancestry Group	Total No. (in thousands)	Percentage of Persons by *kind of ancestry*	
		Single	Multiple
Total	179,078	53.9	46.1
German	51,649	33.2	66.8
Irish	43,752	22.3	77.7
English	40,004	28.7	71.3
Afro-American, African	16,193	53.9	46.1
Scottish	14,205	11.4	88.6
French	14,047	21.7	78.3
Spanish	12,493	78.1	21.9
Italian, Sicilian	11,751	52.0	48.0
Polish	8,421	41.5	58.5
Dutch	8,121	16.8	83.2

Adapted from Table 1, p. 7.

Table 4

Nativity of Italian-Americans by Kind of Ancestry:

November 1979

Nativity	Percent of Persons by *kind of ancestry*			
	Single		Multiple	
Total	100.0	(6,110)	100.0	(5,622)
Native of native parentage	42.7		89.5	
Foreign birth or parentage	57.3		10.5	
native of foreign or mixed parentage		44.1		9.9
Foreign born		13.1		0.6

Adapted from Table 3, pp. 10-11.

Table 5

Educational Attainment of Total Population and Italian-Americans By Kind of Ancestry, Sex:

November, 1979

| Sex | Percent of persons by kind of ancestry | | | |
| | Single | | Multiple | |
	Total Pop	Italian-American	Total Pop	Italian-American
Females, 25 years and over				
Total	110.0 (67,206)	100.0 (2,332)	100.0 (22,732)	100.0 (900)
Elementary: 0 to 8 years	16.9	23.0	9.2	5.4
High School: 1 to 3 years	14.5	16.6	12.6	10.8
4 years	41.0	43.8	43.8	49.4
College: 1 or more years	27.7	16.5	34.4	34.3
Percent high school graduates	68.6	60.4	78.2	83.8
Males, 25 years and over				
Total	100.0 (59,249)	100.0 (2,237)	100.0 (17,625)	100.0 (801)
Elementary: 0 to 8 years	17.9	20.6	10.5	5.1
High School: 1 to 3 years	13.4	16.8	11.1	9.5
4 years	32.8	34.1	33.4	35.2
College: 1 or more years	35.9	28.6	44.9	50.2
Percent high school graduates	68.9	62.7	78.3	85.5

Adapted from Table 3, pp. 10-11.

Figure 1

Rank Order of Ethnic Groups By
Educational Attainment (Percent High School Graduates)

Single Ancestry				Multiple Ancestry			
Males		Females		Males		Females	
Scottish	(81.2)	Scottish	(78.1)	Italian	(85.5)	Polish	(84.0)
English	(74.6)	English	(76.7)	Polish	(84.5)	Italian	(83.8)
German	(72.4)	German	(72.0)	Scottish	(81.5)	English	(81.8)
Irish	(68.8)	Irish	(70.0)	English	(80.9)	Scottish	(81.0)
French	(67.0)	French	(65.7)	German	(79.8)	German	(80.5)
Polish	(64.4)	Italian	(60.4)	French	(77.2)	French	(76.6)
Italian	(62.7)	Polish	(59.1)	Irish	(74.6)	Irish	(75.5)
Spanish	(42.5)	Spanish	(40.5)	Dutch	(68.5)	Dutch	(68.0)
				American Indian	(62.4)	American Indian	(61.3)

Adapted from Table 3, pp. 10-11.

Figure 2

Rank Order of Ethnic Groups By
Educational Attainment (Percent College, One Year or More)

Single Ancestry				Multiple Ancestry			
Males		Females		Males		Females	
Scottish	(50.0)	Scottish	(39.7)	Polish	(52.2)	English	(40.0)
English	(41.8)	English	(34.1)	Scottish	(50.9)	Polish	(39.9)
Irish	(35.3)	Irish	(26.1)	Italian	(50.2)	Scottish	(39.2)
German	(34.6)	German	(25.6)	English	(48.6)	French	(34.7)
French	(30.7)	French	(22.7)	German	(44.8)	Italian	(34.3)
Polish	(29.8)	Polish	(21.4)	French	(42.9)	German	(33.9)
Italian	(28.6)	Italian	(16.5)	Irish	(40.6)	Irish	(30.6)
Spanish	(20.3)	Spanish	(13.3)	Dutch	(31.5)	Dutch	(25.8)
				American Indian	(24.5)	American Indian	(17.9)

Adapted from Table 3, pp. 10-11.

Notes

1. Sections II, III, and IV are adapted from my paper "Family Values and Educational Attainment: Intergenerational Change Among Italian-Americans," *Eastern Sociological Society* (Philadelphia: March, 1982).
2. For an overview of Italian immigration see Alexander DeConde, "The Contadini Go To America," in *Viewpoints: The Majority Minority,* ed., Drew Stroud. (Minneapolis: Winston Press, 1973), pp. 63-72; Patrick J. Gallo, *Old Bread, New Wine.* (Chicago: Nelson-Hill, 1981); Richard Gambino, *Blood of My Blood.* (New York: Doubleday, 1974); Lawrence Pisani, *The Italians in America.* (New York Exposition Press, 1957); Andrew Rolle, *The American Italians: Their History and Culture.* (Belmont, California: Wadsworth, 1972); S.M. Tomasi, and M.H. Engle, *The Italian Experience in the United States.* (New York: Center for Migration Studies, 1970).
3. "Race, Ethnicity, and the Achievement Syndrome," *American Sociological Review,* 24 (1959), 47-60. For a similar discussion see Fred Strodtbeck, "Family Interaction, Values and Achievement," in *The Jews: Social Patterns of An American Group,* ed. Marshall Share. (New York: Free Press, 1958), pp. 147-165.
4. *The Italian Americans: Troubled Roots.* (New York: Free Press, 1980), p. 137.
5. Maxine Seller, *To Seek America: A History of Ethnic Life in the United States.* (Englewood, New Jersey: Jerome S. Ozer, 1977), p. 141.
6. *The Social Background of the Italian-American School Child.* (Totowa, New Jersey: Rowman and Littlefield, 1972), pp. 403-404.
7. "Twenty Million Italian-Americans," *New York Times Magazine.* April 30, 1972.
8. *Italian or American? The Second Generation in Conflict.* (New York: Russell and Russell, 1943), p. 58.
9. *American Minority Relations.* (New York: Ronald Press, 1966), p. 401.
10. *Italian Americans* (New York: Random House, 1970), pp. 153-161. For further discussion of these issues see Humbert S. Nelli, *Italians in Chicago: 1880-1930: A Study in Ethnic Mobility.* (New York: Oxford University Press, 1970), pp. 67-68.
11. Lopreato, p. 155.
12. *Strangers to These Shores: Race and Ethnic Relations in the United States.* (Boston: Houghton Mifflin, 1980), p. 203.
13. "The Italian Americans," *The Center Magazine.* July 1974, pp. 31-43.
14. Miriam Cohen, *From Workshops to Office: Italian Women and Family Strategies in New York City, 1900-1950.* Doctoral Dissertation, (University of Michigan, 1978).
15. *The Urban Villagers.* (New York: Free Press, 1962), p. 169.
16. "Trends in Schooling: Demography, Performance and Organization," *Annals.* 453 (1981), pp. 98-99.
17. *The American Catholic: A School Portrait.* (New York: Basic Books, 1977), pp. 58-60.

18. "The Twilight of Ethnicity Among American Catholics of European Ancestry," *Annals.* 454 (1981), p. 94.

19. "Religio-Ethnic Efforts on Attainments in the Early Career," *American Sociological Review.* 46 (1981), p. 94.

20. Bureau of the Census, "Characteristics of The Population By Ethnic Origin: March 1972 and 1971," *Current Population Reports.* P-20, No. 249. (April, 1973).

21. Bureau of the Census, "Ancestry and Language in the United States: November 1979," *Current Population Reports,* P-23, No. 116 (1982).

Chapter **18** EDUCATIONAL ATTAINMENT
AND EDUCATIONAL VALUES
OF ITALIAN AMERICANS
OVER GENERATIONS
Jerome Krase
Brooklyn College, CUNY

There are as many myths as there are realities regarding education and Italian-Americans. Often myth and realities are mixed in such a way as to make differentiation difficult, if not impossible. It seems that the major reason for the present day confusion between fact and fiction is the paucity of research on the social status of Italians in American society. It is difficult enough for social scientists, educators and Italian-American community leaders to get a handle on the complex problem of educational mobility among the ten million or so persons of Italian descent in the United States without it being made more bewildering by the absence of a substantial body of easily accessible and relevant data. This situation is further aggravated by the lack of support for those willing and able to do what is necessary to fill the information void. At present the expert and non-expert alike are forced to rely on pat generalizations, historical stereotypes, personal observation and intuition. Such comment and "insight," when put into practice, is frequently patronizing or otherwise destructive. One of these stereotypical burdens, and the substantive focus of this paper, is the view that Italian-Americans do not take advantage of opportunities for higher education and that somehow, Italian cultural values (high or low culture) are responsible for this situation. Egelman (1982), Greeley (1977), Alba (1981), and others have argued that the first of these preceding statements does not stand up to scrutiny. It then must follow that the second statement demands some close attention as well. As noted by Egelman (1982), analysis of data from the last few U.S. Census reports have shown that persons of Italian descent have scored at or above the national average for educational achievement. Perhaps Italian values are responsible for this fact.[1] In any case the theoretical focus of this paper is the relationship between cultural values, educational achievement and aspiration. This essay will not solve all the problems or correct all the misperceptions concerning Italians and education in American society, but I am certain that it will contribute some important points in the required reappraisal.

There are two main operating generalizations about Italian-Americans and education — especially higher education — both of which are contrary to the limited evidence available. The first of these is the perception, almost accepted as a truism, that they are disinclined toward educational and professional career mobility. "Italian-Americans do not have the high aspirations of other Americans.," is the common phrase. The second generalization, related to the first, is that there has been little change in regard to actual achievement and aspirations since the onset of mass immigration. Much of this is due to the stereotype of Italians and Italian-Americans as only lower class, working class, or peasant, rural, backward collectivities who are still adapting to the modern world. Put very simply; when people look to study the Italian-American community, they tend to identify those who have achieved the least and who are least like "normal" Americans. Needless to say, this last, generally positive stereotype of high achieving "normal Americans" is equally uninforming. Certainly a significant segment of the Italian-American population might be educationally deficient but it is far from the majority and therefore much more steretypical than typical. Egelman (1982), Gans (1962) and Dyer (1979) have commented on the variations and changes in educational achievement among Italian-Americans. William F. Whyte (1943) in his classic study of Italian-Americans in "Cornerville" pointed out that even in the worst time of the Great Depression a significant proportion of the Italian-American population aspired toward higher education and high status career mobility. Unfortunately, readers are more likely to remember the less mobile and motivated "Corner Boys", and the racketeers than the "College Boys" whom Whyte described. Another related problem is the view of the "Old World," that is; Italy and the Italian population have not changed much since the mass diaspora of the Late 19th and Early 20th Centuries. Italy in the minds of many people, including Italian-Americans of later generations, is still educationally and technologically backward. The most common vision of Italy, aside from the tourist attractions, has been one of backwardness. Again, without a doubt there are parts of modern Italy in which education is still difficult to obtain, or where because of circumstance or cultural values, discouraged, but most of the modern Italian immigrants to the United States are far from the mostly illiterate itinerants of almost a century ago. Related to this last point, some social scientists are beginning to argue that perhaps even the mass of early Italian immigrants were not as educationally, economically and socially backward as is currently believed. In sum, a great deal of research remains to be done on early as well as contemporary Italian-Americans.

Milton Gordon (1964) has provided a model to study the adjustment of immigrant groups to American society. The wide spread use of his model is based primarily on its simplicity and therefore its utility in studying different ethnic groups in our complex and diverse nation. He notes that the overall assimilation process by which new groups are absorbed, or fitted, into the dominant society can be neatly divided into two theoretically distinct but historically integrated phenomena. The first of these inter-related processes is "cultural assimilation," or the adaptation of the im-migrant culture to the dominant culture; sometimes called "acculturation." The second of these processes is "structural assimilation," or the more ob-jective movement of the new people into the socioeconomic structure of the dominant society. Culture includes the norms, values, language, styles or "ways of life" of society, while structure refers to the statuses, positions, strata, and institutions of society. Gordon argued that cultural assimilation is usually an easier and more rapid adjustment but that both processes oc-cur simultaneously so that a "lag" between the two is common; i.e., most ethnic groups are assimilated more speedily culturally than structurally. Different groups have different rates of adaptation or absorption which are influenced by such factors as the degree of difference between the dominant and minority societies and the relative receptivity of both to each other.

In this paper we are focusing on the adjustment of Italians to American society's cultural values regarding educational attainment and assimilation. Educational achievement, and related movement into profes-sional and white collar careers by Italian-Americans is seen as the result of the "Americanization" process by which Italian anti-educational values and attitudes are slowly transformed over the generations, until they are replaced with American pro-educational ones. This, in turn, results in the occupa-tional mobility of Italian-Americans. Italian values have been seen as im-pediments to higher educational achievement (Egelman, 1981).

As noted by virtually all observers of Italian and Italian-American life, the central cultural and structural entity is the family (Tomasi, 1972). Educational and general socioeconomic mobility in American society is most accurately described however as a more individualistic phenomenon. At least at the level of mythology and folklore, achievement in America is primarily the result of individual effort, whereas for Italians, success of in-dividuals must be tempered by concern and respect for the family and its demands. The classic example of Italian mobility is the young man or woman who forgoes educational or career opportunities in order to stay "closer to home." "Closer to home" has both a geographical and sociocultural meaning. Often opportunities for advancement exist at great distance from the locus of the family or its extension, the neighborhood. In some working-class Italian-American areas there appears to be some justification for this perception. Among Italian-Americans who have already passed into the white-collar world, the reluctance is more frequently overcome or somehow accommodated. More intensive research would be needed to substantially document both extremes. It should be noted before continuing that the immobility of Italians is, *prima facie,* false; at least as it relates to the historical record. The record shows that Italians have been one of the most voluntarily mobile groups as evidenced by their vast diasporic experience, seeking economic opportunities in places scattered across the world. However, even this extraordinary movement is tempered by concern for family and kin.

In general "closer to home" means family obligations. Another meaning of the term refers to specific values and relations within each family itself. For example Sennett and Cobb (1972) have noted in their studies of working class culture that some see the educational or socioeconomic advancement of offspring and siblings as rejections of the family itself. Direct and indirect pressure may be placed on the young not to succeed or to seek advancement, if it is interpreted as a rejection of the family. Achievement is channeled to "acceptable" areas. This might be subconscious rather than conscious activity of parents who might ridicule or otherwise demean the "airs" of their children. In any case, children sense even the unspoken fears of their parents that they might be lost to the outside world. These children in turn become chronic underachievers.

Since a common stereotype of Italian-Americans is as a working class group it deserves special attention here. It is this view of Italian-Americans that spurs the concern for creating new and more "American" role models for Italian-American youngsters. There are however several ways in which the role of the Italian family in educational attainment can be interpreted, if in fact it is an accurate impression. The most direct route is to take this impression for granted and to try to effect not only changes in the family, but in the educational system itself so that they are both less of an impediment to achievement. Very simply put; making it possible for opportunities for higher education to exist "closer to home," both geographically and culturally. In other words, making higher education less of a threat to the family by making the institution more a part of family and neighborhood life. That segment of the Italian-American population, then, with the greatest resistance can be accommodated and be able to take advantage of opportunity. It should be noted that Stryker (1981), Abramson (1973) and others have noted the positive effect of Catholic private school experiences on Italian-American achievement. In this context, parochial schools may be more in conformity with Italian cultural and family values.

It is my firm belief, supported by impressions, personal experiences, interviews with educators, parents and students, and finally real data such as that present here, that when "real" opportunity for higher education exists for Italian-Americans of all socioeconomic and cultural backgrounds it will be taken advantage of with great gusto and success. This is true regardless of their misunderstood values and attitudes. What is needed at this point is a reinterpretation of Italian and Italian-American values *vis a vis* education.

Let us, for now, accept the fact that some, perhaps many, people of Italian descent do not take advantage of opportunities for higher education.

Let us further accept the proposition that, above all, Italians are family-oriented and that they expect educational institutions to respect their traditions and concerns. Additionally, let us agree that some are not convinced of the value of educational achievement. What then could be done to take these factors into account and create a situation wherein even the "hard core" will allow themselves and their children to pursue socioeconomic advancement via college education? When these questions are addressed, the reinterpretation of values becomes clearer.

Higher education must be made a part of Italian-American life. It must be made to complement rather than conflict with traditional values. If higher education is a family value, then Italian-Americans would become leaders in achievement. The reality is that for already successful Italian-Americans, higher education has become a family value. For them education and achievement is "closer to home." This is true despite the common experiences of many Italian-American achievers of being unwelcome at many institutions of higher learning because of anti-Italian, anti-working class, and/or anti-Catholic biases, which are often acceptable in American intellectual and academic circles (Greeley, 1969). Italians for the most part have employed the strategy of low visibility on college campuses to avoid conflict. At public colleges, such as the one which is the locus of this research, Italian-American students are unlikely to participate as Italian-Americans in campus affairs. Militant ethnicity or ethno-nationalism is not part of the Italian-American scene. Except for the more recent immigrants from Italy, Italian-American students are not likely to perceive the vast contributions of Italy to the university curriculum as a part of "their own" heritage. Working class Italian-Americans tend to see their own cultural heritage in a college environment as "alien." Conversely, professors find it difficult to connect Italian-American students to the Italians who produced much of what they teach and study. This combination of misconception and misperception is part of the reason for the discomfort that the young feel when they are first in their family to enter college. In order to feel "at home" in the college environement it is necessary for students to find things which are familiar and which they can bring back and make part of their family and neighborhood life.

We shall now turn to consider some recent empirical evidence which can be used to support some of these preliminary arguments and which will bring some important points into clear focus about Italian-Americans. First of all, as to overall Italian achievement in America Greeley (1977) and Egelman (1982) clearly showed that they have achieved at or above national averages for educational achievement, occupational status and income. Despite these facts, based on Census and national survey data, the view of Italian-Americans as underachievers still persists. When the facts are truly appreciated undoubtedly the explanation will be that they have therefore become "Americanized," as the theory of assimilation predicts. Few will question the common perception of Italian values as perhaps being erroneous in the first instance.

Although the data to be presented here are far from sufficient to adequately test the general theory of assimilation, it does provide some sociological food for thought regarding some of its assumptions about American life in general, and urban working-class Italian-Americans specifically. In other words the theory is adequate although the facts were not. The data, and other observations made by the author suggests that for Italian-Americans career and educational mobility has occurred without the hypothesized cultural change. This finding places emphasis on the structure of opportunity as being more crucial to socioeconomic mobility, independent of attitudinal and value change. More directly—Italian-Americans do not have to be less Italian in order to achieve.

The 1970's provided a great, perhaps even noble, experiment in higher education policy in New York City—"Open Enrollment," at the City University of New York. During "Open Enrollment" every high school graduate was guaranteed access to higher education. An added incentive was that for some years tuition was also free. In anticipation of the experiment's onset, educational policy "experts" predicted the major beneficiaries of the program would be Blacks and other "deprived" minorities. In fact, Open Enrollment was designed as a mechanism to compensate minorities for past discrimination. Contrary to expectations, the ethnic group which perhaps took greatest advantage of the opportunity was Italian-Americans. The Open Enrollment—Free Tuition policy removed the most basic obstacles to higher education by even the most reluctant of Italian-Americans. When resistance to higher education is translated into dollars, the free tuition made the point moot. Geographically, City University colleges were within easy commuting distance to most Italian-American neighborhoods and further, they offered many programs at the two and four-year levels which were clearly translatable into practical advantage: preparation for jobs. As noted in an earlier paper by this author Italian-American women, in large numbers, took advantage of the opportunity, upsetting convenient stereotypes. For example, at Brooklyn College, almost half of the Italian-American students who came were female. How much did Italian-Americans change in a few months so that all of a sudden they were interested in higher education and social mobility? My own sense is that they did not change and that their behavior was consistent with their values. The data and discussion which follows, I believe, will show this, as well as bring to the fore some even more interesting aspects of educational values and experiences. The discussion should stimulate further research on Italian-Americans as well as other ethnic groups, who are often understood less than we think. We shall pay special attention to the differences and similarities between generations of Italian-American students, as indicated by their parental backgrounds, and their own experiences and attitudes regarding higher education and social mobility.

The primary data for this discussion were collected during 1975 at Brooklyn College and analyzed at subsequent times. A preliminary report was published in 1976 (Krase and Fuccillo) and another paper focusing on the differences between male and female students at Brooklyn College by this writer was published in 1978. In 1982, a grant from the Italian-American Institute to Foster Higher Education made it possible to further analyze the data for this paper.

Based on a random sample of 290 cases, in 1975, we obtained this general profile of the Italian-American students who took advantage of the open enrollment opportunity. None of the findings were inconsistent with common assumptions about urban Italian-Americans. The "surprising" fact was that they were attending college. About 63% of the students' fathers held blue-collar jobs and 46% of their mothers were also employed outside the household. Despite the fact of free tuition and parental employment, at least half of the students worked an average of 15 hours per week, continuing the tradition of Italian youth employment and self-sufficiency. About 40% came from families of five or more persons and the vast majority had parents who never attended college themselves (only 8% of the fathers and 3.8% of the mothers had earned a college degree). These students were often the first in their families to pursue higher education. Almost a third of the students had at least one parent born in Italy. As expected, the study showed that the students were job-oriented and viewed their education from a career-based perspective. Also not surprising; the students spent little of their spare time at the college in extra-curricular activities. The students were evenly divided between those graduating from public and parochial high schools.

More to the point of attitudes and values, the study showed that the Italian-American students, although doing well at school, felt alienated and did not take advantage of on-campus opportunities because of the perceived "coldness" and lack of personal touches. In other words the college did not operate in the Italian-American fashion of intimacy. The lack of other persons "like them" in the administration and on the faculty also left them feeling at times, isolated, and they either clustered in small groups or returned home to their easily identifiable Italian-American neighborhoods for primary relationships.

With this general picture of the Italian-American student in mind we shall turn now to the specific issues of differences and similarities between generations and how they relate to attitudes toward educational and career mobility. We will also use this data to discuss whether Italian values change and therefore make higher education possible or whether the change in the opportunity itself makes the difference. The assimilation model predicts that the longer any group is in America the more they will express "American" values. Therefore we should expect great differences between cases in which grandparents were born in America versus those cases in which parents have recently emigrated from Italy. The data are presented below patri- and matrilineally, which may also sugest the relative impact of fathers' or mothers' nativity in value changes. Although the data collected and analyzed includes all grandparents, reported in these tables are only father's father and mother's mother.

Because of the limitations of the sample, statistical analysis with any great degree of confidence is not possible and therefore not attempted here. The data presented here is exploratory and suggestive in nature. For example, when we speak of differences between generations of students it should be noted that 63.4% of the students' fathers, 8.2% of their father's fathers, 72.2% of students' mothers and 19.0% of their mother's mothers were born in the United States. The total sample size in this analysis is only 273 and therefore making absolute statements about differences between generations would be too ambitious. The number of fathers and mothers born in Italy is 73 and 46 respectively. The number of father's fathers and mother's mothers born in the United States is 24 and 52 respectively. It should be noted that the figures for grandparents born in Italy include students whose parents were born in Italy as well:

Table 1

Nativity of Students'
Parents and Grandparents

	Nativity			
	United States	Italy	Other	Don't Know
	n	n	n	n
Fathers	171	73	19	10
Mothers	198	46	27	2
Fathers Fathers	24	230	18	1
Fathers Mothers	40	210	22	1
Mothers Fathers	38	188	45	2
Mothers Mothers	52	171	48	2

N = 273

Our findings give us an indication of the relative degree of educational and occupational attainment of the families from which our Italian-American student sample came. The data show that the more "Americanized" parents have to a much greater degree attained at least minimal levels of education, as compared to the less Americanized. The mothers and fathers, whose own mothers and fathers, were born in the United States are much more likely, for example, to have completed at least 8 years of education (primary school). Of those born in Italy, 35% of fathers and 43% of mothers had only 8 years or less education, versus 9% and 2% respectively for those whose own parents were born in America. Similarly, the more Americanized were more likely to have graduated from high school. This advantage does not, however, hold true at the level of college education where the two groups are virtually equal in educational attainment.

Interestingly, the advantage that the more Americanized parents have in educational attainment seems not to have been translated into the same degree of occupational achievement. If we group occupational levels and look at the highest and lowest prestige strata we find that the fathers born in Italy are more likely to have high status jobs (Professional, Technical and Administrative) than those fathers whose own fathers were born in the United States. The less Americanized are also more likely to hold low status positions as Operatives, Service workers and Laborers. If we look at fathers born in America, including those whose fathers were born in Italy, we are further confounded. This group has attained more than either the least or most Americanized groups in high status positions, but did worse in low status jobs. How can this be explained?

Although the data presented here is limited, some informed discussion is possible. It is suggested that these complex findings are related to the characteristics of different immigrant cohorts — a sizable proportion of more recent (post-1965) immigrants from Italy are employed in higher status occupations. This conforms to the findings on educational attainment where we saw that at the highest levels of education Italian-born fathers compared favorably with their more Americanized counterparts. This suggests that since the earliest periods of mass migration, 1890-1910, a large and significant proportion of the immigrant population had higher socioeconomic status. This might mean several things: One, higher status Italians have increased their interest in coming to America. Two, there is a higher proportion of higher status persons in the Italian population, reflecting increased opportunity over the decades in Italian society. Three, lower status Italians were less likely to choose America as a destination. Four, some combination of these developments. What is certain is that Italy is not the backward country it is assumed by many to be and that we should expect that some changes in the characteristics of immigrants would have taken place over the past nine or so decades. Unfortunately, most people continue to be under the assumption that Italy offered the United States only low-status migrants.

Noting the differences in the "structural" changes in the Italian and Italian-American population we should then expect that the generations are not so different from one another as previously posited. We should not expect such a great advantage to persons of Italian descent who emigrated to America during the earlier periods of mass movement. Descendants of early migrants might be more Americanized but this might not consistently and directly translate into advantages in educational and occupational achievement. If I might be allowed to specuate at this point, I would suggest the possibility that for early Italian lower-class immigrants the American experience was more socially and economically debilitating than for counterparts who stayed at home and benefited in a more culturally hospitable environment by the eventual modernization of Italy.

We have noted earlier the necessity of seeing Italian-Americans from the perspective of family versus individual attainment. Therefore we should look at higher education in a family context and compare more and less Americanized student family settings. The data collected on college education of family members, other than the student him or herself shows that if parents were born in Italy then it is more likely that other family members are either presently attending college or have college degrees. In other words those whose grandparents were born in the United States are less likely to have other family members presently in college or with degrees. Of further interest is the fact that it seems as though American born grandmothers are more associated with higher education than American born grandfathers. In general American nativity is of greater advantage to females than to males, although Italian-American females still do not achieve as well as Italian-American males. In other words; if you are female it is better to be American than Italian, but in all cases it is best to be male.

Let us turn now to a consideration of the self ethnic identification of the sample. Students were given the option of writing their ethnicity or nationality in the following form; "Italian", "Italian-American", "American-Italian" and "American". As might be expected, there were noticeable differences based on the students' generation. The differences in ethnic identification are not, however, absolute. For example, if one's father or mother was born in Italy one was more likely to respond "Italian" then if one's grandfather or grandmother was born in America. The proportions were 54% and 59% versus 38% and 30% respectively. The "American" designation is more interesting. 2% of students with Italian born fathers and no students with Italian born grandfathers identified themselves in this way, while none of the students with Italian born mothers and 10% of those with American born grandmothers gave "American" for their ethnic group. The intermediary designations — "Italian-American" and "American-Italian," conformed closely to expected generation. What is of greatest significance in these responses is the small proportion who answered "American" alone in any case, and the high proportion who answered "Italian." Despite this high rate of Italian identification, it should be noted that in an earlier report by this author (1975) only 19% of the sample reported more than "occasional" use of the Italian language at home. Language use is often given as an indication of cultural identity and commitment. This identification of "Italian" is then much likely to be a response to a question which offers little variation in response than a true indication of cultural similarity. It suggests that Americans are likely to identify themselves by national roots regardless of their awareness and facility with their original national culture. This is not, of course, peculiar to persons of Italian descent.

The students in the survey were also asked to offer what they thought would be the "Major Obstacles" to their attaining career or professional goals. Some interesting observations can be made regarding their responses. About 40% of all students reported "no major obstacles," but the most optimistic were those with American grandfathers and the least optimistic those with Italian-born mothers. The more Americanized were more likely to offer "Race" as an obstacle, while "Ethnicity" was seen as an equal problem by both groups. Interestingly, those with American born grandmothers and Italian born mothers were most likely to see "sex" as a problem. Overall, the less Americanized saw "Age" as a major obstacle to goals. In both groups "Religion" was mentioned the least.

The students' "Long Range Occupational Goals" are also reported. Because of the lack of variety in their responses to this question, it is not possible to make very fine distinctions. Most noteworthy is the fact that those with American born grandfathers and Italian born mothers were most likely to cite professional long range goals. Those with American grandfathers and grandmothers were also most likely to be "undecided." Since professional careers require graduate education the data on "Immediate Plans After Graduation," ought to indicate similar findings. The data show that students with American born grandparents more often plan to attend graduate school immediately after graduation, whereas the least Americanized are more likely to plan to go to work. This might mean, however, that the less Americanized are going into professions which do not require as much, or as immediate, graduate education. This may also indicate that the less Americanized are planning to work full time and go to graduate school on a part-time basis. The data on the type of graduate program students intend to pursue seems to confirm this expectation as there was little difference in intention to go for a graduate program between more and less Americanized respondents. Students with American born grandmothers and students with Italian-born mothers are the most likely to indicate "Medical" programs, while those with American grandfathers and grandmothers are much more likely to be interested in "Law" programs. Those with American born mothers and fathers are also most likely to indicate interest in Masters Degree programs.

We will now look at how the students responded to questions concerning college education in general and the amount of moral support they receive from their parents. If we look at profiles of attitudes toward college education and values associated with higher education, we find that the more and less Americanized students are very similar. Their responses in all cases are in the same general direction and differ only in degree of response. In general all students are practical and pragmatic and do not view the college as a social or cultural opportunity. The students are in other words; serious minded. It is interesting to note that in the early 1970's this was only beginning to be "typical" of American college youth, as reported by Yankelovich (1974). More recent surveys have been reported in the media that the practical, non-idealistic trend in college and youth values has continued. Does this mean that American youth values have changed, while Italian and Italian-American values have not? If I could be allowed to be facetious here, I would state that it appears that American youth have been Italianized over the past generation. Although the attitudes of the generations toward college education are remarkably similar, some observations can be made regarding even slight, but regular, differences between the most and least Americanized groups.

In reference to the objectives of all students in their college education the following are considered "very important" by the majority of all students and could be ranked, most to least important, in the following order: "Grades," "Intellectual Pursuits," "Course Work," "Job Training," and "Earning Money." Conversely the following were regarded as least important in the same order: "Solving Social Problems," "Social Activities," "Cultural Activities," and "Student Government." It should be noted here that 40% of the students thought solving social problems was very important while proportions range from 20% to less than 10% for the other activities. With few exceptions, the responses of the most and least Americanized are almost identical. The least Americanized seem more practical and those with Italian born mothers the most practical of all. It must be repeated, however, that the differences may not be statistically significant. This practical orientation is shown by the fact that almost three quarters of the students neither engage in college extra-curricular activities nor off-campus activities. The more Americanized participate on campus more often and the least Americanized participate more often off-campus.

When asked to agree or disagree with certain statements about the college, many more students "totally disagreed" than "totally agreed" with the statements; "I come to Brooklyn College in my spare time," and "If I could get a good job I wouldn't go to college." Students were slightly less emphatic about the latter statement than the former. Interestingly, those with more Americanized fathers and mothers are most likely to agree with the second statement.

The final data to be discussed herein are those reporting on the importance of college education to the students themselves and how important they perceived their education is to their parents. Students were asked to indicate their degree of agreement with statements: "My college education is important to me; my father; my mother." We have focused here only on those responses which indicate "total agreement" with the statements.

As we might expect their education is most important to student themselves. It is virtually identical for mothers and fathers; although the perceptions of mother's support is greater than for fathers'. Those with Italian born parents or American born grandparents seem to receive the greatest support, as represented by total agreement to the statements. In almost all cases, American-born grandfathers and Italian-born mothers seem to give the students the greatest sense of support.

Although the data presented here has severe limitations from a statistical point of view, in combination with other data and studies I believe many important points concerning Italian-Americans and achievements can be made. It is also possible to question some important aspects of general theory about structural and cultural assimilation, and Americanization in general. As noted earlier, much of the problem is due to a lack of understanding of what has occurred in Italy since mass migration to America. From the author's point of view, the greatest problem is that our expert notions of Italians and Italian-Americans seem to be stuck in a turn of the century scenario.

Bibliography

Abrahmson, Harold J.
   1973   Ethnic Diversity in Catholic America. New York: John Wiley and Sons.
Alba, Richard
   1981   "The Twilight of Ethnicity Among American Catholics of European Ancestry," Annals 454 (March): 86-97.
Child, Irwin L.
   1943   Italian or American? The Second Generation in Conflict. New York: Russell and Russell.
Covello, Leonard
   1972   The Social Background of the Italo-American School Child. Totowa, New Jersey: Rowan and Littlefield.
Dyer, Everett D.
   1979   The American Family: Variety and change. New York: McGraw-Hill.
Egelman, William
   1982   "Italian-American Educational Attainment: An Introductory Analysis Utilizing Recent Current Population Survey Data."

American Italian Historical Association Annual Meeting, October 30. Jamaica, New York: St. John's University.

Egelman, William and Constance DeVito Egelman
1981   "Ethnicity and Education: A Review of the Italian-American Experience." Preventing Psychosocial Malfunctioning in Ethnic Families: An Interdisciplinary Symposium. Brooklyn, New York: Brooklyn College. April 11.

Gans, Herbert J.
1962   The Urban Villagers, New York: Free Press.

Gordon, Milton
1964   Assimilation in American Life. New York: Oxford University Press.

Greeley, Andrew M.
1977   The American Catholic: A School Portrait. New York: Basic Books.

Krase, Jerome and Vincent Fuccillo
1975   Italian-Americans and College: A Survey of Student Experiences At Brooklyn College. Brooklyn, New York: Center of Italian-American Studies.

Krase, Jerome
1978   "Italian-American Female College Students: A new Generation Connected to the Old." in Betty Boyd Caroli, Thomas F. Harney and Lydio Tomasi (eds.) The Italian Immigrant Woman in North America. Toronto, Canada: Multicultural Historical Society of Ontario: 246-51.

Krase, Jerome
1982   "The Mediterranean-American Neighborhood." Proceedings of the Mediterranean Sociopsychiatric Association, Second Mediterranean Congress of Social Psychiatry. Udine, Italy.

Sennett, Richard and Jonathan Cobb
1972   The Hidden Injuries of Class. New York: Alfred A. Knopf.

Stryker, Robin
1981   "Religio-Ethnic Effects on Attainments in the Early Career," American Sociological Review 46 (April):212-31.

Tomasi, Lydio
1972   The Italian-American Family. Staten Island, New York: Center for Migration Studies.

Whyte, William F.
1943   Street Corner Society. Chicago: University of Chicago Press.
Yankelovich, Daniel
1974   Changing Youth Values in the 70's. New York: McGraw-Hill.

Chapter **19** ITALIAN-AMERICANS AND
PUBLIC HIGHER EDUCATION:
THE COUNSELING PROGRAM AT
THE CITY UNIVERSITY
OF NEW YORK
Joseph V. Scelsa
Italian-American Institute of C.U.N.Y.

The Program

On March 19, 1980 The City University of New York officially announced the formation of a Specialized Counseling Program for Italian-
American students at C.U.N.Y.

This announcement was directly preceded by the Chancellor of The City
University of New York's (C.U.N.Y.) decision to request on October 10,
1979 from the Chief Budget Examiner of the New York State Division of
the Budget permission to allocate the sum of $150,000 appropriated for 18
counselor positions under the Italian Studies Institute in the 1979-80 senior
college adopted budget. In his letter the Chancellor outlined the general role
of these counselors as well as the rationale for their existence.

> The role of these counselors would be to recruit students for the
> University and to advise students after they are enrolled on
> financial aid and various aspects of college life. Special atten-
> tion is required in these activities to the unique needs of minority
> and ethnic groups.[1]

The Chancellor went on in his letter to outline how he intended to
deploy these counselors:

> It is our intention to assign up to half the counselors to the
> Italian Studies Institute. These individuals would not duplicate
> the work of the Institute but complement its ongoing activities.
> After a review of college needs, programs and enrollment, the
> positions would be assigned on a project basis to those cam-
> puses where the need is greatest. The remaining positions would
> be permanently assigned to the individual senior colleges.[2]

226

On October 31, 1979 the State of New York Division of the Budget in a letter to the Chancellor approved, with specific provisions, the allocation of the $150,000 reapportioned in Chapter 53 of the Law of 1979 for the support of counseling positions at The City University of New York.[3]

Although the Chancellor had requested 18 counselor positions, half of which were to be assigned to the Italian Studies Institute, the division of the Budget ruled that only ". . . nine counselor positions may be allocated to individual senior college campuses the full annual salaries of which must not exceed the amount reappropriated for 1979-80."[4] The rationale given for only allowing C.U.N.Y. to appoint nine counselors instead of the 18 which had been requested was that "Since this appropriation was made specifically to the public agencies — the City of New York on behalf of the senior college division of the City University of New York — not to the private, non-profit Italian Institute supported through a contract with the State Education Department . . . , it would not be appropriate to direct a portion of the $150,000 appropriated to support a function located at, or assigned to, the Italian Institute already funded at the $500,000 level."[5]

Concomitantly, during the month of October 1979 a special recruitment was conducted under the auspices of the Chancellor's office by the Italian-American Institute to Foster Higher Education, Inc. Counselors were recruited from the community at large as well as the Counselor Education Programs in and around New York City and Professional Counseling Associations in New York State. The general criteria for these positions were a minimum of a Masters Degree in counseling and a demonstrated interest, ability and knowledge, as well as an effective sensitivity to the target population.

By November 1, 1979 the names of 18 candidates who had been recruited by the Italian-American Institute were submitted to the Chancellor's office for review by his personnel and budget committee. During the month of November 1979 those candidates were reviewed and on December 5, 1979 the Chancellor made his initial selection.

Due to candidates' availability as well as administrative checkpoints, the nine counselors were not appointed until January 28, 1980. The following is the job description which they were given along with their letters of appointment:

> Under both the general administrative oversight of the Office of Student Affairs and the direct supervision of a designated college official, the Assistant for Specialized Counseling will provide a coordinated, multi-dimensional service that will incorporate both outreach and on-campus aspects and relate to the following areas: career exploration, academic advisement, financial aid, recruitment, and general counseling. Through direct liaison with the Italian-American Institute, the activities of the Assistant will

focus primarily on the needs of the Italian-American student population but will also be open to the community and campuses at large. Responsibilities will include maintenance of records and logs submission of weekly activity plans, participation in ongoing orientation sessions, and workshops with the Institute, and other tasks as appropriately assigned.[6]

Despite the diversity reflected in the specific functions of these counselors on their respective campuses, the services provided can be broken down into four general categories. These categories are (1) the administration of career inventories (tests); (2) outreach efforts; (3) individual counseling sessions; and (4) group counseling sessions.

The career inventories administered were of the paper and pencil type for the purpose of career awareness through a program of guided self-exploration. Some of the instruments were The Strong-Campbell Interest Inventory, The Hall Occupational Orientation Inventory, The Self-Directed Search and Kuder D. D. During the first year of operation of the program a total of 654 of these inventories were administered.[7]

The outreach visits made by the counselors were for the purpose of C.U.N.Y. recruitment. They included contacts with agencies and institutions such as local public and private high schools and community colleges, fraternal organizations, unions, parents associations, senior centers and youth organizations. During its first year of operation, 130 such outreach visits were made with a potential 1,248 students contacted.[8]

The individual counseling sessions were of the kind traditionally associated with campus counseling centers. These sessions were conducted on a one-to-one basis on matters related to career exploration, academic advisement, financial aid, and general counseling.

The group counseling sessions involved a variety of group settings (counseling formats, meetings and workshops) in which students were provided information related to college orientation, employment opportunities, student life, consciousness raising, study skills, changing sex roles, standardized tests, financial aid, and career-life planning. During the first year of operation the combined number of individual and group counseling sessions conducted was 2,582 which serviced approximately 5,825 clients.[9]

The next section will deal with the political events prior to 1980 which impacted on The City University of New York and ultimately led to a policy decision to establish a specialized counseling program for Italian-Americans at C.U.N.Y.

A Decade of Political Activity

Covello in his book "The Social Background of the Italo-American School Child" describes the southern Italian society of the last decade of the

19th century and the first decade of the 20th century as the remnant of a feudal system with basically a two-class structure: the landed class, the "latifondo," and the propertyless peasants who worked for them known as the "contadino."[10] He goes on to describe this social structure as one with rigid class boundaries. A result of this structure was the contadino's concern with maintenance of a state of equality with other peasant families rather than upward mobility which for them was impossible. It was the contadino social class which immigrated to the United States in the last decade of the 19th century and the first decade of the 20th century bringing with them their values and attitudes. The descendants of these illiterate peasants, their children, and grandchildren, were to become the faculty and student bodies of The City University of New York which will be discussed here.

Strictly speaking in social anthropological terms, these descendants are not considered to be a group, that is ". . . a corporate body with a permanent existence; a collection of people recruited on recognized principles, with common interests and rules (norms) fixing the rights and duties of the membership in relation to one another and to these interests."[11] However, to the extent to which these descendants are distinguished from the native-born population and are conscious of their differences they can be considered an ethnic group. Therefore, Italian-Americans as a group are herein defined as an ethnic group by virtue of the fact that they have distinguished themselves from others and the native-born population.

During the decade of the 60s, The City University of New York was in a period of unprecedented expansion; new colleges and campuses sprung up all over New York City bringing the University system to a total of 18 campuses by the beginning of the 70s: Baruch College, Borough of Manhattan Community College, Bronx Community College, Brooklyn College, The City College, Hostos Community College, Hunter College, John Jay College of Criminal Justice, Kingsborough Community College, LaGuardia Community College, Lehman College, Medgar Evers College, New York City Technical College — Brooklyn Campus, New York City Technical Colege, Queens College, Queensborough Community College, The College of Staten Island, and York College. These, as well as older institutions, had never been experiencing increased enrollments due to the post-war baby boom, and they needed additional faculty to teach the ever-increasing student bodies. As is the custom in academia, these new faculty members started at the bottom of the academic ladder filling the ranks of Instructor and Assistant Professor. In time, they hoped to advance to the rank of Associate and Full Professor during the course of their tenure. Within the ranks of these increasingly new faculties, members of minority and ethnic groups started to become visible at C.U.N.Y. One of the ethnic groups to have its members included was the Italian-American. These were the first generation of the contadini to receive a higher education and to pursue academic careers.

At first these Italian-American faculty members met socially to discuss matters of mutual interest, but when a number of them started to be denied tenure (C.U.N.Y. has a five-year policy on tenure — either you get it at the end of your fifth year or you leave) or promotions, they decided to form the Italian-American C.U.N.Y. Faculty Association for mutual support and assistance. They soon turned their attention toward matters of affirmative action and later discrimination.

The president of the newly formed faculty association focused his attention on affirmative action. He attended numerous meetings with the Chancellor during 1971-1973 while other faculty endeavored to enlist the support of outside agencies as well as State legislators. In December of 1971 the executive director of Americans of Italian Descent, Inc., an organization whose letterhead reads "United and Dedicated to Combat Defamation," charged C.U.N.Y. with de facto discrimination against Italians in higher education in an article published in *The Challenge*. In June 1973 correspondence with the New York State Division of Human Rights confirmed that C.U.N.Y. had been discriminatory in its hiring and promotion policies and practices in its dealings with Italian-Americans. Then in October of the same year members of the New York State Assembly invited interested persons to testify as to under representation at C.U.N.Y. of Italian-Americans.[12]

During this same time period Italian-American faculty began gathering information for a report on the extent of discrimination at C.U.N.Y. In late 1973 they presented their preliminary findings: ". . . despite the fact that Italian Americans constitute 25% of the population of New York City, and despite a progressively increasing number of Italian-Americans graduating with doctoral degrees, the representation of Italian-Americans at The City University of New York was at a low 5% level."[13] However, it was not until May 1976 that these findings were published.

Concomitantly, with the Italian-American faculty complaints of discrimination, Italian-American students at the various campuses of C.U.N.Y. were beginning to complain of improper counseling as well as inequitable distribution of student fees. They formed a C.U.N.Y.-wide student association and they, too, sought the support of State officials. As a result of the combined efforts of both the faculty and students, the Chancellor was prompted to address their concerns, which he did in a letter dated March 17, 1975. This letter was sent to all C.U.N.Y. college presidents and stated the following:

> Over the past ten years the City University has moved aggressively to offer the possibility of a higher education to populations previously excluded. Beginning with College Discovery, then SEEK and finally, through open admissions,

the opportunities of the University were expanded to even larger segments of the City's youth.

Among those which have entered the University in ever-growing numbers are Italian-Americans, young people from all sections of the City. I would like to call your attention to this expanding component of the University's enrollment and to urge you to consider ways in which their particular needs can be served better.

The young Italian-Americans come to us with a proud and rich cultural tradition in literature, music and the arts. They also carry with them customs and values that flow from their ancestral homeland, their religious heritage, and their American experience. It is important to them and their communities that the University represent a congenial, understanding and sympathetic environment. If this is to be so, it behooves, all of us — faculty, administration, and staff — to recognize, understand and respect traditions, customs and beliefs of this large and important component of our academic community.[14]

The Chancellor then outlined seven specific points for consideration:

Point I

The development of a series of programs that draw upon the cultural and the folk tradition of Italy and the Italian-American community.

Point 2

The encouragement of student and faculty organizations on the campus that are oriented toward the preservation and promotion of academic, cultural or spiritual values of importance to Italian-Americans.

Point 3

The development of academic programs and/or courses that appropriately reflect the contribution made by Italians to history, literature, science and the arts.

Point 4

The encouragement of outreach programs to serve the special needs and aspirations of those Italian-American communities within the natural orbit of the college.

Point 5

The development of orientation programs for counselors designed to sensitize them to the cultural, social and spiritual heritage of Italian-Americans. In establishing such a program every effort should be made to draw upon the resources of the community and its leadership.

Point 6

The creation of advisory committees to the President with which you can consult as to how the college and its various components can improve their services to Italian-American students and the communities from which they come.

Point 7

Periodic consultation with the Italian-American faculty and student organizations on the campuses so that you can be alert to incipient problems and through which you may ascertain ways in which the college can more effectively fulfill its obligations to its students and faculty.[15]

This letter laid the groundwork for two important elements of the Specialized Counseling Program for Italian-Americans. Point 4 stated the need for specialized outreach — an area which was to become a major thrust of this counseling program. Point 5 provided the rationale for the specialized orientation which the counselors were to receive at the Italian-American Institute some five years later. In justification and explanation for the above-stated remedies, the Chancellor stated, "We are concerned here with the City's largest minority and one which, like other minorities, has over time suffered the degrading effects of bigotry, misunderstanding and neglect."[16] However, this letter did not address the faculties' primary concern: inclusion as an affirmative action category.

In May 1976 the second faculty report on the status of Italian-Americans at the City University was published. In this document entitled *Italian-Americans: The Neglected Minority in City University,* jointly sponsored by the Italian-American Center for Urban Affairs and The Association of Italian-American Faculty of C.U.N.Y., they called for affirmative action to be extended to Italian-Americans. "We are asking the University Administration to redress the grievances of Italian-Americans, as well as those of other minorities, without pitting one group against the other."[17]

Prompted by this publication and the ever-increasing activities of the faculty, the Chancellor addressed this issue in a memorandum to the C.U.N.Y. Council of Presidents dated December 9, 1976.

It is my belief that the present situation requires the University to take positive action to assure that qualified persons of Italian-American ancestry are identified so that they can be considered fairly along with other candidates for positions that might become available at the University. I am equally concerned that the processes of the University are such that Italian-Americans receive fair consideration in the processes that lead to promotion and tenure within the University.

To this end I am designating Italian-Americans as an affirmative action category for this University in addition to those so categorized under existing Federal statutes and regulations. I also have instructed the Affirmative Action Office to include Italian-Americans in the data collected for affirmative action purposes.[18]

Now, having been designated an affirmative action category by the University one might think the fervor of the Italian-American community might subside — not so. Under the leadership of the Chairman of the Italian-American Legislative Caucus, New York State Senator John D. Calandra, a series of legislative hearings were conducted at the City University of New York during the months of December 1977 and January 1978. As a result of these hearings a new report was published in January 1978 by the New York State Senate. This report entitled *A History of Italian-American Discrimination at C.U.N.Y.* analyzed the current state of affairs concerning Italian-Americans at the University. It also made specific recommendations that an institute be established at C.U.N.Y. for Italian-Americans which would provide the academic community with guidance and cultural and international services.[19]

Following this report two items were added to the 1979-1980 State budget: one would create an Italian-American Institute to be housed at C.U.N.Y. and the other would provide funding for 18 University counselor positions — these new counselors to provide services to the Italian-American community, be funded through the C.U.N.Y. central office, and be permanently assigned to campuses throughout the system. Thus, the Specialized Counseling Program for Italian-American students at C.U.N.Y. was created.

Discussion

What did the Chancellor of C.U.N.Y. accomplish politically by his policy decision to create a specialized counseling program for Italian-Americans at C.U.N.Y.? Essentially, he was able to appease all three concerned parties — the faculty, the students, and their supports in the New

York State Legislature — and he did this with the least amount of structural change to the system.

The faculty wanted affirmative action instituted for Italian-Americans. The students wanted counselors sensitive to their Italian-American experience. By his offer to hire 18 counselors who were experts in Italian-American attitudes and values (essentially counselors of Italian descent), the Chancellor overtly demonstrated that he was sensitive to both of their concerns and that he had a limited plan to address some of them. The students gained the most by the creation of this program. They wanted culturally skilled counselors, and they got them. The counselors hired were all professionally trained personnel, sensitive, willing, and eager to work with them. Unfortunately, the positions these counselors were hired to fill are part of an administrative series known as Higher Education Officers (H.E.O.) which are non-tenure bearing tracks. In addition, they were hired by the C.U.N.Y. central office and then placed on their respective campuses. This effectively circumvented the traditional academic hiring process whereby faculty selects its own colleagues. Whether or not the Chancellor did this for expediency purposes is not as important as the internal and external political ramifications of this policy decision. Internally, in the eyes of C.U.N.Y. academia, these new counselors were second class members of their community since they did not have the same rights and privileges as regular faculty, and they had no part in their selection processes. Externally, the Chancellor succeeded in diverting the focus of the Italian-American communities' political activities away from the central office and on to the campuses. Thus, while the Chancellor's creation of these counselor positions overtly addressed the concerns of the Italian-American community, it also redirected and diffused their political momentum as well. It is important to note here that the inherent structural weaknesses of the program may lead to strife between the faculty and the Italian-American legislators who may be called upon to defend their constituents again in the future. However, this scenario is yet to unfold.

Notes

1. Letter of Chancellor Robert J. Kibbee to the Chief Budget Examiner of New York State, Mr. Paul Veilette dated October 10, 1979.
2. *Ibid.*
3. Letter from the Deputy Budget Director, Mr. Michael Finnertly, Executive Department, Division of the Budget to Chancellor Robert J. Kibbee dated October 31, 1979.
4. *Ibid.*
5. The Italian-American Institute to Foster Higher Education Inc. (I.A.I.) a not-for-profit private corporation received a grant of

$500,000 from the New York State Education Department for the contract year beginning August 1, 1979 and ending August 1, 1980. During this period the Institute was housed at Queens College, one of the 18 campuses of the City University of New York.

6. Candidates actual starting dates differed due to individual availability subject to prior work commitments (January 28, 1980 through March 15, 1980).

7. The C.U.N.Y. Assistance for Specialized Counseling Program. 1980 Annual Report, p. 12.

8. *Ibid.,* p. 14.

9. *Ibid.,* p. 15.

10. Leonard Covello and Francesco Cordasco, *The Social Background of the Italo-American School Child.* Leider: E.J. Brill, 1972.

11. Lucy Mair, *An Introduction to Social Anthropology,* New York: Oxford University Press. 1972. p. 15.

12. John D. Calandra, *A History of Italian-American Discrimination at C.U.N.Y.,* New York: The New York State Senate, 1978, pp. D-1, D-2, and D-3.

13. *Italian-Americans The Neglected Minority in City University,* New York: Italian-American Center for Urban Affairs, Inc. and Association of Italian-American Faculty of C.U.N.Y. 1976, p. i.

14. John D. Calandra, op. cit., pp. C 1-3. Letter from Chancellor Kibbee to all College Presidents in C.U.N.Y. March 17, 1975.

15. *Ibid.,* p. C-2.

16. *Ibid.,* p. C-3.

17. *Italian-Americans the Neglected Minority in City University, op. cit.* p. ii.

18. John D. Calandra, *op. cit.,* Appendix B. Affirmative Action Directive Memorandum from Chancellor Kibbee sent to C.U.N.Y. Council of Presidents, December 9, 1976.

19. *Ibid.,* p. 27.

EPILOGUE

The 1982 Covello Award Paper

FUNERALS, FAMILY
AND FOREFATHERS:
ITALIAN-AMERICAN
FUNERAL PRACTICES*

Daniel David Cowell, M.D.
National Institutes of Health

I. Introduction

Flowers are everywhere, a house full of flowers — the scent of hundreds of chrysanthemums, carnations, roses, and lillies leave an unforgettable olfactory imprint which tells me this day is different from all the rest. What can I make of this day? Where can I hide? How can I shut out the death of my grandmother, wasted by years of struggle against a killer thyroid, when she has lain throughout the night in the upstairs bedroom next to grandfather's bed? (a "wake" the adults call it.) Why has our house been transformed into a place of choking sadness covered with a pall of joylessness? What are those shadows in that ghostly bedroom at the top of the stairs? I'd better not go up there ... perhaps grandmother will awake ... maybe she is not dead but only sleeping, keeping grandfather company.

Three times in the first 20 years of life I experienced this kind of ritual farewell involving members of my immediate family to whom I had been very close and have never forgotten. This paper represents a serious effort to understand these experiences with insights afforded by relevant anthropological, sociological, psychological and historical considerations. No attempt will be made in this paper to examine all aspects of the Italian-American, Roman Catholic funeral ceremony such as the development of cemeteries or the religious ritual itself in the New World as contrasted with the Old. Rather, I focus on the thesis that the ritualistic observance of death I experienced had its roots in Old World traditions, was modified by the conditions of American social patterns and funeral customs and was further shaped by the particular psychosocial dynamics of our own family. These factors are what this paper seeks to address in coming to terms with and better understanding those emotion-laden experiences. To these ends, I

---

* 1982 Covello Award Paper

have added selected material consisting of personal reminiscences and recollections by others on the Italian American funeral practices they had known or funeral practices they had heard about in Italy.

The otherwise extensive immigration literature contains few references to the sociology of immigrant funeral ceremonies and practices. This paper approaches this neglected area by surveying at least some of the more prominent English language sources pertaining to general funeral practices in the Old World, paying particular attention to the few that relate specifically to the Italian experience. The next sections deal with aspects of evolving funeral practices in the social culture of the New World and how these shaped Italian-American funeral practices. The concluding section briefly relates the experience of home funerals in my family of origin to the larger societal practices described.

II. Old World Funeral Customs and Cultural Values

Unlike its neighbors, France and Switzerland, Italy had no national laws affecting funerals and interments until after the country became fully unified in 1870. Before then, the larger municipalities generally controlled the exterior aspects of the burial of the dead, such as the hearse and carriage transportation and earth or mausoleum burial. Private undertaking firms, available only in the cities, would be engaged by families to assist in the "interior" arrangements such as the decoration of the inside of the home and the arranging of personal and religious ceremonies. [1]

The situation in the rural areas of southern Italy was, however, different than the practices which were developing in the large cities of the north. Geographically, linguistically, and socially fragmented, the young Republic was also rich in local funeral beliefs and customs; not surprisingly, these varied with region and village, reflecting the persistence of local mores and customs, folk religions and *campanilismo* (intense village loyalty and parochialism) whose origins were lost in the mists of time and mingled with the tramp of conquerors.

Generally, when death occurred in the home, windows were blacked out and candles lighted in the room in which the body lay. Embalming would not have been practiced:

> Home funerals were common. No embalming was done so the body would have been unburied for only twenty-four to thirty-six hours . . . the body was washed and dressed by the family. The family would be coming and going offering support, prayers and the preparation of food. . . . There would be a wake and the priest would officiate at the initial funeral service in the home before accompanying the body to church for Mass [2]

In the peasant world of the 1850's, the deceased would have been "layed out" in his house on a bed or table, in clean clothes with a simple cross of flowers nearby. The vigil, "wake" or lying-in state, was itself derived from ancient Hebrew practice, being a precaution against a premature burial, an act of piety and an occasion of prayers for the dead. It also provided an opportunity for those who had been present at the death to clear themselves of the suspicion of foul play; and a chance for all interested parties to witness whether an equitable distribution of property had been made.[3] Burial clubs composed of guild members, which formed in larger Italian cities in the middle Ages, helped defray the expenses of funerals, prayed (motivated by the Catholic doctrine of purgatory) and showed respect for the deceased and family.

Following a wake, the body would be placed in a pine box, carried on the shoulders of friends to the church cemetery, preceded by a village band if available, and buried by the family who also marked the grave with a small stone or cross.[4] All this would likely have been the case in the tiny hill town of Montella, near the city of Avellino, in the Campania where my maternal grandfather was born in 1867 before emigrating to America in 1886. There would have been no burial club in such a small community.

A closer examination of the situation indicates that the *contadini,* or peasants, of southern Italy, who comprised the majority of the Italian immigrants to America, lived according to the centuries-old way of life, being not as affected by the ideological and technological developments sweeping across Europe in the late 19th century. Their folk religion, according to Vecoli, was a syncretic melding of ancient pagan beliefs, magical practices and Christian liturgy. Cult and occult were admixed in a closely held, magico-religious world view characterized by a belief in a thin margin of physical survival and vulnerability to instant calamities, especially to those caused by malevolent spirits. Each moment and event were thus infused with religious and magical significance.[5] It is likely that the people of Montella would have been influenced by these or similar belief systems.

Further consideration of specific funeral patterns among southern Italians is enlightening in understanding the ways in which these patterns changed in the New World. In her study, Mathias has emphasized the extent to which even the poorest south Italian peasant family would go in order to pay for funerals. In this connection, Mathias believes the importance of these sacrifices and the sense of urgency in following specific rituals involving the care and burial of the dead were all related to the prescriptions of folk religion involving the peasants' pervasive and profound dread of the return of the soul of the deceased. It is toward the prevention of this return that she believes nearly all peasant funeral rituals were directed. In consequence, behavior surrounding death and burial so permeated daily life in the rural south that the peasants were described by Moss and Thompson as "death-oriented".[6]

Perhaps reflective of this sense of vulnerability and the underlying apprehension about the soul among the villagers was the scrupulous attention paid to the Roman Catholic sacrament of Extreme Unction and to the dying person in particular:

> A vigil was always maintained without interruption with the dying person . . . physical contact was always kept so as to ease the transition from the physical to the supernatural world. Death was talked about as if it were a *thing*, a feared and evil being ("the Angel of Death"), not a biological event.[7]

In effect, according to Mathias, various components of the funeral and burial rituals functioned to placate the soul, render its reluctant, usually involuntary and frequently violent departure from this world as amicable as possible and to forestall any possibility that it might return to disturb those who remained behind. Useful objects such as matches and small change would be placed near the body and objects of which the deceased had been particularly fond were put in the pine box. The body would be carried out of the house feet first: by not "seeing" the door as it left, it would not be able to locate it later. The procession to the cemetary would traverse various paths, returning to the house by a different route to confuse the soul's sense of direction; the wailing and lamenting which had begun at the time of the death were forbidden upon the return trip lest the soul be distracted from its other-worldly journey and return.

> I recall that when grandfather died in 1955 at the age of 88, his wake was held in the home and the funeral was begun there. He looked dignified in the vested suit which he made in the years when he had fashioned then-Governor Woodrow Wilson's clothes. Small change was placed in his pocket, as well as other mementos of the Knights of Columbus, Fourth Degree, the Sons of Italy and other fraternal societies of which he had been a member. It had always seemed to me that in our family there was held the belief that no one ever died a "natural" death: there was always someone or something "responsible," some act of omission or commission — which, despite all evidence to the contrary, was unaccountable. Hence, I always sensed a pervasive sense of guilt mixed with the sadness and the unforgettable scent of those legions of flowers. I recall having read about one person who said, "I never forget the smell of those flowers. They, more than anything else, gave me the chill of death."[8]

With the funeral over, the mattress of the deathbed was taken out and washed and a meal prepared by neighbors for the family and friends. Thus were the funeral activities concluded until the Day of the Dead (November 2) when a mass would be celebrated, the grave visited and food left out on the table (in a hospitable gesture should the soul happen to return). Since the soul was thought capable of observing and experiencing what transpires on Earth and its departure had been a forced one, it sought constantly to return and thus had to be coaxed and persuaded to remain in the next world. Perhaps it is in this connection that one of the lesser acknowledged purposes of the aforementioned prayer societies was to pacify the reluctant soul and hasten its arrival in heaven from purgatory—where it would be so gratified that it would no longer seek to return to Earth.

An amplification of the world view from which these practices derived has been provided by Vecoli. While the *contadini* generally regarded themselves as Christians, he reminds us that their brand of folk religion had little to do with the polity of the church, or its dogmas of sin, atonement and salvation. The peasants' fearful respect for the clergy's imputed arch-magician powers and their indispensability for the sacraments may have surpassed actual reverence for them or for the church as an institution. In fact, according to Lopreato, the people in southern Italy have generally never been pious, the family being the primary influence in their lives. Viewing the church as a traditional exploiter along with the landholding or signorial class, the *paesani* existed in an uneasy relationship with the village priest who, often with contempt, regarded himself as their temporal as well as spiritual superior. Thus through the centuries, asserts Lopreato, a chasm developed between the church and the working masses. The latter believed in God and the various saints, even availing themselves of the church at critical periods of their lives; "but the private conception of religion was nevertheless heavily strewn with all sorts of beliefs in the forces of good and evil and included faith in various sorts of magical practices; at the heart of such beliefs and practices was the religious *festa* [feast, Saint's day] which later in the New World would come in for a great deal of criticism from the Irish-dominated Catholic Church."[9]

The spirit of *companilismo* of each *paese* [native village] was expressed in these *festa,* the veneration of local patron saints and madonnas. Patronage with a compulsive, magico-religious quality to a particular local saint or saints, *clientelismo,* ensured protection or the miraculous fulfillment of favors requested. According to Vecoli, supernatural practices extended beyond the rites sanctioned by the church; since the *contadini* believed that even the ministrations of the priests could not reach certain areas of the spirit world, the *mal'occhio* [evil eye] or intervention of other malevolent forces could only be countered by various charms, amulets potions and incantations. In extreme cases there would be resort to a *mago* or *strega* [magician or witch]. He concludes that folk religion for the *contadini* was no "Sunday affair" but rather a total system of deeply held beliefs and practices of great significance which were employed in coping with the harsh and often tragic realities of daily existence.

Thus as Cornelisen aptly commented with reference to the Mezzogiorno, "there was a sense of magic in religion and a sense of religion in magic".[10] The immigrants, notes Vecoli, carried this religion oriented world view with them as they went out in search of bread and work. "Together with the other aspects of southern folklore," Vecoli notes, "the magico-religious world view followed the immigrants to the new shores and stayed with them for several generations".[11] Funeral rituals involving the pacification of the departed soul were, in fact, brought to the New World by the early immigrants.

As will be seen in the next section, Mathias has traced this continuity through the modifications imposed by New World social practices, funeral customs, and the opportunity for social competition made possible by improved socioeconomic conditions of the *contadini* in the New World. It is not difficult to imagine that this familiar world view would be employed by the *contadini* in organizing the novel, bewildering and stressful experiences they faced in adjusting to their adopted land.

III. The American Way of Death

The family centeredness, funeral customs, and cosmology the Italian immigrants brought with them to the New World were modified by the evolutionary forces at work in that dynamic and heterogenous society. Thus, according to Farrell, between 1830 and 1920, there was a growing trend toward urbanization of the American population, industrialization and increasing specialization and professionalization on the part of many kinds of service providers. These combined with changes in transportation, science, medical practice, religion, philosophy psychology, aesthetics, and domestic life to shape American beliefs and behavior concerning death.[12] The skilled furniture or cabinet maker, for example, for whom making plain, pine-box coffins had been a sideline, gradually came to make these his specialty; he began to professionalize both his demeanor and services, while beautifying death and burial. Given these forces at work in society, Farrell's study lays out the mainstream of American death practices which developed between 1830 and 1920. Except in a few instances, these practices became the accepted and established American way of death thereafter. Thus while the focus of this paper remains on Italian-American funeral practices, it is necessary to consider pertinent aspects of the societal context and the value systems concerning death within which the immigrant practices flourished in the New World.

Farrell states that betweeen 1830 and 1920 American conceptions of death changed in a manner referred to as "the dying of death" — the cultural circumvention of the formality, gloom and dread of death which can be attributed to a variety of factors. Not the least of these he points out were the growing American hubris and confidence in the power of technology and science to demystify life, and control the environment—perhaps even death; the secularization of life; and a corresponding mitigation of the medieval, church-engendered theology of death ("the disappearance of hell from popular theology").

According to Farrell's analysis, in the 19th century general changes in religious thought took place. These were inherited from the Enlightenment and developed as a response to Romanticism. In addition they were adapted from scientific naturalism which strongly influenced the development of rural, picturesque, garden-type cemeteries; death was characterized as a repugnant process of decay and "scientific," biological interpretations of death were substituted for religious and spiritual ones. Moreover, he asserts that a developing faith in American medicine, the growing sanitary movement, the "expertization" and professionalization of the sciences (providing models for aspiring morticians), and the emergence of psychology as a social science emphasizing the psychological effects of death upon survivors—all influenced the attitudes toward death in America in the 19th century. The general growth of capitalistic enterprise in this period also fostered the industrialization of the fledgling funeral service business, the development of an insurance industry ("insuring" against death), and stimulated the competition for prospective customers among cemeteries which were beginning to base their own activity upon "modern business practices".

All these changes worked in the direction of "sterilizing" death, commercializing it into a burgeoning American industry while intensifying the elements of social status which were associated with the various services the young industry was beginning to provide: artful embalming became more common, for example, and plain wooden coffins were being replaced, by 1880, with decorative, more "luxurious" and ever-more expensive caskets; funeral directors capitalized on the difficulties involved in conducting home funerals from cramped, vertical tenements and offered "parlors" in their own "homes" for funerals.

For all these and other reasons, it was posited by DeTocqueville that American middle-class minds turned to the maintenance of appropriate etiquette, uniformity and order in the meaning and management of death.[13]

Native American southerners and immigrants in general did deviate from the patterns of the American Way of Death. In the case of the former, the low level of southern income and the slow growth of cities long hindered the concentration of moneyed markets for the products and services associated with the "dying of death." In the case of the imigrants, as has been shown by Kalish and Reynolds, ethnic variations persisted, although the ethnic subculture came to be influenced by and to adopt the middle-class American Way of Death for its own use.[14] More will be said about this in the case of Italian-Americans in the next section.

American funeral practices came to be influenced in four aspects as a net result of all the societal, technological and attitudinal changes mentioned: 1) the care of the body; 2) the container for the deceased; 3) the place of the funeral; and 4) funeral procedures. The cumulative effect of these changes in funeral practices shifted the focus from the finality of death, decay of the body and apprehensions about the soul to one which emphasized bodily preservation and comfort for the survivors.

In the first place, as noted, the traditional preparations of the corpse by family and friends came to be replaced in the 19th century by nonfamily members, who began to assume more of the traditional family functions, becoming "undertakers" in the process. Embalming became the primary standard of professionalism and was well accepted by 1900, being favored as a means of preservation of the corpse for shipment (especially during and following the Civil War), for "naturalization" or improving the appearance of the corpse; disinfection; protection from long-term decay; and definitive resolution of the premature burial issue. The underlying spirit of these rationales was well illustrated by one undertaker (known as "Funeral Directors" by 1883) who advised colleagues that "one idea should always be kept in mind, and that is to lay out the body so that there will be as little suggestion of death as possible."[15]

Coffins traditionally conforming to the general shape of the human body began to be replaced by more elaborate containers, constructed in uniform rectagonal shape that directed attention away from the singular individuality of death. The concentration upon the body which the costly conversion from coffin to casket implied would have been unthinkable to impoverished *paesani* whose focus and efforts were directed to the pacification of the soul and the prevention of its return.

Before the turn of the century, funerals were ordinarily held in the home of the deceased; the common alternative was one which began in the home with a vigil and a viewing of the body followed by a procession to the church for the main ceremony, completed by the conventional trip to the cemetery and the committal service. A number of factors, however, combined to change the locus away from the deceased's home. The funeral directors of the time contended that there was a need to consolidate clinic, home and chapel and serve as a central receiving point for the interstate shipment of bodies in the post-bellum period.

In an effort to induce patronage, by 1920 funeral homes were beginning to be made as cheerful, pleasant, aesthetic and fashionable as possible, directing attention away from the centrality of death and emphasizing the proper appearance of the deceased. This final segregation of the funeral from its domestic context tended to confirm the contemporary role of the funeral director and the indispensability of his services. For Farrell, it culminated a distancing of death that had proceeded previously within the middle-class American home. He refers to the use of the "parlor," which in Victorian homes (and in the one in which I grew up), was viewed as somewhat of a formal room which lent itself to the solemnity of a funeral.[16]

It was not a big change, apparently, to completely exteriorize the funereal aspects of parlors (and later parlors themselves) by relegating this unhappy occasion to the "parlors" of funeral directors; the domestic parlors became transformed into "living rooms." Even where the funeral remained in the home, flowers (with the encouragement of the floral industry) replaced somber black drapery in an attempt to create a more cheerful environment for the funeral proceedings and to mitigate the sting of the loss suffered.

> When we first arrived in Trenton in 1908, there were no funeral parlors. They only developed later so the wake had to be conducted from the home by the funeral director. Even so, the family would have been shocked to let their beloved dead go to a cold lonesome place to stay before the funeral. They were kept at home and a member of the family stayed up all night on guard. This was an accepted procedure. This was respect.[17]

Changes in the funeral service itself accompanied the other changes, becoming in general briefer, less doleful and somber, stressing consolation for the survivors while the family and friends of the deceased assumed more passive roles as comforted spectators. To some extent, observes Farrell, the ensuing privatization of grief also carried with it a suppression of grief; it was "as if grief were a contagious disease," a needless and shameful woe, a manifestation of abnormal self-indulgence, and a sinful objection to the Divine Will.[18] Memorial observances in terms of the length of the period of mourning clothes, for example, were abbreviated.

In summary it is not difficult to conclude that all these attempts to reduce the gruesomeness and fearfulness of death and to stress its beauty and beneficence also acted to reduce its reality as well as its sting; they created an unfamiliar, aesthetic climate of funeral practices compared to the crucial, life-integrated funereal rite of passage which the effusive Italian immigrants had long accepted as imperative.

IV. The Immigrant Funeral in the New World

Mathias has focused on the funeral practices of the Italian community of south Philadelphia. As a packed, encapsulated ghetto, this community once included my maternal grandfather who was also a parishioner of Saint

Mary Magdelene, the first Italian Catholic church in America (1852). She suggests that the isolation which these immigrants felt from the larger community along with the internal factions which were indigenous to them inevitably fueled old rivalries and intensified the drive for differentiation and status with the funeral being a public stage for competitive display: the better the display, the higher the admiration for the family. According to Mathias, the immigrants remembered the pattern and form of funerals of the wealthy landowners in southern Italy, and adopted that approach as a basic, status-oriented model for funerals in the New World. That approach, I think, was compatible with the contemporary native American interest in more impressive material objects and displays in connection with funerals encouraged by the developing funeral service industry and the other societal factors already described.

Thus, she asserts that basic funeral patterns of the *signori* were followed and the Old World peasant customs embellished by means of resources at hand in the New World: the number of floral wreaths were increased; a funeral band led the procession to the church and/or the cemetery; a cart or horse-drawn hearse was used in place of strong shoulders; a wooden casket substituted for a pine box; mourners were hired; an elaborate bier in the home was substituted for a plain board or bed; embalming became the usual practice; announcement cards were distributed; monuments as elaborate as circumstances allowed replaced small stones or wooden crosses; porcelain pictures began to adorn the grave stones as was the custom among the *signori* in southern Italy; and graves were tended by the families who used the occasions for Sunday socialization (and for comparing the impressiveness of the grave stones).[19] Available accounts of those old funerals are illuminating and moving:

> The funeral was a large and orderly affair . . . the two story house was jammed full of mourners at the meeting hour and the whole Italian quarter was sitting out on the doorsteps watching the gathering. The Christopher Columbus Society turned out one hundred seventy strong with white gloves and badges with black over them. Undertaker Crawford was in charge and his black-plummed hearse was drawn by four jet black horses. The funeral cortege did not pass directly to the church but up Hudson, back to Clinton and then the full length of Mott Street so that its length and splendor could be fully appreciated by the quarter. This is said to be the custom whenever anyone dies there.[20]

In Chambersburg (the old Italian community in Trenton, New Jersey) the wake always lasted three days. The corpse was *never* left alone. Everything was very solemn . . . jewelry, rosary beads and rings were always left in the coffin — as was anything else that touched the coffin . . . there was a fear — a superstition some would say — that unless care was taken Death would follow the mourners back from the cemetery to claim other victims. Friends would stop at a public place before going home from a funeral so as not to bring Death home with them. A picture would never be taken of a sleeping person — it was thought that Death might be tempted to claim that person . . . a funeral band would play in the procession and the group would swing by the house one last time ("the last visit") . . . we went as families to the cemeteries on Sundays to talk, to visit and tend the graves. There was a different attitude toward grief than today; it was *terrible,* a *hopeless abyss* [emphases added are mine] . . . there was no hope, no consolation.

When leaving a home funeral or parlor you must stop before going to your home and buy something. If unable to buy, you must walk around outdoors for a while before going to your home . . . widows were expected to scream and carry on; at the grave site they scratched their faces and tore their hair. They were prevented from jumping into the open grave. In returning from the cemetery only the family and very close relations returned to the house and no refreshments were offered. People came to console — you came to grieve. Mirrors were covered and draped in black; you were not allowed to look at yourself.[21]

In summary, through all of these embellishments, the overt emphasis as with the native American society generally, gradually shifted away from a concern with the soul to the body of the deceased and its proper display. The basic characteristics of the peasant funeral of simplicity, family control and the fear of the soul of the departed were modified by reversion to the prestigious funeral patterns of the *signori* — and were reinforced by the trend toward "naturalization," standardization, social display and minimal personal expression in the course of the evolving American funeral practices. It should be mentioned that although Mathias' thesis is neat, it is certainly possible that the immigrants would eventually have accepted the American Way of Death even if there had *not* been a signorial model as a handy prototype to fall back on. Acceptance of the new model for managing death could have reflected gradual acceptance of middle-class values rather than the recollection of an earlier, familiar funeral pattern or have represented discomfiture in the new society over the more superstituous elements in the older observances.

V. The Contemporary Italian-American Funeral

By 1940, Italian Americans generally accepted embalming with the funeral director taking the body from the hospital or house to his establishment for preparation before returning it to the home for the "laying out" to which all friends of the deceased, however remote, were expected to attend. According to Mathias, folk rituals were (and still are) practiced although sublimated to the pressures of the new model for standardization, modernization and proper display.[22] According to Vecoli, the trend toward de-emphasis of traditional devotional and communal practices is discernible in the changing Italian-American funeral; what had been a set of rituals for dealing with death, including the custom of night vigils and anguished lamentations came to be largely discarded. The use of bands at funerals and photographs on the tombstones have been proscribed by the church since 1955 and 1944 respectively. "The old people are hushed when they mourn and few bodies are laid out at home; the padded luxury of the funeral parlor has become the scene for the drama of the last hours with the body of the deceased and the funeral director has taken over the duties which had once been performed in the peasant culture by the family alone."[23] Elaborate bronze caskets came to replace wooden ones; the paid mourners are a thing of the past; announcement cards have been replaced by newspaper notices; and an anonymous system of "perpetual care" has largely replaced the communal function and the central obligation of the family for the care of the gravesite in this ever-changing, mobile society.

> When our ancestors felt like laughing you could hear them all over the county and when they cried, glory, how they cried! This is as it should be. If we weren't meant to laugh and cry and tear our hair in anguish when we felt like it, then we wouldn't be human beings, but leaves or stones . . . they don't have wakes like they used to anymore; at least not Italian wakes.[24]

Private insurance plans are now common but fraternal benevolent societies are still active in supporting the family, defraying expenses and praying for the deceased. The old custom, perpetuated by various ethnic groups, of bringing money to the wake, is described by Grieco in the following passage:

> I imagine there are a lot of people who don't know how Italians insured themselves when they came to this country in the early part of the century . . . when one of them died all the other Italians would bring a certain amount of money to the wake, so that the family could pay for the burial. The name and amount

of money were duly recorded in a book and this became a debt of honor for the bereaved family . . . I can remember going to Italian wakes and seeing very poor people go proudly into the back room to donate their few dollars toward easing someone else's burden. They were responding not to a semiannual bill but to the understanding in their hearts.[25]

Mathias believes that the emphasis of the *paesani* upon the journey of the soul has actually only gone underground, emerging symbolically in other guises such as the characteristic floral forms resembling those used by the *signori*. Perhaps it is also accurate to theorize that the apparent change in America away from fear of the returning soul has become sublimated but displaced onto another more symbolic (and culturally acceptable) form — fear of loss of status. Certainly there is sufficient basis for this proposition in a society which, as it must have appeared to the immigrants, places such emphasis upon the acquisition of material goods, competition, individualism, the trappings of worldly success, secularist beliefs and the demystification of life. One piece of suggestive evidence in favor of this hypothesis would be the obligatory character and the force behind the fear of loss of social status in this society which appears as strong as the concern of the *paesani* over the return of the soul. My own impression is that:

Despite these changes, what remains of the intense experience of funerals in my youth is the reaffirmation of family ties in the coming-together of the family members at those times; some of them may not see one another from one funeral to the next. Our family (the extended, not the immediate family) puts out a veritable banquet of refreshments for all immediately after the committal service and old times are recounted, but soon most people slip away to resume the rhythm of their own lives. The sense of loss and sadness are certainly present, but it seems neither as oppressive nor as profound as once was the case — as if the event which has occurred is indistinguishable from other important events, occurrences or changes. Few — at least outwardly — seem to express themselves fully on what has been lost. The funerals, although solemn and not pleasant in any sense, feel more impersonal and more "managed"; they are far less leaden, less awesome, and no longer constitute such a dreaded ordeal. I recall by the time funerals were over in the old days, you *knew* the deceased was dead. As my mother remarked, "Sentiment played a big part in those early days; it wasn't he or she is gone — forget it. Not then — grief was *real*." [emphases mine].[26]

V. The Ronca Family

Given the foregoing background, the funeral experiences of my mother's immediate family can be placed in perspective. A brief review of those experiences provides the basis for related observations.

My grandfather's death in 1955 seemed to mark a key transition: there have been no further home funerals despite 13 family deaths since. Perhaps the simplest explanation for this is that of the closure of a chapter—a last sign of respect, a gesture of the heart at the final passing of the maternal grandparents and the era they represented; an accommodation (perhaps with relief) to the American Way of Death.

Coincident with the passing of the immigrant generation went substantially the lest vestige of the old-style funeral, the family structure with which it seemed related, as well as the pall of grief which it imposed upon the bereaved. With the passing of that generation went the last tie to the Italian parish which had been a point of reference for the family for a half century. And finally that passing brought to a final contraction a large intergenerational family of the type seldom seen today. For the first time since they were married, my own parents were challenged by the opportunity to experience themselves and their son as a nuclear family unit.

There has appeared to be no difficulty in the subsequent exteriorization of funerals to funeral home. Since 1955 there have been "laying outs" or "viewings" but no wakes (no reason for them since the bodies are no longer in the home). Funeral services have been brief. The role of clergy has been a small one, fraternal organizations are no longer present and no bands have played. The caskets have been elaborate (even "comfortable" as described by one funeral director). Mourners have been restrained although sad. Fees associated with Perpetual Care have been dutifully paid. I regularly visit cemeteries where family members are buried and such visits remain a felt obligation for most family members.

After 1955 the earlier insistence upon home funerals—perhaps related to respect for the older generation, as a subconscious demonstration of that generation's pride of home ownership or as a reflection of a sense of guilt associated with exteriorizing the funeral—gave way fully to the American Way of Death.

Floral arrangements were, and still are, very elaborate and include the "pillow," "blanket" and the "cross" but no "pillar" or "clock." The crucifix attached to the coffin is never buried but is removed and retained as a tangible remembrance displayed in the home. The women are "layed out" in white gowns with hands enfolded around a prayer book or rosary beads; no other objects are placed on the person of the deceased or in the coffin and I can never recall the use of salt as a preservative. The men, as was my grandfather, are dressed in freshly pressed suits.

On the morning of the funeral, the closing of the casket is no longer preceded by a kiss of the deceased by each member of the immediate family as was the case when our funerals were held in the home. I remember the experience well: it did not seem frightening or unpleasant, but rather an affectionate or respectful farewell (the hard, unyielding flesh served as a vivid reminder of the embalmer's art and the infinite distinction between life and nonlife).

The last funeral mass, I can recall, with the casket in church and involving a eulogy was in 1955. Since then only brief Catholic services have been conducted in the funeral home both the night before and the morning of the procession from the funeral home to the cemetery. Pallbearers continue to be recruited from among the able-bodied males in the family as they have always been. It is interesting to note in this connection that the gloves they wear are removed and still left with the casket for internment: the old precaution about leaving with the dead anything which has come in contact with them seems to have persisted. I have not personally observed anyone who goes first to a public place before returning home, but there may be some among the older mourners who do. I have often seen the funeral procession take a final turn by the home of the deceased before going to the cemetery — which seems to indicate that at least in that respect there is no fear of the soul's return. Mourners are invited to the home following the brief committal service for an extensive meal.

Grave markers have always been modest, without adornments or florid sentiments, and have usually not been emplaced until years after the death. Whether this phenomenon represents a reluctance to spend hard-earned money for that purpose, the inertia of depression and weariness or a denial of the finality of the death, is difficult to say. No special religious services are now held upon the succeeding anniversaries of the deaths and formal religious ceremonies are not a prominent part of remembrances which now tend to be personal and private in nature. The mourning periods of my youth which ranged up to a year and which were very strictly observed are now much abbreviated.

In retrospect, I conclude that my family's funeral practices have followed the general progression outlined by Mathias and, at least since 1955, have conformed to the American Way of Death. Whatever superstitions may once have existed have gradually disappeared and even their derivatives are not now much in evidence. Changes in the family's funeral practices also appear to be related to the evolution over time of the family itself in America: this has been characterized by a shift toward the nuclear family, a strong sense of civic responsibility and citizenship, a greater mobility and an emphasis upon education, acculturation and assimilation of middle-class values.

Finally as the "latency" period of the 1950's gave way to the turbulent decade of the 1960's, so my grandfather's passing in 1955 marked the irretrievable end of an era beyond which already acculturized offspring would carry the process of middle-class assimilation still further. This process included the family's funeral practices. Whether we have lost something valuable in the process of having our deaths packaged and managed in the newly prescribed manner, can be disputed; there is no doubt, however, that significant and permanent changes in our practices have occurred in line with the new model.

Notes

1. R.W. Habenstein and W.M. Lamers, *Funeral Customs the World Over.* (Milwaukee, Wisconsin: Bulfin Printers, Inc., 1960), p. 515-26.
2. Rev. C. Donanzan, Pastor, Holy Rosary Catholic Church, Washington, D.C., interview, July 7, 1981.
3. R.W. Habenstein and W.M. Lamars, *The History of American Funeral Directing.* (Milwaukee, Wisconsin: Bulfin Printers, Inc., 1955), pp. 106-08.
4. E. Mathias, "The Italian-American Funeral: Persistence Through Change," *Western Folklore* 33 (1974), pp. 35-50.
5. R.J. Vecoli, Jr., "Cult and Occult in Italian-American Culture," in R.M. Miller and T.D. Marzik (eds.), *Immigrants and Religion in Urban* America (Philadelphia, Pennsylvania: Temple University Press, 1977), pp. 25-47.
6. L. Moss and W.H. Thompson, "The South Italian Family: Literature and Observations," *Human Organization* 18 (1959), pp. 35-41.
7. I. DeAngelo, daughter, former Italian Counsular Agent, Felice Ronca (the author's greatuncle), Trenton, New Jersey, personal interview, July 22, 1981.
8. G. Cautella, "Italian Funeral," *American Mercury,* 15 (October, 1928), pp. 200-06.
9. J. Lopreato, *Italian Americans,* (New York: Random House, 1970), p. 87-9.
10. A. Cornelisen, *Torregreca: Life, Death, Miracles,* (New York: Dell Publishing Co., Inc., 1969), p. 29.
11. R.J. Vecoli, *op. cit.,* pp. 11-29.
12. J.J. Farrell, *Inventing the American Way of Death,* (Philadelphia, Pennsylvania: Temple University Press, 1980), pp. 3-135.
13. A. DeTocqueville, *Democracy in America,* (New York: Vintage Books, Alfred A. Knopf, 1945), pp. 266-67.
14. R.A. Kalish and D.K. Reynolds, *Death and Ethnicity,* (Los Angeles, California: University of Southern California Press, 1976), p. 218.
15. J.J. Farrell, *op. cit.,* p. 160.
16. *Ibid.* p. 175
17. T. Cowell, mother of the author, personal interview, July 23, 1981.
18. J.J. Farrell, *op. cit.,* p. 179.

19. Mathias, *op. cit.,* pp. 40-50.
20. Trenton (New Jersey) *Daily True American,* description of the funeral of Leonardo Covello (the author's paternal grandfather), October 20, 1899.
21. Personal interview with T. Cowell and I. DeAngelo; loc. cit.
22. Mathias, *op. cit.,* pp. 43-44.
23. Vecoli, *op. cit.,* pp. 41-44.
24. R. Grieco, "They Who Mourn," *Commonweal,* 57 (March 27, 1953), pp. 628-30.
25. *Ibid.*
26. Personal interview with T. Cowell; loc. cit.

Index of Names

Subject Index

American Italian Historical Association Proceeding Series

1968
Ethnicity in American Political Life:
The Italian-American Experience
Salvatore LaGumina, Ed.

1969
The Italian American Novel
John M. Cammett, Ed.

1970
An Inquiry into Organized Crime
Luciano Iorizzo, Ed.

1971
Power and Class: The Italian
American Experience Today
Francis X. Feminella, Ed.

1972
Italian American Radicalism: Old
World Origins and New World
Developments
Rudolph J. Vecoli, Ed.

1973
The Religious Experience of
Italian Americans
Silvano Tomasi, Ed.

1974
The Interaction of Italians and
Jews in America
Jean Scarpaci, Ed.

1975
The Urban Experience of Italian
Americans
Pat Gallo, Ed.

1976
The United States and Italy: The
First Two Hundred Years
Humbert Nelli, Ed.

1977
The Italian Immigrant Women in
North America
Betty Boyd Caroli, Ed.

1978
Pane E. Lavoro: The Italian
American Working Class
George E. Pozzetta, Ed.

1979
Italian Americans in the Professions
Remigio U. Pane, Ed.

1980
The Family and Community Life
Of Italian Americans
Richard N. Juliani, Ed.

1981
Italian Immigrants in Rural and
Small Town America
Rudolph J. Vecoli, Ed.

1982
The Italian Americans Through
The Generations
Rocco Caporale, Ed.

1983
Italians and Irish in America
Francis X. Femminella, Ed.

To Order Copies Or For Information Write To:

AIHA National Office
209 Flagg Place
Staten Island, New York 10304